BRAMLEY
MOORE DOCK

Bob Waterhouse

BRAMLEY MOORE DOCK

From Slavery to Football at the New Home of Everton FC

First published by Pitch Publishing, 2025

Pitch Publishing
9 Donnington Park,
85 Birdham Road,
Chichester, West Sussex,
PO20 7AJ
www.pitchpublishing.co.uk
info@pitchpublishing.co.uk

A CIP catalogue record is available for this book
from the British Library.

ISBN 978 1 83680 202 0

Printed and bound on FSC® certified paper in line with
our continuing commitment to ethical business practices,
sustainability and the environment.

Typesetting and origination by Pitch Publishing

Printed and bound in India by Replika Press Pvt. Ltd.

CONTENTS

Introduction 9

Everton's Search for a New Home 11

John Bramley-Moore – The Epitome of a Slaver 41

History of the Port of Liverpool 53

Regeneration of the Docks: A New Future for
Liverpool's Dockland 101

Is The Bramley-Moore Stadium a
Potential Threat to the Dockland Heritage
or a New Future? 123

Everton FC's Historic Links to Slavery 154

Conclusion 180

Notes 184

DEDICATION

I would firstly like to dedicate this to my wife and two sons for their endless support in writing this book. Finally, I would like to thank retired academic Philip Garrahan for his endless help in editing, advising and inspiring the book.

INTRODUCTION

THE BOOK will consist of seven chapters documenting the history of the site of Everton's new ground, including its original links to slavery. It will also set this history in the context of the broader history of the rise and decline of the Liverpool docks. It will look at how those docks have regenerated over the last 40 years and examine what role the new stadium could play in future regeneration of north Liverpool. The book will also document the club's historic links to slavery.

The first chapter will examine Everton's over-20-year history in looking for a new stadium. The second chapter will look at the life of John Bramley-Moore, who created the dock that is the site of the new stadium and made a large percentage of his wealth from slavery. The third will focus on Liverpool's long history as a maritime port, including the building of the Bramley-Moore Dock, which opened in 1848. The fourth will look at the regeneration of the docks since the 1980s – for Liverpool City Council, Everton's new stadium is intended to be part of this. The fifth chapter will look to the threat to Liverpool's dockland heritage in the light of the 2021 UNESCO decision to withdraw its World Heritage status to the Liverpool waterfront – the approval of the stadium project was a key reason for this decision. The sixth chapter also looks at how the new stadium could help regenerate north Liverpool. The final chapter will examine the club's historic links to both slavery and the abolitionist movement. One interesting aspect of my research has been to find a direct link between the name of the original Methodist chapel that founded the club with slavery.

EVERTON'S SEARCH FOR A NEW HOME

AT THE start of the 2025/26 season, Everton Football Club will move out of their home of 133 years, Goodison Park, and make the short trip of a mile or so up to the docks and move into their purpose-built stadium of Bramley-Moore Dock. The new stadium will seat 52,888, potentially rising to 62,000. It will occupy the site of the old Bramley-Moore Dock, which was drained and infilled with sand from the Irish Sea to form the base supporting the new stadium structure. As well as being a home to Everton FC it will host international football; in October 2023 it was announced that the stadium would be one of the grounds hosting Euro 2028. It is also intended that the stadium, out of season, will host arts and cultural events like pop concerts.

The American architect Dan Meis, who has designed the stadium, wanted to it to be built in sympathy with its surroundings:

'Bramley-Moore is a site steeped in Liverpool history. It gives the opportunity to draw on that context ... we were striving for a building that was both familiar and yet awe-inspiring, historic yet futuristic.'[1]

The conservation issues surrounding the new stadium will be a major feature of this book.

The club had been searching for a new home for over 20 years. Goodison Park was dated, with the Bullens Road stand being built in 1926 and the Gwladys Street stand being completed in 1938.[2] Also, there was no room for expansion, as the ground is hemmed in by numerous terraced streets.

In the mid-1990s, controversial chairman Peter Johnson – he had previously been chairman of Tranmere Rovers and was a self-confessed Liverpool fan – first began the search for a new stadium. In 2001, plans were announced for a 55,000-seater stadium in the Kings Dock area beside the newly renovated Albert Dock.[3]

The stadium would have a retractable roof and be used for concerts all-year round. However, the club had insufficient funds to proceed with the project and, in 2003, it was shelved. According to Paul Gregg, a former Everton stakeholder and business partner of the late Everton chairman Bill Kenwright, the latter pulled out of the stadium as he wasn't prepared to borrow another £30m to fund a stadium that the club wouldn't own. It would be owned by the council, who were prepared to put in significant funds to secure the stadium.[4]

The site eventually became the home of the M&S Bank Arena, venue for the 2023 Eurovision Song Contest. It was a prestigious site in a prime riverside location and the failure to relocate there was seen by most Everton fans as a lost opportunity.

Peter Johnson eventually sold his stake in the club to the Bill Kenwright consortium in 2009. That year, under fire from the fan pressure group Keep Everton In Our City, the club board dropped their proposal to move the ground out of the city to nearby Kirkby.

In December 2006, Everton joined the rush to move stadia to generate more income. The board announced the possibility of a move in conjunction with Knowsley Council and Tesco. The 50,000-seat stadium would be part of a £400m development. The club argued the move would develop the Everton FC brand, would take advantage of multi-use facilities and would create a media-friendly stadium. It must also be said that the stadium would have enormously expanded the club's income. For Tesco, it would help construct a socially responsible corporate identity and build a brand community.

Showing a desire to consult the fans and being aware of a growing opposition to the out-of-city stadium concept, Everton chairman Kenwright announced a ballot and the fans conducted a fierce debate. A grassroots organisation, Keep Everton In Our City, was formed and lobbied private and public institutions in the local area and wider region.

In August 2008, the secretary of state for communities and local government, Hazel Blears, ruled that the proposals breached local and regional planning policy and ordered a public inquiry.

In November 2009, as a result of the inquiry, Blears's successor, John Denham, agreed that the project breached local and regional area planning policy and would encourage business away from the city centre. The proposal was dropped and the club committed itself to finding a new site in the city.[5]

At the same time, the club were also examining a possible ground share with Liverpool FC on

Stanley Park. The project received the enthusiastic support of the then-City Council leader Warren Bradley, as the stadium would be part of England's bid to host the 2018 World Cup.[6] The project was never popular with a majority of both sets of supporters. The project was finally quashed in 2016 when Liverpool announced plans for its new main stand, showing that its owners, the Fenway Group, were committed to redeveloping Anfield rather than building a completely new stadium.[7]

Mindful of the failure of all previous proposals to gain the support of the fans, Everton FC was careful to adopt a much more consultative approach to the proposal to relocate the club's ground to the Bramley-Moore dockside site. Revealingly, the new stadium project was called 'The People's Project' by the club, which intended to undergo extensive fan consultation to prevent the previous mistakes in the search for a new stadium.

In October 2018, the club announced a two-stage public consultation process about moving to the new ground. The first three-week consultation started on 15 November that year. This took the form of a series of exhibitions across Liverpool. The second stage came in the summer of 2019 when the club submitted detailed plans including homes, health and business facilities.[8] Everton's then-chief executive Denise Barrett-Baxendale said: 'This consultation marks a very significant moment as we progress with this project. We would like as many people as possible – and not just football fans – to take part and let us know their views.'[9]

The club received 43,000 responses to the second-stage consultation, which was believed to be the largest commercial undertaking in the city's history. It also had 20,000 responses to its first-stage consultation. The second-stage tour events were attended by 15,000 people including 2,726 non-Everton fans, 24 per cent of whom had no interest in football. Overall, 98 per cent of respondents supported the club's plans.[10]

The consultation process was praised by independent outsiders such as Chris Daly, the head of the Chartered Institute of Marketing, who said: 'Strong brands put their customer at the heart of everything they do, and Everton's stadium consultation is a shining example of this. The club has not assumed, but asked fans what it is they want, inviting Evertonians and the wider public alike to play a meaningful part in the process.'[11]

The consultation process also won awards. In November 2019, 'The People's Project' was named as the 'best property and construction campaign' at the Northern Marketing Awards.[12] In 2020, it won the 'stakeholders in planning' category at the National Planning Awards.[13]

'The People's Project' was unanimously supported by Liverpool City Council's planning committee and was later approved at government level when, in March 2021, secretary of state for housing, communities and local government, Robert Jenrick, gave it the green light.

On 31 May 2017, Liverpool City Council announced that it had voted in favour of a special purpose vehicle company acquiring the land and leasing the stadium, which in turn would be subleased back to the club for 200 years.[14]

In March 2022, the club announced that it would no longer receive funding from the council and that it had alternative funding. Two months later, it paid back £502,000 of the £841,000 costs the council had incurred in exploring the loan.[15]

In the meantime, the club got on with the stadium's construction, which began in September 2021 with the draining of the dock through the depositing of silt from the Irish Sea.

One possible snag occurred in July 2021 when UNESCO announced that the building of the stadium, along with other dockside developments, would end Liverpool's status as a World Heritage site. However, despite this, the stadium continued to be built with the support of local political authorities.[16]

At the time of writing, despite numerous questions about future funding, the stadium continues its rise above the River Mersey, apparently on schedule to be finished in December 2024 for opening at the start of the 2025/26 season. By mid-February 2024, the stadium was structurally complete, with the final concrete terracing panel being installed.[17]

The financing of the stadium has been a complicated story, despite the original utterances of club owner Farhad Moshiri in 2019 that: 'I'll throw as much money as needed. It is no luxury; we have to get it done. If we want to have a big club, we need a modern stadium and we will get it.'[18] By April 2022, he had contributed £100m for the enabling works (the dock infill and preparatory work).[19]

Initially, the club had a £30m naming rights option with Moshiri's business partner, Alisher Usmanov. However, this was cancelled due to his sanctioning in March 2022 following the Russian invasion of Ukraine.[20]

In 2017, the city council agreed to partly fund the stadium through acting as guarantors for £280m – expected to rise to £500m. In January 2018, city mayor Joe Anderson proposed to borrow £280m from the city's public loans work board and lend it to Everton. Ultimately this plan was dropped by both council and club as it was found to be unworkable and undesirable to both parties.[21]

By June 2023, it was announced that the cost of building the new stadium had risen by 50 per cent and the search was on for new investors to secure the completion of the building contract. It seemed to come down to one of two American finance companies – MSP Sports Capital or 777 partners. The former was in negotiations for a 25 per cent stake in the club and had already provided a loan which would secure £100m in funding, which could later be converted into shares.[22]

By August 2023, MSP Sports Group withdrew its offer for a 25 per cent stake in the club after its bid was opposed by one of the club's existing lenders, Rights and Media Funding Ltd from Cheshire. However, MSP's £100m loan to the club would remain, but not as convertible debt.[23] The money was expected to give the club breathing space to ensure an allocated budget for the new stadium, as well as freeing resources for general funding. It was also expected that some of the money would be used to repay a loan of £40m from AJ Bell.[24]

The withdrawal of MSP paved the way the following month for the club to be taken over by 777 Partners, subject to approval by the Premier League, the FA and the Financial Conduct Authority. This time, there was no opposition from Rights and Media Funding. It was understood that it gave the club interim financial funding, and the deal would see Moshiri cut his ties with the club after seven tumultuous years.[25]

It seems that 777 calculated that the media rights for the Premier League were likely to double in ten years. This was in stark contrast to the other European clubs where 777 had an interest. In Italy, Genoa's share of a recent media rights offer shrank while in France, Red Star FC had to be part of a re-tendering process when no firms came forward with the desired $1bn rate.[26]

The takeover was controversial given that 777 already had stakes in other European clubs, some of whom had seen fan protests opposing 777 investment. At Hertha Berlin and Standard Liege, the protestors alleged that 777 had had a negative effect on both the running and competitiveness of the teams. The former *Daily Star* journalist Paul Brown even claimed that he had yet to speak to anyone in football who believed the group had the capability of running a Premier League club and that it may be more interested in adding value to its portfolio rather than in owning Everton.[27]

In response to growing fan concerns at Everton, the group sent them a message of reassurance in October 2023. According to a post on the fansite Royal Blue Mersey, it seemed to have a degree of success. The nine-paragraph statement hit all the right notes as far as Evertonians would be concerned, talking about *Z Cars*, the fans' incredible support and using words like 'effort' and 'accountability', terms that many fans claimed could not be associated with the previous regime.[28] The group initially gave the club £81m towards the cost of the stadium building. This was expected to reach £100m by the time the takeover was completed.[29] Should the deal not go through, there were, according to former chief executive Keith Wyness, 'investment groups out there, that I know of, who are interested in the club and in the stadium asset'. He put particular emphasis on the stadium as being of interest to future investors.[30]

By February 2024, the club takeover still had not been approved after 22 weeks of consideration, even though the much smaller 25 per cent stake Sir Jim Ratcliffe acquired in Manchester United had been approved after only a month and a half. In the meantime, the club were becoming more dependent on life support loans from 777. One of the possible causes of this delay was the sustained negative publicity surrounding 777. Throughout all this, 777 honoured its commitment to keep the club afloat.[31]

On Friday, 17 November 2023, Everton learned they had been hit with a ten-point deduction by the Premier league (this was subsequently reduced to six points). According to Dave Powell of the *Liverpool Echo*, this was unlikely to deter 777 partners from its purchase of the club as the group had already 'priced in' all potential penalties and points deductions. He did recognise that the price 777 would have to pay for the club may now be subject to change, presumably a lowering.[32] However, an article two days later by Simon Mullock in the *Sunday Express* claimed that the penalty could prompt 777 to walk away from the takeover.[33]

The penalty was caused by the club breaching the maximum debt levels clubs were allowed by the Premier League for the 2021/22 season. The debt of £124.5m was higher than the £105m allowed. The cost of borrowing to finance the new stadium was a key factor in breaking these limits. The club believed that there were some key mitigating factors behind the debt level, such as having to pull out of a lucrative naming rights deal for the stadium with Alisher Usmanov's USM company after the Russian invasion of Ukraine. They also believed that the loans taken out to finance the stadium build should not count in the penalty, as infrastructure projects sat outside the Premier league's profit and sustainability rules. Consequently, the club appealed against the penalty.[34]

The appeal was successful in clawing back four of the lost points. By May 2024, after Everton were hit with a further two-point deduction relating to financial breaches for the 2022/23 season, 777 partners remained in play but had still not received Premier League approval. The 'miracle week' in late April 2024 of three successive victories, including a 2-0 derby victory over Liverpool, saved Everton's Premier League status and things appeared to be looking up for the club and their future stadium. However, concerns about 777 were magnifying and there was even talk of the club going into administration. An article by Matt Slater of *The Athletic* which summarised a report on 777 by the London investment firm Leadenhall even concluded that: 'This must surely be the end of 777's almost eight-month attempt to complete its purchase of Everton, and very possibly the end of 777, too.'[35]

The report documented that 777 and its associated companies were the subject of 16 different lawsuits over unpaid debts totalling $130m. Leadenhall itself claimed it was owed $600m by the group. It also alleged that the group owed a further $2bn to strategic insurance investor A-CAP.[36]

This report led to the Everton FC Shareholders' Association insisting that majority shareholder Farhad Moshiri recognise that '777 Partners are not fit and proper prospective owners of the club'.[37] According to *Liverpool Echo* journalist Joe Thomas, the Leadenhall report added further pressure on the Premier League whose decision on this case 'will be viewed as a landmark decision and come under heavy scrutiny by lawmakers debating whether it can operate in the best interests of the sport'.[38] Concerns over this report led to Moshiri having a face-to-face meeting with 777. The club subsequently announced that, should the deal with 777 partners collapse by the end of May – an increasingly likely occurrence – plans were in place to progress alternative scenarios.[39]

Later in the month, much of 777's international stable appeared to be in serious financial circumstances, with late payments from 777 causing extreme disquiet among fans at clubs under its ownership. Belgian club Standard Liege were hit with a transfer ban, Vasco da Gama of Brazil had their 777 ownership overturned by a judge and Germany's Hertha Berlin were struggling to recover after being relegated from the Bundesliga. Even among 777's more successful acquisitions, there were significant issues, with Italian club Genoa being docked a point due to tax irregularities and 777 facing mounting anger from fans of Red Star Paris.[40] The group's football assets in Belgium were seized by a Belgian court due to non-payment of a second payment owed to Standard Liege, which had led to non-payment of players' wages in April. In Brazil, the two 777 members on the board of Vasco da Gama were removed from the board due to a court order. In April, the 777-backed Australian budget airline Bonza entered voluntary administration and ceased operating.[41]

A more positive development, in late May 2024, was the apparent interest in Everton from the US digital media entrepreneur John Textor. His successful companies were worth $9bn and he seemed to have had equal success with his football investments in three global clubs. Botafogo of Rio de Janeiro were having their third successive season in the Brazilian top flight, Lyon had just finished sixth in France's Ligue 1 to qualify for the Europa League and, crucially, Textor's 45 per cent stake in Crystal Palace had paid off, with the London club achieving their joint highest Premier League finish of tenth place. Textor had expressed dissatisfaction with being unable to be the controlling influence at Palace and voiced a desire to have such influence at another Premier

League club. He expressed a vocal preference for Everton:

'Everton represents the best of English football: the struggles, the glory, the *want*. I love that it's out of London. Everybody should want to buy Everton right now. That kind of club is what I'm referring to. How great would it be to take one of these great English clubs back to sort of glory?'[42]

Firstly, he would have needed to sell his Palace stake, which might not have been possible in the timescale, with the 777 Partners bid expiring by the end of the month. He was also still keen on gaining a controlling influence over Palace.[43]

By the start of June 2024, after the 777 partners deal deadline had expired, *The Athletic* journalist Matt Slater believed that the two most likely scenarios for Everton were entering administration or the club's main creditors taking control. If the club went into administration, it would incur an automatic nine-point deduction, effective from the start of the 2024/25 season – potentially precipitating the nightmare scenario of inaugurating the new stadium in the Championship. Another key argument against going down this route was that Laing O'Rourke, the contractor building the stadium, would almost certainly have insisted on a clause requiring the club to renegotiate its contract in the event of the club going into administration. This would have substantially pushed up the remaining building costs. For these reasons, Slater believed that the most likely scenario was for the club's main creditors to take control. MSP Sports Capital had the right to seize 51 per cent of Everton's shares from Moshiri for 777's failure to repay the £158m loan it made to Everton the previous summer.

However, they could have done this already and had so far not done so. There was also a possibility that the Cheshire-based company Rights and Media Funding could bid for the shares – or that there could be a joint bid from the two companies.[44]

By early June 2024, according to *Liverpool Echo* journalists Joe Thomas and Dave Powell, the battle to take control of the club was between MSP Sports Capital and the Everton-supporting millionaire duo of Andy Bell and George Downing. However, the proposed bid from major Crystal Palace shareholder John Textor was also a possibility. The latter bid was jeopardised by his need to divest himself of his shareholding in the Selhurst Park club.[45] Bell's Blythe Capital played a role in the securing of funding for the stadium in 2023 and both he and Downing were prominent in MSP Sports Capital's bid for a 25 per cent stake in the club. Bell's commitment to the club could be judged by his setting up of a new vehicle called Toffee Venture, which was a private company listed with Companies House as a business within the bracket of sports and recreation education. Downing's commitment to the city could be seen by his company taking over the historic Port of Liverpool building, one of the city's waterfront Three Graces buildings, at which he was implementing a multi-million-pound restoration.[46] The joint bid was also apparently being backed by Michael Dell, the tenth richest man in the world worth about £120bn, according to *Times* journalist Paul Joyce, who claimed talks between the pair and the club were at an advanced stage.[47]

By now, John Textor was apparently out of contention due to the difficulties he faced in selling his Crystal Palace shares. However, *Bloomberg* reported that the situation remained fluid and that Textor should not be completely ruled out of the race.[48] The situation also became more complicated with the apparent interest in the club from Roma owner Dan Friedkin, who had a fortune of £4.8bn.[49] Yet another bid was received from London-based businessman Vatche Manoukian, who was fronting a rumoured

£400m offer to buy the club. The bid reportedly involved several international investors, including a member of the Saudi royal family. This offer was an all-equity one which would not take on additional debt, thereby aiming to create a sustainable long-term strategy.[50] By mid-June, the bid by 59-year-old US billionaire Friedkin appeared to be the clear frontrunner. He was said to be on the brink of signing an exclusivity deal with the club. News of this bid appeared to prompt the Manoukian group to pull out of the race. It posted the following statement:

'Everton fans deserve to be competing for trophies once again and we hope this deal delivers success for the club on and off the pitch. I want to thank our world-class investors for their support and we are excited to turn our focus to new opportunities to take great clubs to the next level.'[51]

According to the *Goodison News* website, Friedkin, unlike 777 Partners, wouldn't encounter any problems in passing the Premier League's owners' and directors' test due to his successful four years of running AS Roma, the Italian club having won the Europa Conference League in 2022 before then reaching the last four of the Europa League in successive seasons, finishing as runners-up in 2023.[52]

On 21 June, the club announced that the Friedkin Group had been granted a period of exclusivity to progress discussions with a view to acquiring a majority shareholding in the club. This was expected to take between 30 and 60 days but could be extended if required. There was no guarantee that the deal would go through, particularly in view of the three previous deals with Maciek Kaminski, MSP Sports Capital and 777 Partners failing to complete.[53] However, the Friedkin Group, unlike 777 Partners, had a proven track record in football. It also had a reputable financial background that was easy to access. This, according to the Everton correspondent for the *Liverpool Echo*, Joe Thomas, would all help the Friedkin Group pass the Premier League's owners' and directors' test.[54] If this bid went through, which most informed commentators believed would happen, the future of the stadium seemed to have been secured, with the first home Premier League game to be staged in August 2025. Clear demonstrable proof of the veracity of this statement happened four days later when one of Friedkin's companies, TDF Capital, took a charge against the new stadium. This signified that the old MSP loan for the stadium build had been repaid, with TDF acting as security agent for the transaction, with the new stadium as collateral for the loan. This deal was significant, as failure by 777 Partners to repay the MSP loan had been a key factor in the Premier League refusing to agree to its proposed takeover of the club.[55]

According to *Liverpool Echo* journalist Chris Beesley, Friedkin was likely to feel that Everton was actually in a stronger position than Roma, due to the respective progress of the two clubs' new stadia. Bramley-Moore was six months from completion when Friedkin was given exclusivity over Everton. However, the proposed new Roma stadium, despite being planned two and a half years before Bramley-Moore, had not got off the ground due to opposition from the local political authorities. Ironically, the new Roma stadium plans were the work of US architect Dan Meis, the designer of the new Everton stadium.[56]

On 19 July 2024, there was a fresh twist in the takeover saga when the Friedkin Group pulled out due to concerns over the financial exposure the club had to 777 Partners, who Dave Powell, writing in the *Liverpool Echo*, described as a 'stricken investment firm'. The Friedkin Group was particularly concerned about several legal cases 777 was involved in, some including allegations of fraudulent activity, and that A-CAP was wanting to reduce its exposure to 777. However, the Friedkin Group was insistent it was not in a rush to seek repayment by the club of the money spent on repaying the MSP loan.[57]

In mid-August, it was reported that the club appeared to have turned full circle, returning to John Textor and giving him a period of exclusivity with a view to a future purchase of the club.[58] One would assume that he was thoroughly prepared to resolve the issues left by the 777 group.

Finally, though, in late September, the situation appeared to be resolved. The Friedkin Group issued a joint statement with Farhad Moshiri's Blue Heaven Group. With the two parties apparently prepared to put aside their previous concerns about the outstanding 777 Partners' debt, it was announced that the Friedkin Group had acquired the 94.1 per cent of the club owned by Moshiri. The deal was subject to approval from the Premier League, the FA and the Financial Conduct Authority. *Business of Football* writer Dave Powell predicted the Friedkin Group would have no problems in passing these tests and would have the funds to complete the deal.[59] Throughout the preceding months, it had been clear that the Friedkin Group was the best placed financially to take on the club and there was no stumbling block like the one Textor faced regarding his shareholding in Crystal Palace. Friedkin, who made his fortune in the car industry, was financially secure, having recently been listed by Forbes as the 383rd richest person in the world. Encouragingly for Everton fans, since taking ownership of AS Roma in 2020, the Friedkin Group had invested £830m in the Italian club, helping them to compete at the top end of Serie A and to enjoy success in Europe.[60] Now, with the announcement of the Friedkin deal, both the future of Everton Football Club and the development of the new stadium appeared to have been secured.

JOHN BRAMLEY-MOORE –
THE EPITOME OF A SLAVER

IN AUGUST 2021, after several months of painstaking work in preparing Bramley-Moore Dock for the building of Everton's new stadium, the club announced they would be creating a memorial on the site highlighting the dock's historical connections with the slave trade. It was this history which was behind the decision not to name the club's new ground the Bramley-Moore Dock Stadium.[61]

A club spokesman commented: 'What happened across Liverpool in terms of slavery should not be airbrushed out of the city. It is a huge part of our history and we have to face up to that. You only have to look around the docks, the neoclassical and the Georgian buildings around the city, to see that. There is an absolute desire from Everton to ensure what happened is commemorated in some form, whether that's a plaque or in the hydraulic tower at the docks, which will be a visitor centre.'[62]

Dr Joe Mulhern, who has written extensively about the Brazilian slave trade, including John Bramley-Moore's involvement, has welcomed the Everton's decision to commemorate the stadium's links with slavery:

'I hope it will lead to more awareness of the city's connections to slavery including those, as in the case of Bramley-Moore, which lasted long beyond the abolition of slavery in the British Empire in 1833.'[63]

Liverpool Museums also welcomed Everton's announcement over a memorial and their historian in residence, Lawrence Westgaph, commented:

'It's really positive that Everton will be highlighting the links of Liverpool and the history of slavery. Football hasn't had the best history with incidents of racism. Things aren't perfect but it has come a long way since those dark days. It is absolutely fantastic to hear this news from Everton.'[64]

Everton's decision to include a memorial on the new stadium site was the latest example of the city recognising an unsavoury chapter in its history. In 1994, Liverpool's Maritime Museum in the Albert Dock created a specific section dedicated to Liverpool's role in the slave trade. By the millennium, growing interest in this section led to a specific Museum of Slavery being set up in 2007.

So, who exactly was John Bramley-Moore and what part did he play in the history of the city? In 1846, Bramley-Moore was the chairman of the Liverpool Town Council dock committee which convinced the council to finance the construction of new docks to the north of the city's existing dock area. The biggest of these would be called the Bramley-Moore Dock.[65]

John Bramley-Moore was born in Leeds in 1800. As a young man, he spent time as a merchant in South America, marrying Seraphina Hibernia Pennell, daughter of the British consul general for Brazil.[66] When he was in Brazil, he was initially only known as John Moore, only adding Bramley in 1841. There seems to be some evidence that the name change was deliberately made to enhance the status of the relatively low-born John Moore and seal the marriage.[67]

He had arrived in Brazil in 1820 and quickly set up an import-export business. Unlike in England, where slavery had been banned in 1807, slavery was still legal in Brazil and was flourishing at this time. In the 1820s alone, slave traders forcibly trafficked more than 500,000 Africans to Brazil to work as slaves on plantations and in a range of rural and urban contexts. Aside from trading in slave-worked exports such as sugar and coffee, Bramley-Moore himself was a slave owner, making use of forced labour in both his commercial establishment in the centre of the city and on his 'extensive and prettily situated' country estate (*chácara*) at Alto da Boa Vista, a property containing 5,000 coffee bushes.[68] The estate was situated a few miles inland from Rio de Janeiro, a city where two million captive slaves arrived between the 16th and 19th centuries. In 1996, during renovations of a family home, an 18th century burial pit was discovered containing the bones of 30,000 bodies of slaves who didn't survive the two-month journey across the Atlantic to Rio de Janeiro. It is now the site of the Memorial of the New Blacks, a research centre and museum to preserve the history of slavery in Rio de Janeiro.[69] Despite slavery being abolished in Brazil by 1831, an extensive illegal trade existed until the mid-19th century. British firms – including Moore's – were actively involved in this illegal trade, as the historian Joe Mulhern documented:

'British firms played a central role in the resurgence of the trade through the supply of manufactured goods on lengthy credit terms, which allowed the traffickers to make repayment on the return of their clandestine voyages. These arrangements were so lucrative to British merchants, many with branch houses in Liverpool, that it caused HM Chargé D'Affaires in Rio to admit in 1839 that "very many, nay most of our countrymen in Brazil, are more or less openly, advocates and supporters of the slave trade".'[70]

In 1835, Bramley-Moore left Brazil and was back in Liverpool. However, his company continued in Brazil and, according to Mulhern, it had one of the clearest links with slavery of any British firm. In 1839, it signed an attestation of good character to Manoel Pinto da Fonseca, who had already organised slave traffic and would go on to be one of the most notorious slave traders in the 1840s. Mulhern documents a later incident which could have endangered the firm's fortune:

'The most flagrant example of Bramley-Moore's complicity in the illegal slave trade.

though, was the capture in March 1840 of the *Guiana* by a Royal Navy cruiser off the coast of West Africa. The *Guiana*, part owned by Bramley-Moore and another Liverpool merchant, was then taken to Sierra Leone, where it was condemned by the vice-admiralty court for aiding and abetting the slave trade. The court's suspicions were well-founded; the vessel had been chartered by well-known *traficante* Manoel Francisco Lopes while at Bahia, where John Moore & Co had an office, with the intention of supplying the "coast goods" typically employed in the illegal trade.'[71]

However, this incident did little to hinder Bramley-Moore's political career. By 1841, only a year after the *Guiana* incident, he was elected to the town council and became a member of the dock committee, subsequently being elected chairman, which gave him considerable power.[72] In fact, within a year, he embarked on the dock project which would bear his name. As chairman of the committee, he was deputed to negotiate with Lord Derby for the purchase of the land two and a half miles north of the city centre to allow the building of six docks.[73] Both in his council role and as a Conservative MP – he was elected in 1854 – he continued to promote trade with Brazil, which was still heavily involved with slavery. He was also chairman of the Liverpool Brazilian Association.[74] His party politics were clearly illustrated by his attitude to the Chartist movement – which campaigned for greater rights for the working class at the time – when, in 1848, he discharged 600 dock labourers who had refused to be enrolled as special constables to combat Chartism.[75]

Bramley-Moore was far from the only prominent Liverpool politician involved in the slave trade. In fact, one of the two owners of the first recorded slave ship, *The Merchant*, to depart from Liverpool in December 1699 for West Africa (probably Angola) was William Clayton, who would go on to become lord mayor of Liverpool and an MP.[76]

However, when questioned, Bramley-Moore always denied links with slavery. He was aware that it would have damaged his career had his involvement in the trade become widely known. Bramley-Moore maintained an unsullied public reputation to the extent that the satirical magazine *Porcupine* named him, after he achieved the go-ahead for the dock extension, as 'the ablest, or at any rate, the most enterprising and successful dock chairman Liverpool ever had'.[77]

There is a feeling within the city that Bramley-Moore's name and his true role in Liverpool's history has been hidden to some extent. Simon Hughes, the Merseyside football writer for *The Athletic*, feels that this is because he didn't rise to the heights of another Liverpool politician, William Gladstone, and become prime minister. Jimi Jayne, a black writer who grew up in Toxteth, suspects it is part of the city playing down its links with slavery.[78] However, Hughes and Jayne agree that the club has an opportunity, and an obligation, to educate people about the city's history of slavery. Hughes fears that the lack of a current permanent name for the stadium may lead to local people calling it the Bramley-Moore Stadium, which could lead to similar protests seen in Bristol when the Edward Colston statue was thrown into the river.[79]

Everton Football Club are aware of the stadium site's links with slavery. They have no plans to keep the name Bramley-Moore and are planning to have these links remembered in the hydraulic tower and engine room, which is being restored as part of the new stadium development. There are plans for a visitor centre within the building or, at the very least, a plaque commemorating the site's links with slavery.[80]

Others would like the club to go further, with features such as a commemorative walkway being incorporated into the development. Jimi Jayne feels that the club have a unique opportunity as a potential major local influencer to educate the local public on the slavery issue.[81]

The next chapter will look at the wider history of Liverpool as a port, including the opening of the Bramley-Moore Dock in 1848. It depicts a city growing rich off the profits of illegal slavery, from which John Bramley-Moore successfully kept a public distance. The city continued to thrive, often, although not exclusively, from the products of the slave trade, such as the importation of cotton and tobacco from the plantations of the southern states of the USA for the Lancashire cotton mills and Liverpool tobacco factories, as well as from sugar produced on West Indian plantations and imported to famous Liverpool factories such as Tate & Lyle. Other products, such as coal imports, that the Bramley-Moore Dock was centrally involved in were the products of the British Industrial Revolution, itself often financed from the earlier slave trade. Other aspects of the docks' expansion, such as emigration and the luxury passenger trade, were developed due to the growth of the US economy.

HISTORY OF THE PORT OF LIVERPOOL

THE CITY began life as a tidal pool off the River Mersey. It was probably called the 'lifer pool', meaning 'muddy pool'. It wasn't mentioned in the Domesday Book but was founded by King John as a port in 1207. England had recently conquered Ireland and he needed a port to send men and supplies across the Irish Sea. He later built Liverpool Castle to protect the town. The port imported some wine from France, but the main trade was with Ireland, importing hides and skins and exporting iron, salt and wool.[82]

In medieval England, Liverpool wasn't regarded as a great port. During Edward I's reign

(1272-1307), it was recorded that Bristol had 26 ships, Hull 16 and Liverpool only one.

Initially, Liverpool's growth as a port owed a lot to the salt trade. Many of the future slave traders, such as the Ashton family, had acquired salt works or traded in salt before becoming involved in the slave trade. John Ashton's investment in the Sankey Canal in the 1750s allowed more coal to be brought to his salt works. Crude brine salt was made in Liverpool as early as 1611. Salt was also used as part of an earlier triangular trade with the West Indies as it was exported to Newfoundland to use in the cod fisheries. Some of the fish was exported to the West Indies in exchange for rum, tobacco and sugar. Thus, the pattern was set for the future slave trade.[83]

In 1666, a ship called *The Antelope* left Liverpool, loaded with linen, nails and coal. It sailed way beyond the port's normal furthest shores of Spain and Portugal. A year later, she entered the port loaded with sugar cane from Barbados. This voyage started the port's long association with the Americas and the sugar trade. It is worth saying that the slave trade changed goods imported into Liverpool, like sugar and tobacco, from being luxury items to those accessible to the whole population.

Liverpool first gained an entry to the West Indies market through its supply of Manchester cloth goods to the Spanish colonies, therefore bypassing the 300 per cent tax paid for equivalent goods from Spain.[84] In the early days, this just meant that British goods such as herring, beef, horses, butter and Kendal cotton were traded for sugar. The plantations were initially manned by British slaves, who were sent there to work. These included criminals, orphans and even 800 West Country supporters of the Duke of Monmouth's 1688 'Glorious Revolution', who were 'exported' by Judge Jeffreys. A typical white slave would be an 'indentured' white servant who, in return for a free passage and a strip of land, bound themselves to work for the plantation owners.[85]

The first actual slave ship recorded to have sailed from Liverpool was *The Blessing* in 1700. She sailed to Guinea and then discharged 220 black slaves in Barbados. There, the ship loaded up with sugar, cottons and ginger.[86]

In 1709, the world's first commercial wet dock was created in the form of the Old Dock, originally the Thomas Steers Dock.[87] The wet dock involved encasing the pool in stone while the upper reaches were filled in.[88] When it opened in 1716, it allowed ships to be unloaded in a day and a half, significantly undercutting the old process of unloading old boats at sea into smaller boats to transport the cargo to shore, a process which could take up to two weeks. Soon, the dock was oversubscribed, which led to the rapid construction of newer and larger docks for a growing size of ship.[89] The petitioning of parliament for the building of the dock was undertaken by Sir Thomas Johnson, who is sometimes referred to as 'the founder of modern Liverpool'. He was elected mayor in 1695 and became an MP in 1701. He was also one of the city's slave trade pioneers, financing some of the earliest slave voyages and being involved in the 'Viginia Trade' of slave-produced tobacco. He gives his name to the current St Thomas Street.[90]

The dock allowed Liverpool to become a great port in the 18th century. In the early 18th century, the writer Daniel Defoe commented: 'Liverpool has an opulent, flourishing and increasing trade to Virginia and English colonies in America. They trade round the whole island (of Great Britain), send ships to Norway, to Hamburg and to the Baltic, as also to Holland and Flanders.'[91] Calling at Liverpool in 1770 whilst touring some of the northern counties, Arthur Young, described Liverpool docks as 'far superior to any mercantile ones in Britain'.[92]

The port's success was also helped when the Sankey Canal – and, later, the Leeds and Liverpool Canal – threw open the Lancashire coalfields to Liverpool. The trade with the West Indies and, eventually, America led to the dramatic growth of the port. By 1752, there were 124 ships trading with America and the West Indies, 88 with Africa and 125 with Ireland.[93] In the 18th century, the port was intimately involved in slavery. The pattern of trade was documented by Liverpool historian Ken Pye, who described how goods like pottery, jewellery, fabric and knives would be traded for slaves in West Africa. The survivors of the journey to the West Indies would then be exchanged for rum, cotton, tobacco and sugar cane. The latter products would then be shipped back to Liverpool and reprocessed and sold to the rest of Britain and the Empire.[94]

Liverpool developed this trade because of its proximity to the sort of goods that sold well in Africa such as textiles from Lancashire and Yorkshire, brass, copper and pottery from Staffordshire and guns from Birmingham. Crucially, its merchants also developed the expertise for dealing with African traders on the West African coast.

The trade then dramatically increased during the 18th century, as depicted in an article by Liz Stewart, the lead curator of archaeology and the historic environment at the Liverpool Museum:

'For Liverpool merchants, of course, success was often at huge human cost: much of the mercantile trade involved the trade in enslaved African people, abducted in West African countries and forcibly transported across the Atlantic. Through the 18th century, around 200 merchants controlled this trade in Liverpool and a further 1,400 invested in them or were employed through them. A wider network of mercantile activity was built on slavery and the products of the work of enslaved people. Liverpool's economy was so intricately linked to slavery that, in 1806, it was described as "the metropolis of slavery". The first graving dock in Liverpool – which now no longer exists – was built in 1718 and was overseen by Richard Norris, who was a slave trader.'[95]

By 1750, Liverpool had overtaken both Bristol and London to be England's biggest slaver port. It had partly managed to do this through undercutting both ports in the sale price of slaves by paying their crews less and paying their sellers an annual salary rather than by the number of slaves sold; this made selling a more stable occupation. Faster sailing ships were also built on the Mersey, which extended Liverpool's dominance. The city was also helped by a 1750 Act of Parliament which allowed for its extension of the trade through the setting up of the African Company of Merchants.[96] When the African Company was formed to administer and control the British forts on the west coast of Africa, 100 Liverpool merchants paid the entrance fee. Many more joined later, although others chose not to.

F.E. Sanderson has also identified 200 Liverpool merchants who, between 1788 and 1807 had investments in the slave trade.[97] By the 1790s, it controlled 80 per cent of the British slave trade and 40 per cent of the European slave trade.[98] In total, almost 5,000 slaver ship voyages were made from Liverpool and carried something like 1.5m slaves.[99] By 1792, Liverpool had 131 transatlantic slave-trading ships compared with 22 operating from London and 42 from Bristol. This meant that one in five captured African slaves crossing the Atlantic were transported on ships based in Liverpool.[100] In 1797, the poet William Bagshaw Stevens wrote of Liverpool: 'Throughout the large built town, every brick is cemented to its fellow brick by the blood and sweat of negroes.'[101]

Liverpool's key role in the slave trade was commemorated on 23 August 2007 when it opened its International Slavery Museum at the Albert Dock. This date was specifically selected, as it marked the bicentenary of the Emancipation of Slavery Act.[102] In 2021, plans were announced to expand the museum as part of a ten-year plan to redevelop the city's waterfront. It will have a new entrance through the old Dock Traffic Office, now the Dr Martin Luther King Jr Building. The museum hopes that this will place it at the centre of national and global conversations about racial inequality and the legacies of transatlantic slavery. The site has a particular poignancy, as it was the site of the dry dock to fit out, clean and repair slave ships.[103] On 23 August 2024, the city marked the 25th anniversary of its annual Slavery Remembrance Day. It was part of a week-long programme of events which also coincided with the anniversary of the Haitian slave revolution of 22 August 1791. The most significant event on Slavery Remembrance Day was a Walk of Remembrance, which started at Williamson Square and weaved its way through the city.[104]

One of the most successful slave traders, Richard Watt, had sugar plantations in Jamaica and invested in slave voyages. At the time of his death, he was one of the richest men in the country with a fortune of more than £600,000. He started out as a carriage driver but was educated by his employer and eventually appointed to supervise a trip to Jamaica, where he settled and made his fortune.[105] He is commemorated with a memorial in the city's Anglican cathedral. He also purchased and renovated Speke Hall, which is now owned by the National Trust and is one of the finest Tudor mansions in the country.[106]

Many of the mayors, councillors and MPs of the city invested in the trade and profited from it. One three-time mayor, Thomas Leyland (1752-1827), was a banker and multi-millionaire who traded with Grenada, Jamaica, Barbados and Havana. He traded slaves for rum, sugar, palm oil, hides and indigo.[107] The city's key role in the slave trade is today still clearly illustrated at the city's town hall, with the *Historic England* website description of the Grade I Listed building noting:

'The building has an exterior decorative frieze showing African faces, elephants, crocodiles and lions – references to the slave trade where Liverpool gained much of its wealth. All of the city's mayors between 1787 and 1807 were involved in the slave trade.'[108]

In the 19th century, many of these elected public officials with links to the slave trade actively campaigned against the ultimately successful campaign to abolish it.[109] In 1788, Liverpool Council, under the influence of the slave ship owners, petitioned parliament to oppose a proposed bill on the better regulation of slave ships.[110] This campaign failed and, slavery was abolished, first in England in 1807 and then throughout the Empire in 1833.

Within parliament, one of the most vigorous opponents of abolition was William Gladstone, who was born in Liverpool, and became the Liberal prime minister in the late 19th century. He would later become a fierce anti-slaver.

Gladstone's father had made enormous sums of money from the slave trade, as explained by the *Historic England* website:

'John Gladstone (from 1764 to 1851) made his fortune investing in West Indian plantations. As a result, his wealth increased from £40,000 in 1799 to over £500,000 in 1828.

'John Gladstone began trading in sugar and cotton in 1803. He purchased several estates including the Belmont estate in Demerara, Guyana, and the largest one, Vreedenhoop, which had 430 slaves. Throughout the 1820s, John Gladstone ignored the growth of the anti-slavery movement.

'William Gladstone used his maiden speech in the House of Commons in 1833 to argue against the immediate emancipation of slaves. After 1834, when slavery was abolished, the Gladstone family received over £90,000 in compensation.'[111]

Gladstone successfully argued for compensation for his father's slave-owning business and received a very favourable deal for him, as explained in a 2021 article by journalist Sanchez Manning: 'He received £106,769 (modern equivalent £83m) for the 2,508 slaves he owned across nine plantations. His son, who served as prime minister four times during his 60-year career, was heavily involved in his father's claim.'[112]

In 2023, members of the Gladstone family travelled to the Caribbean and issued a public apology for the historical part that their ancestor played in the slave trade. They also indicated that they intended to contribute to a fund to pay for further research into the impact of slavery. Charlie Gladstone, William Gladstone's great, great grandson and president of Gladstone's Library in Hawarden, North Wales, said: 'John Gladstone committed crimes against humanity. He was greedy and domineering. We have no excuses for him.'[113]

The British government borrowed the staggering amount of 40 per cent of its GDP in the 1830s to compensate slave owners for the loss of property and earnings. This figure was only paid off in 2015 and is the equivalent of £17bn today.[114] In total, 46,000 slave owners were compensated. It amounted to the biggest compensation scheme in British history until the bailout of the banks in 2009. The slaves themselves received nothing and were compelled to provide another 45 hours of unpaid labour each week for a further four years after their liberation. They were effectively paying part of the bill for their freedom.[115]

Many of Liverpool's best-known streets are named after slave traders. One of the most famous is, of course, Penny Lane, which was immortalised by the Beatles in their 1967 hit single. It is widely believed that the street was named after the 18th century Liverpool slave trader James Penny who, in 1788, spoke out in favour of the trade to a parliamentary committee investigating it. His ships such as the *Mampookata*, *Count du Nord* and

Enterprise carried between 500 and 600 slaves[116] However, in 2020, the city's International Slavery Museum, after 'comprehensive research', concluded that there was no evidence linking the street name to James Penny. It is not clear where the street name did come from, but the museum is adamant that they uncovered no link to the slaver.[117]

Rodney Street was built between 1782 and 1801, housing many of the town's merchanting elite, including John Gladstone, who made his fortune in West Indian slave plantations.[118]

Joseph Brooks, the builder of the town hall, which was itself funded by the profits of slavery, also had a street named after him and Brooks Alley still exists today. Joseph Brooks was one of six family members actively engaged in slavery. His nephew, Joseph Jnr, owned one of the most infamous slave-trading vessels in history, *The Brooks*. It was immortalised by the Plymouth chapter of the society for effecting the abolition of the slave trade when it created a poster depicting the ship carrying its human cargo. The poster was in wide circulation at the end of the 18th century and played a part in the abolition campaign.

Prior to abolition, the evidence given by the ship's surgeon, Thomas Trotter, led to the act passed by parliament in 1789 which limited the number of slaves a ship could hold to 484.[119]

Parr Street is named after Thomas Parr, whose ship, *Parr*, was equipped to carry 700 slaves. It was reported to have exploded off the coast of West Africa in 1798, possibly due to carrying gunpowder in return for slaves. At 57 Parr Street, he built an elegant warehouse behind his townhouse and this was used to store iron, from which products were made and used to buy slaves.[120]

Many of these names, including Gladstone and Brooks, invested some of their wealth in founding the Liverpool Royal Institution in

1819, which was a forerunner institution of the University of Liverpool.[121]

In 2019, Liverpool City Council formally apologised for its role in the slave trade.[122] The following year, Liverpool mayor Joe Anderson identified the first 20 streets and squares in Liverpool which, having been named after people connected with slavery, would be recognised with plaques explaining their links. This was partly a reaction against some councillors requesting that the streets be renamed. Famous streets such as Bold Street, Renshaw Street and Clayton Square were on the list.[123] The first of the plaques was unveiled on William Brown Street in April 2021 outside Central Library. The city is also committed to erecting nine more plaques at sites including Bold Street, Parr Street and Tarleton Street, all of which were named after Liverpool traders involved in the slave trade.[124]

Interestingly, the general area of Bold Street is called the Ropewalks because the length of Bold

Street was used to measure rope for sailing ships, including those for the slave trade.[125]

The city's adviser on this policy, Lawrence Westgaph, while supporting the plaque scheme, wants the city to go a stage further and erect a memorial to the slave trade.[126] One city institution has already decided to try to eradicate its own links to slavery.

In 2022, the Blue Coat Grammar School decided to change the names of five of its six houses to remove the names of those connected to slavery – the names Blundell, Shirley, Graham, Bingham and Syth. These houses have been renamed, with one of them being named after prominent local historic anti-slavery campaigner William Roscoe. [127] Another institution, the University of Liverpool, decided in 2021 after a Black Lives Matter campaign by its students, to change the name of its Gladstone Hall to Kuya Hall in honour of Dorothy Kuya, who was the city's first community relations officer and helped establish the International Slavery Museum.[128]

In the early days of the slave trade, slaves were occasionally sold in shops, warehouses, coffee houses and on the steps of Custom House.[129] However, when slavery was abolished, many freed slaves, other black people and sons of African leaders chose to settle in the city, giving it the oldest black community in the country.[130]

Liverpool isn't the only slave trading port trying to cope with its historical heritage. The case of Bristol sprung to prominence in 2020 when protesters threw a statue, erected in 1895, of Edward Colston into the river. The statue was subsequently recovered and it is planned to exhibit it in a museum without removing the protestors' ropes and graffiti.[131] In the late 17th century, Colston was a senior executive in the Royal African Company which, at the time, held a monopoly in the English trade in African slaves. Prior to the statue incident, the charity which ran the city's large concert hall had already decided to change its name from the Colston Hall to the Bristol Beacon.[132] In November 2023, Bristol University announced that it would remove the dolphin emblem of Edward Colston from its logo. However, it wasn't prepared to rename some of its buildings named after businesses historically profiting from slave labour on its plantations, such as the tobacco company Wills and chocolate manufacturer Fry's. Other buildings retaining their names would be the Goldney Hall, named after a family who produced metal exchanged for slaves, and the Merchant Ventures building named after a guild that played an active role in the slave trade and included Edward Colston as one of its members. The university pledged £10m to 'address racial injustice' in the university and the city.[133]

A recent article in the *Glasgow Times* listed 62 streets and areas in the city with links to the slave trade. One of them was the Gallery of Modern

Art on Queen Street, which was formerly the home of Lord William Cunninghame, who had made a substantial fortune in the 18th century from the importation of tobacco from the southern US slave plantations.[134] In the summer of 2020, the statue of the Duke of Wellington situated in front of the old Cunninghame mansion had on its usual traffic cone-bedecked head the Black Lives Matter slogan and, in the surrounding streets, the names of slave traders were replaced with those of black activists, martyrs and Celtic Football Club supporters.[135] There were attempts to rename streets such as Buchanan and Dunlop, also named after tobacco companies profiting from the slave trade. There have been suggestions of having some of the George Square statues removed as at least ten of the 12 have some links with historic slavery including that of James Watt, who worked both with his father, who had business interests in the West Indies and North Carolina, and with his business partner, Matthew Boulton, whose joint production with Watt of steam engines was financed by slave-derived wealth and whose products were used on Caribbean plantations.[136] Boulton and Watt's factory was based in Birmingham where other factories supplied guns, neck collars and chains to slavers in the Americas.[137] By the early 1800s, Glasgow became known as the 'Second City' of the Empire, with much of its trade based on colonial trade from Caribbean sugar plantations. Two figures had played a key role in this trade. Colonel William Macdowell and Major James Milliken. In the early 18th century, Macdowell was described as 'the most notable figure in Glasgow'. Both he and Milliken had made their fortunes through the ownership of several sugar plantations in the West Indies. Macdowell eventually diverted the route of some of his sugar ships to Glasgow, where he bought shares in the South Sugar House. There is evidence that he was a particularly frugal planter, providing his slaves with little food and shelter. Consequently, many died from starvation when storms affected the importation of their main diet, imported slated herring from the Clyde.[138]

Newcastle, although much less involved in the slave trade, is also planning to rename two of its streets in the light of the Black Lives Matter protests. They are Blackett Street and Colston Street. There is some doubt, however, about whether the latter is named after Bristol slave trader Edward Colston.[139] In Plymouth in 2020, the council attempted to rename Hawkins Square, named after the slaver and explorer Jack Hawkins, and call it Jack Leslie Square in honour of a black footballer who played for Plymouth in the 1920s and 1930s. This proposal was withdrawn after a road near Plymouth Argyle's Home Park stadium was named in Leslie's honour. The latest proposal is to rename it Justice Square.[140]

In Hull, which was represented in parliament by the abolitionist William Wilberforce, the director of the Wilberforce Institute for the study of slavery and emancipation has argued for a strategy of using the place names to draw attention to the complexities of the issue.[141]

A similar strategy seems to have been adopted in London, where Mayor Sadiq Khan has committed £500m to develop a slavery memorial at West India Quay in the capital's Docklands. The area is home to warehouses that were built to receive the products of slavery, the only remaining buildings of their kind in the city. The money will also fund educational programmes related to the victims and their descendants in the city.[142]

However, it must be recognised that some of the Liverpool's prominent merchants were also active opponents of slavery. The Rathbone family, who had made their money in timber, and the packet steamer owner James Cropper joined lawyer William Roscoe and blind poet Edward Rushton in forming a group of prominent Liverpool anti-abolitionists. Rushton publicly sang about the plight of the slaves in the city and wrote West Indies eclogues about the iniquities of the slave trade. He had previously been a mate on a slave ship and became blind aboard it. He had a bookstore in the city and was shot at because of his anti-slavery sentiment.[143] In 1809, Roscoe and his friends rescued nine Portuguese slaves from a ship in the port and they later became free men.[144] In 1787, Roscoe wrote the poem 'The Wrongs of Africa' and donated to the newly formed Society for the Abolition of the African Slave Trade. The society claimed Liverpool made £300,000 annually from the slave trade.[145] Some of the anti-abolitionists also have their names commemorated in Liverpool today. One of my favourite Liverpool pubs, the Roscoe Head is named after William Roscoe and Rathbone Road is in the Wavertree district. There is also an argument to commemorate these names with street plaques. There is some evidence that they played a crucial role in the national abolition movement, as prominent national campaigners such as William Wilberforce and John Barton cultivated and valued their friendship.[146]

There was the occasional person with a foot in both camps. One of the most famous of these was John Newton, the author of the hymns 'Amazing Grace' and 'Glorious Things of Thee Are Spoken'. The former is closely associated with the African-American community in the USA, but it started out being penned by a slave captain. He lived in Liverpool between 1755 and 1764, although he was born in London. Before he came to Liverpool, he served as a mate on several slave ships. Whilst on board the Liverpool slave ship *The Brownlow*, he witnessed the horrific mistreatment of slaves. There is some evidence that Newton helped administer the cruelty. When the ship returned to Liverpool, he was promoted to captain of the slave ship *Duke of Argyle* and later *The African*. After he left seafaring due to illness, he became the tide surveyor living at Edmund Street in the city. Ironically, the UNESCO commemorative plaque at the site makes no mention of his role in the slave trade. It was during his time as tide surveyor that Newton seems to have had a spiritual conversion and he was subsequently ordained as an Anglican priest.[147] While he was a curate in Olney, he appears to have come under the influence of the anti-slavery poet William Cowper.[148] When he became rector of St Mary Woolnoth in London, he became an ally of the chief abolitionist, William Wilberforce MP. In 1788, he published his 'Thoughts Upon the Slave Trade', which was sent to every MP. In 1807, he lived just long enough to witness the passing of the act abolishing the international slave trade. He died in December of that year.[149] Full abolition of slavery didn't happen until 1833.

The research of F.E. Sanderson suggests that Liverpool recovered very quickly from abolition. Due to the diversification and expansion of trade which had begun in the late 18th century, the problems were shortlived.[150] One area of diversification in the early 19th century was the cotton trade from America to the mills of Manchester, which led to a further increase in trade, with more than 500 voyages being made a year to America by the 1840s.[151] This trade, at the time, was created by the slave owners of the American Deep South. One of the principal benefactors of this trade was William Brown, who was one the biggest importers of cotton; by 1844, he held one sixth of the total trade. He subsequently donated £40,000 for the building of the city's museum and public library, which now stand on William Brown Street, named after him.[152]

These buildings are just two of the numerous sites of the city's architecture to be financed by slavers. Alex Robinson gives a sense of the scale of this legacy:

'... public walks, crescents, and leisure gardens, ... churches, schools, theatres, the music hall, the first gentlemen's library, the Lyceum – they were all endowed by the merchant community within which the names of slave traders were prominent.'[153]

Ironically, in a city whose wealth stemmed from slavery and trade with the slave-owning American south, visiting American sailors such as the 19th century writer Herman Melville were surprised how racially tolerant the city was. He was amazed to see black American sailors arm in arm with white girls and that the only beggars were white and mainly Irish.[154]

This racial tolerance also calls into question the belief that Liverpool was a great supporter of the Confederacy during the American Civil War. The research of Jim Powell suggests that Liverpool had a more nuanced relationship with the Confederacy than is often assumed. In fact, political meetings in the city concerning the war were overwhelmingly supporting the North. It is true that the highest circulating newspaper, the *Liverpool Mercury*, did appear to support the Confederacy, but this appears to be no more than sharing the dominant view of the British press that the South would inevitably win. For Powell, the dominant view of Liverpool, as exemplified by the views of both of its MPs, was to support British neutrality. This also was the view of the British government and was endorsed several times during the war by the Liverpool Chamber of Commerce, despite it containing one of the leading propagandists for the South, James Spence. It is true that two ships were built on Merseyside for the Confederate navy. However, there is also some evidence that John Laird, whose company built one of the ships, was also considering building ships for the Union, as he submitted plans for their construction. Powell also questions the view that many Liverpool merchants were involved in blockade running by suggesting that much of it was done by American firms and, overall, it was a negligible trade.[155]

Nothing illustrates better the continuing success of Liverpool as a port city in the post-abolition era than the expansion of the docks including the opening of Bramley-Moore Dock in 1848. In John Bramley-Moore's speech to the Liverpool Town Council in January 1846, he outlined how the mid-19th century growth of trade at Liverpool eclipsed all the major ports in England at the time. Compared to the whole of the London docks from 1843 to 1845, Liverpool was shipping 383,819 tons of goods compared to London's 154,378 tons. It was also comfortably outstripping both Hull and Bristol, whose relative trade growths were less than a third and fifth respectively. There was also a corresponding growth of revenue, with £6,076 more taken in the final half of 1845 compared with the first half. In appealing to the entrepreneurial side of the council's leaders, he also highlighted that the railway companies, which would need to demolish existing buildings on the site, would contribute £68,000 of the proposed overall cost of £531,000. Only 246 houses needed to be pulled down to build the new dock Liverpool dock compared with 1,300 when St Katharine Dock was built in London. He also demonstrated that, with the dock committee's surplus of almost £100,000, it would be able to borrow up to £4m, more than enough to expand the docks. He recommended that the council apply for a bill to be approved and ratified by parliament to build the dock.[156]

The land was purchased from Lord Derby, as the 1796 map of Liverpool shows. Twelve months after Bramley-Moore's famous speech to the council, its dock committee gave its approval to the scheme and sealed the crucial expansion of the docks. Bramley-Moore Dock was opened on 4 August 1848 as part of the northern expansion of the Liverpool dockyards. Its area of water space was more than nine acres and its gates were 60ft wide.[157]

The expansion was supervised by Jesse Hartley, who was superintendent of the dock estate. In total, he oversaw the building of 17 new docks between 1830 and 1859.[158] On the same day in August 1848, the Nelson, Stanley, Collingwood and Salisbury docks were also opened. This was only two years after Prince Albert had opened the dock in his name situated more closely to the city centre.[159]

When the Bramley-Moore Dock opened, it was the most northerly part of the dock system. It was designed to accommodate the largest steamships of the era.[160] Its core trade was in coal. It exported coal from the South Lancashire coalfield and facilitated the use of some of this coal as bunker coal for steamships in port. A key reason why the coal trade increased so quickly was Liverpool being connected to the railways shortly after the opening of the Bramley-Moore Dock. The Lancashire and Yorkshire lines were both subsequently connected to the docks.[161] A spur of the railway was used to enable the transfer of coal from the trucks. A new bridge, which could be raised or lowered hydraulically, carried the line over the Dock Road. This was eventually replaced by the overhead dock railway.[162]

The dock was in operation for over 140 years. Because it was mainly used for the export of coal and the use of coal for steamships it explained the open plan nature of the site as there was no use for warehouses. The opening of the dock ensured that Liverpool would continue to be a dominant British port city for the next 100 years.[163]

In the 19th and early 20th century, Liverpool was the largest emigration port in the world. From 1830 to 1930, more than nine million emigrants sailed from Liverpool for a new life in the USA, Canada and Australia. Many of them came from mainland Europe including Scandinavians, Poles and Russians.[164] They would often travel via Hull, as it was often cheaper to travel from Liverpool than from a domestic port.[165] In the 1840s and 50s, Liverpool also became a port of transit for two million Irish people fleeing the potato famine and attempting to emigrate to

America. Tens of thousands of them could not afford to travel further than Liverpool and began to settle in slum-type conditions in Vauxhall and Kirkdale. This laid the basis for the large Catholic population in the city. Most of the immigrants came through Clarence Dock just to the north of the city. This spot is today commemorated with a small plaque.[166] On the plaque, the inscription reads: 'Throughout these dock gates passed most of the 1,300,000 Irish migrants who fled the great famine and "took the ship" to Liverpool in the years 1845-52. Remember the Great Famine.'[167]

The importance of Liverpool as a port was recognised in the 1850s when the government created the Mersey Docks and Harbour Board to oversee port activities. At its peak, the docks employed as many as 60,000 people and indirectly almost as many again in the processing and manufacturing industries created through the port's import trade, such as the Bryant & May match factory.[168] By this time, Liverpool was among the four greatest ports in the world and was handling a third of Britain's exports, double that of London, and a quarter of its imports. It owned a seventh of the world's registered shipping, creating a wealthy class of owners, merchants and bankers who lived in the burgeoning suburbs of the region and in the city where tidy rows of stone-stepped houses resembled Manhattan. Lord Street shops and St Johns Market stocked a wide selection of American goods and the city was known as 'the New York of Europe'.[169] Research by W.D. Rubinstein showed that at its peak (1880-99), Liverpool produced more millionaires than Greater Manchester, West Yorkshire, the West Midlands, Tyneside and East Anglia combined.[170]

The French historian Hippolyte Taine, who visited the Mersey docks in 1863, marvelled at their enormity, scope, and ingenuity: 'The spectacle of the Liverpool docks is, I think, one of the greatest in the whole world.'[171]

The author of *Moby Dick*, Herman Melville, wrote in his 1849 novel *Redburn*:

'In magnitude, cost and durability, the docks of Liverpool surpass all others in the world … for miles you may walk along that riverside. Passing dock after dock, like a chain of immense fortresses.'[172]

He had also previously compared the Liverpool docks to the Great Wall of China and the and the pyramids of the Pharaohs.[173]

When the Liver Building was opened in 1910, its clock mechanism was the largest in the world and its owner ate dinner on one of the clock faces before it was installed.[174] However, by the 1890s, the Liverpool docks began to decline. The chief cause of the decline was the narrow river basin, which increasingly failed to accommodate the larger iron and steel boats. More and more shippers turned away from Liverpool in favour of the of the UK's deeper and more modern ports. [175] One attempt to reverse this trend was the opening of Gladstone Dock in 1913, which was finally completed in 1927. It would be capable of accommodating the largest ships then to be constructed, as it had the largest area of enclosed water of any dock in the world.[176]

Liverpool has had a long history of transatlantic cruise liners. The first transatlantic passenger service started there in 1840 with the wooden paddle steamer *Britannia*, owned by Samuel Cunard.[177] At just 1,154 tons and carrying only 115 passengers, it could fit into the Britannia restaurant of today's *Queen Mary 2*.[178] Five years later, the port's pre-eminence in this market was sealed when IK Brunel's SS *Great Britain* made her maiden voyage to New York from Liverpool. It was an important voyage because the liner was propeller-driven, which set the pattern for every passenger ship which followed.[179] In the 1840s, the famous American author Nathaniel Hawthorne was based in Birkenhead whilst working at the American Consul in Liverpool.

He regularly observed transatlantic passenger services coming up the Mersey and he captured the vibrancy of the trade:

'Once a week comes a Cunard steamer, with its red funnel pipe whitened by the salt spray; and firing off some cannon to announce its arrival, she moors to a large iron buoy in the middle of the river … Immediately comes puffing towards her a little mail-steamer, to take away her mailbags, and such of the passengers who choose to land; and for several hours afterwards, the Cunarder lies with smoke and steam coming out of her, as if she were smoking a pipe after some toilsome passage across the Atlantic.[180]

It did host renowned liners like *The Lusitania*, *The Mauretania*, *The Aquitania* and the Canadian Pacific *Empress* liners.[181] On 7 May 1915, a German U20 submarine torpedoed *The Lusitania* en route from New York to Liverpool. Of the 1,959 passengers 1,195 perished. The sinking was crucial in bringing the USA into World War

One two years later.[182] *The Mauretania* and *The Lusitania* were Cunard's attempts to match the German kaiser class of ships, as well as those from the White Star Line. Both ships were the latest line in luxury. *The Mauretania* also won the blue ribbon award for the fastest transatlantic crossing and survived World War One before finally being scrapped in 1935.[183] Liverpool's intimate links with the transatlantic luxury passenger liners had already been illustrated in 1912 when the Titanic sank in the North Atlantic. The ship was owned by the White Star Line, which was based in Liverpool, and ten per cent of the crew came from the city.[184] White Star pioneered luxury travel from Liverpool when, in 1871, it introduced first-class cabins and dining saloons amidships so they were subject to less engine vibration.[185] At its height, the Liverpool landing stage was so busy that ships would literally be queueing in the Mersey to discharge and embark passengers. [186] My uncle and aunt emigrated to the USA in the late 1950s on a transatlantic passenger ship and returned on *The Sylvania* in the mid-1960s. The last voyage of *The Sylvania* to Liverpool was on 24 November 1966.[187].

In the 1960s, the Liverpool passenger trade entered a decline that was irreversible. As historian Adrian Jarvis noted, the port authorities were saddled with huge debts in building the Gladstone Dock earlier in the century.[188] In the long term, it failed to reverse the decline of Liverpool as a port. This decline was hastened post-World War Two by the growth of transatlantic air travel. By the late 1950s, aeroplanes were carrying more transatlantic passengers than ships were. The airlines were able to promote themselves as being cheaper overall than ships if the time factor was considered. Two other factors – the introduction of tourist fares and the regular use of faster jet engine planes – ensured that passengers would maximise their transatlantic trips compared to sailing. In 1958, in the first year of service for *The Sylvania*, she carried 1,036,000 passengers. However, this was also the first year of commercial jet airline services between Europe and the USA, with passenger numbers suffering accordingly. In 1966, the chairman of Cunard announced losses of £14m for the past five years. *The Sylvania* was renamed and eventually undertook Pacific and Amazon cruises. [189] By the late 1960s, the chairman of BOAC recognised the reality of the situation when he stated people who needed transport would use the air and that ships were for leisure.[190]

Consequently, the last Cunard service to New York ended in 1966.[191] The last transatlantic passenger cruise was *The Empress of Canada* on 7 November 1971.[192] In the early 20th century, the big cruise lines had started transferring services to Southampton, starting in 1907 with White Star's express services. This was followed by Cunard in 1919. Although, like White Star, Cunard continued to operate its lesser vessels from Liverpool, the transferral of its headquarters to

Southampton indicated the long-term decline of transatlantic passenger traffic from Liverpool.[193]

There had been a brief growth in trade during World War Two when, despite being the second most bombed port after London, there was a dramatic growth of shipping using the port. This was because of the dependence on transatlantic convoys, which shifted the pattern of trade from the south and east and Liverpool became the main transatlantic convoy port.[194] During the war, more than 1,000 convoys safely arrived in Liverpool, bringing in much needed supplies of food, materials, munitions and men.[195]

My father was one of numerous merchant sailors manning the perilous wartime Atlantic convoys sailing from Liverpool. Starting with the SS *Bactria* in July 1941, he would make numerous transatlantic voyages. On the first one, he came under machine gun attack from a Focke-Wulf reconnaissance plane, which was later shot down. This was the first of numerous encounters with enemy fire, all of which he survived. The principal forces of Western Command were in the Liverpool Gladstone Dock.[196] The port was also a major transporter of British and Allied troops with 1,747,505 service personnel passing through the city during the war.[197]

The port was heavily bombed due to this strategic location, as explained by the Liverpool Museums website:

'Liverpool was the most heavily bombed British city outside London. The city was a prime target for attack because, with Birkenhead, its "twin" across the Mersey, it was the country's biggest west coast port. Every week, ships arrived in the River Mersey bringing supplies of food and other cargoes from the USA and Canada. Without these supplies, Britain would have lost the war.

'The German Luftwaffe made about 80 air raids on Merseyside between August 1940 and January 1942. These reached their peak in the seven-night blitz in May 1941. The bombing was aimed mainly at the docks, railways and factories, but large areas were destroyed or damaged on both sides of the Mersey.'[198]

The bomb damage was a factor in the post-war decline in the shipping trade in Liverpool. It also dramatically shrank as the UK's pattern of trade shifted towards the ports of the South-East. This led to a deindustrialisation and a dramatic decline in population. Liverpool's population was at a peak in 1931, with 855,688 inhabitants, and this had declined to 439,476 in the 2001 census.[199] The number of registered dock workers in the city also dramatically declined from 16,085 in 1957 to only 1,100 in 1989. [200] Between 1966 and 1994, Liverpool's share of all ship arrivals in the UK halved as it fell from being the second largest UK port to the fifth.[201]

The Bramley-Moore Dock eventually closed altogether in 1988 as the Lancashire coalfield finally closed after the 1984–85 miners' strike. The walls and the hydraulic tower, however, were both awarded Grade II Listed status, so Everton FC has preserved them and encouraged the new stadium to be built in sympathy with the dock's architecture.[202]

Another factor in the dock's decline was the growth of container transport, which necessitated the building of the Seaforth container terminal in 1971, which also took trade away from traditional docks like Bramley-Moore. Liverpool's tidal range and the decline of smaller freight ships meant that by 1971 the city's southern docks were all closed.

Also affecting Liverpool's decline was joining the EEC, later to become the EU, in 1973. In 2004, Henry Overman and Alan Winters illustrated how ports in the South-East had benefitted from EU membership while those in the North-West had not:

'Most notably, there has been the rise of Dover as a major trading port and the corresponding decline of Liverpool. The former saw its share of both imports and exports increase more than threefold over the 20-year period, while Liverpool saw a decline of similar magnitude.'[203]

Their figures show that from 1970–72 to 1990–92, Dover's share of the UK's exports had risen from 5.8 per cent to 19.4 per cent while Liverpool's had declined threefold.[204]

The first sign of a more optimistic trend was the opening of the Liverpool2 complex in 2016. This was an extension of the Seaforth Dock, whose giant Chinese cranes now dominate the Mersey landscape. This development allowed for two 13,500-ton vessels to be accommodated simultaneously; previously, the maximum was 3,500-ton vessels. The approach to the Mersey channel was also deepened to 52ft to allow access to the new ships arriving from the newly widened Panama Canal.[205]

The legacy of Liverpool's decline as a port and the numerous examples of consequent economic regeneration, including the new Everton stadium and Liverpool2, will be examined in the subsequent two chapters.

REGENERATION OF THE DOCKS: A NEW FUTURE FOR LIVERPOOL'S DOCKLAND

DOCKLAND REGENERATION has been extensive in declining ports in the western world for the last 50 years or so. One of the main inspirations for Liverpool's regeneration was Michael Heseltine, secretary of state for the environment in the early 1980s. On the face of it, he was an unlikely saviour, as the Thatcher government overall was to have a disastrous impact on the city as my second book, *Liverpool Football Club Ruined My Life: Sixty Years of Supporting Everton*, documented:

'For the city of Liverpool broadly, the 1980s was a terrible time for large sections of the population.

The privatisation and deindustrialisation policies of the Thatcher government aggravated the long-term industrial decline of the city, taking unemployment up to record levels. There was endless factory closure such as: the Dunlop golf ball factory in Speke, the Bryant & May match works and the Triumph motorcycle factory. In addition, large plants like British Leyland had just closed in 1978.'[206]

In 1982, the *Daily Mirror* stated that: 'They should build a fence [around Liverpool] and charge people admission. For, sadly, it has become a "showcase" of everything that has gone wrong with Britain's major cities.' [207]

Margaret Thatcher herself and her chancellor, Sir Geoffrey Howe, seemed to be adopting a strategy of 'managed decline' toward the poor areas of the inner cities. In the summer of 1981, Thatcher had seemed to give up all hope of assisting Liverpool: 'We have poured money into big employments in Merseyside; a failure.'[208]

However, Heseltine, as a more centrist member of the administration, had a proven record of supporting government intervention to revive declining inner city areas of the country. He was prompted by a more 'one nation' interventionist approach, which he was allowed to implement when, after the 1981 riots, he was appointed to head a taskforce charged with tackling the issues on Merseyside. He immediately commissioned a report titled 'It took a riot'. In the report, he explicitly espoused an alternative set of policy directions to the managed decline approach of Thatcher and Howe. 'They are based on my beliefs that the conditions and prospects in the cities are not compatible with the traditions of social justice and national even-handedness on which our party prides itself.' [209]

He had already set up the London Docklands Development Corporation in 1981. It was financed from a grant from central government and the proceeds from the sale of land there.[210]

The government also designated the area as an Enterprise Zone in 1982, which attracted inward investment from business due to tax concessions.

The LDDC quickly set up improved transport links, with the creation of the Docklands Light Railway and City Airport. It also facilitated the building of the totemic Canary Wharf skyscraper as a financial centre in 1988, creating 50,000 jobs and 23,00 new homes. In the Royal Docks, the LDDC created the London Exhibition Centre (ExCel) and 7,000 new homes in a development called Silvertown.[211]

Canary Wharf was followed by several skyscrapers, including One Canada Square, which opened in 1991 and was, at the time, the tallest building in the UK. These buildings now dominate the skyline on the outskirts of central London and effectively moved the City of London further eastwards and cemented London's reputation of one of the world's great financial centres. However, the immediate area still retains some of the UK's most deprived communities. As author Michael Collins said of the dockland regeneration: 'It fell short by placing too much emphasis on the private sector and not staying true to its original promise to the public sector.' [212]

Several major British ports have also gone through major regeneration since the 1980s; notably Cardiff. In 1987, the secretary of state for Wales, Nicholas Edwards. set up the Cardiff Bay Development Corporation. It succeeded in creating projects such as the Cardiff Bay Barrage, which stretched from Cardiff Docks to Penarth to create a freshwater lake. The project brought new homes, such as those in Atlantic Wharf, and new office buildings including Crickhowell House, now the offices of the Welsh Assembly.[213]

Dockland regeneration has also been achieved in many other cities in the developed world, such as Brooklyn Park in New York, where a large dockland area of Brooklyn has been transformed through the creation of a large public park, 700 affordable houses and the conversion of the Domino sugar refinery into 3,000 apartments and 6,000sq ft of office space.[214]

Another notable dockland regeneration project in Europe has been that of Bilbao in the Basque region of Spain. In the early 1980s, a 'strategic plan for the revitalisation of Bilbao' was approved by the regional and local authorities. The plan allowed for the transfer of many abandoned industrial sites and old deteriorated neighbourhoods from the port authority to the Ria 2000 organisation, which has transformed the city's port area to include landmark buildings such as the Guggenheim Museum and the Eskalduna Palace. The project also included the canalising of San Anton and the Ribera and building the promenades at Portugalete and Las Arenas.[215]

The first regeneration project in Liverpool was that of the Albert Dock. When it was opened in 1846 it was designed for the sailing ship trade.

That would be a main reason for its undoing. Even by the 1860s, it was beginning to struggle as steamships gradually took over and the dock wasn't big enough to accommodate them because its narrow entrances prevented larger vessels from entering.[216] Instead, it concentrated on the storage and distribution of some of the more valuable goods such as silk, brandy, tea, tobacco, ivory, cotton and sugar. It came to dominate trade with China, with more than 90 per cent of the city's silk trade coming through it. The area where the dock was built was also the hub of the slave trade in the late 18th century.[217] However, by the 1920s, virtually all commercial shipping had finished in the dock.[218] The dock was also severely affected by bombing during World War Two.

A more positive development, in the 1950s, was the granting of Grade I Listed status, which was to have a long-term impact on its future development.[219] Various schemes were suggested in the 30 years following this but came to nothing because of wrangling between the various political bodies in charge of the dock.[220] There were two attempts to demolish it in the 1960s by the Mersey Docks and Harbour Board, but its future was assured in 1976 when the city council declared it a conservation area.[221]

The dock's saviour eventually emerged in the early 1980s in the unlikely form of Michael Heseltine when he was seconded for 12 months as effectively the 'minister for Merseyside'. He succeeded in this role – despite opposition from many senior figures in the Thatcher government – in channelling millions of pounds of government money into urban regeneration schemes like the 1984 Garden Festival and the renovation of the Albert Dock.

As well as the physical regeneration of the dock, the body set up by Heseltine to revitalise the city, the Merseyside Development Corporation, arranged for the new Merseyside Maritime

Museum and the Tate of the North to be based in the dock. The latter's opening was supremely ironic since Tate & Lyle's famous Liverpool dockside plant had only been closed for good a few years before. The area around this plant, situated in Love Lane, was known as 'Sugartown'. At its height, 500,000 tons of sugar was refined here.[222] More than 10,000 workers had worked for the factory in its lifetime and most of its workers, known a 'sugar girls', were female. It had finally closed in 1981. At its height, it was the largest sugar refinery in the world.[223]

The MDC also reclaimed almost 1,000 acres of polluted land for the International Garden Festival. This included the building of 60 miles of new roads and footpaths. The two projects succeeded in creating 22,000 jobs at a time of seriously high unemployment in the city.[224]

The Albert Dock was officially reopened by the Prince of Wales – the future King Charles III – in 1988. In 2004, it was one of the centrepieces of Liverpool's successful bid to have waterfront UNESCO status.

Today, the Albert Dock is the major attraction in a booming tourist industry in Liverpool, which is now the fourth most visited British city for foreign tourists. It welcomes over 54m tourists and 4.8m overnight guests.[225] Heseltine has since commented that his work in the city ranks as his 'greatest achievement'. He used the hospitality industry as a yardstick of this success when he commented: 'In 1980, there were a thousand beds in hotels; today, there are 9,000 beds in hotels.' In 2012, his contributions were recognised when he was awarded the freedom of the city of Liverpool, the only modern Conservative to be awarded this in modern times.[226]

The International Garden Festival wasn't the same long-term success. When it opened on 2 May 1984, it covered 60 individual gardens.[227] This included a Japanese garden and pagodas. Attractions included a Festival Hall, a walk of fame featuring local stars, a yellow submarine built at Cammell Laird's, a light railway system, a statue of John Lennon, a giant model of the *Blue Peter* galleon, the 'Wish You Were Here' tourist sculpture, a red dragon slide, a red bull sculpture and a Kissing Gate.[228] Over the five months following its opening, it attracted 3.4m visitors. But, after 1984, the site wasn't maintained. More than half of the site was given over to housing, while the remainder was left derelict.[229]

However, after 25 years of neglect, work began in 2010 to restore the site. It reopened in 2012 after considerable relandscaping which restored two pagodas, created new lakes and waterways, upgraded pedestrian access to the promenade and delivered new parking.[230] The pagodas were restored thanks to the help of respected Japanese landscape architect Satoru Izawa and the purchase of 5,000 Chinese-sourced decorative tiles for the respective Japanese and Chinese pagodas. The 'moon wall', with its intricate carved stonework, was also restored.[231]

In 2017, Liverpool City Council also took control of a waterfront site at the northern end of the gardens which used to house the exhibition hall. By 2023, after two years of work, 380,000 tons of soil and waste had been removed from the site. The council now has a prime residential site on its hands.[232] The council has development partners Metropolitan Workshop, Shedkm, Mace and Montagu Evans preparing a brief to create 1,500 homes on the site.[233] Some of the soil was used to create the Southern Grasslands Park, a 24-acre green space including more than 5,700 trees and shrubs, 2km of walking paths, and miniature woodlands and meadows. The site was opened in August 2023.[234]

To reverse the long-term decline of cruise ship voyages from the port, the city council announced plans for a new cruise terminal to be constructed at the Prince's Jetty site in 2017. Since 2012 Cruise liners had only been able to do 'port of call' visits to Liverpool. Also, in 2012 a temporary terminal building and a floating landing stage were built for smaller cruise ships.[235] However, the new proposal would enable transatlantic liners to start and finish at the port, which would dramatically increase revenue. The scheme received a severe blow in December 2022 when, in the middle of a financial crisis and with costs rising from £50m to a projected £88m per year, the city council withdrew from funding the project and sought a private sector backer.[236]

In December 2023, the council formally announced that the scheme was to be handed over to the private sector. Negotiations were to be held with the Mersey Docks and Harbour Company to complete the legal formalities of handing back the dock. It had already entered negotiations with a third party with a view to maintaining the current workforce.[237] According to Peel L&P, the strategic land business behind the project, the coming years will see the completion of Prince's Dock with a new cruise liner terminal and hotel, new residential developments and new commercial space.[238]

In April 2024, it was announced that the world's largest cruise port operator, Global Ports Holdings PLC, had signed a 50-year agreement with the Mersey Docks and Harbour Company to operate services at the Liverpool Cruise Port. Global Ports plans to invest up to £25m in the port's infrastructure, which will double its operations. This will include a new floating pontoon, which will increase capacity and allow for the simultaneous berthing of two 300m ships and up to 7,000 passengers a day. A new terminal building will be constructed incorporating retail and hospitality outlets. GPH sees the port as the potential gateway to the growing Northern European, British and Irish cruise markets. In 2023, Liverpool welcomed 102 cruise ships with more than 186,000 passengers. This is expected to grow to 200,000 in 2024 and then to more than 300,000 once the new works are completed.[239]

In 2024, work is planned to continue on the Mersey Tidal Power Project, which the combined authority says could provide the energy to power up to a million homes and create thousands of jobs in its construction and operation. Over the previous six years, the combined authority had undertaken early technical work to develop the potential scope of the scheme, which could be up and running within a decade. It will play a significant role in the region's ambitions to be carbon net zero by 2040.

Liverpool city region mayor Steve Rotherham signed an agreement in December 2022 and since then, the Mersey Tidal Power team has worked closely with South Korea's state water company, K-water, to cooperate and share lessons that could help develop the world's largest tidal power scheme on the River Mersey.[240] This project appeared to have a boost in early 2024 when the then-leader of the opposition, Sir Keir Starmer, visited Liverpool and appeared to endorse the project: 'There are different types of renewables; tidal is one of them. I've looked at some of the tidal projects. I am not going to earmark particular projects that we would fund at this stage, but renewables are really important.'[241]

In March 2024, the actual plans for the scheme were unveiled. The city region mayor, Steve Rotherham, released images of the barrage featuring cycle lanes and trees. It would create the first ever cycling and pedestrian route across the Mersey, as well as tackling future possible effects of global warming, such as managing the effects of rising sea levels. He claimed that the scheme, the first of its kind in the UK, could generate clean and predictable energy for 120 years and create thousands of jobs.[242] Over the last three years, the authority has undertaken early technical work to develop the potential scope of the scheme, which could be up and running within a decade, playing a huge role in the region's push to be carbon net zero by 2040 – at least a decade ahead of national targets. On 19 March 2024, the combined authority started the formal process to initiate the scheme by preparing the scoping opinion to be submitted to the planning inspector for what would be the world's largest tidal power scheme.[243]

The Tobacco Warehouse has also been restored into high-class apartments and welcomed its first residents in October 2021. The apartments are advertised as bringing New York-style 'loft living' to the historic Stanley Dock.[244] When it opened in 1901, the building was claimed to be the world's largest. It retains the title of the world's largest brick warehouse, at 1.3m sq ft and 14 storeys high. It was the largest tobacco warehouse in the world, with a total floor area of 15 hectares. For several years, it was the world's most profitable warehouse. It stopped storing tobacco in the 1980s.[245]

In 2010, it was bought by Harcourt Developments, which had a long-term regeneration project in mind. Firstly, the North Warehouse was converted into the Titanic Hotel and Rum Warehouse Centre in 2014. It has been very successful, enjoying high occupancy rates and winning many awards.[246] In the hotel, bedrooms start at 56sq m and the architecture of the Victorian warehouse has been retained, including exposed brickwork, steel columns, concrete ceilings and the original windows.[247] The building is a Grade II Listed, 19th century warehouse originally designed by Jesse Hartley in 1855. It took just over a year to be transformed from a derelict brick shell to a luxurious hotel. The hotel was the first of a multi-stage redevelopment of the Stanley Dock which will transform the former Tobacco and South Warehouses into a residential, business, educational and leisure complex.[248]

The scheme has acted as a catalyst for the transformation of the area known as Ten Streets, which is being promoted as a new cultural hub which will incorporate the nearby Bramley-Moore Dock area. As part of this cultural hub, it has been envisaged to build the UK's first revolving auditorium theatre, based on a successful venture in Amsterdam.[249] There are also plans for new public spaces including a pedestrian and cycle-friendly avenue in the centre of the area. The city is planning to improve rail connections and to widen the A565 road.[250]

It is worth stating that regeneration and the growth of private sector investment has acted to reverse the trend of Liverpool as a declining port. Even by 2011, it had become a profitable port, moving into the top five ports nationally in terms of tonnage.[251]

By 2020, Liverpool was the fourth main maritime hub in the country behind London, Grimsby & Immingham and Milford Haven. The volume of freight entering the port amounted to 23m metric tons.[252]

Two years later, its container port broke several records. In March of that year, it handled 52,300 containers, beating its previous record from October 2019. In April, the five Chinese cranes were used simultaneously for the first time and in February, the port's Terminal 1 brought two additional cranes into operation, boosting its quayside capacity by 30 per cent.[253] The next phase will include the installation of another three ship-to-shore cranes and ten cantilever rail-mounted gantry cranes. There will also be a second container terminal. This will effectively double the container capacity of the port. By 2023, it had become the country's fourth busiest container port. It handled around 900,000 20ft equivalent units of cargo. It now dominates cargo traffic with North America and serves more than 100 non-EU destinations. It is also the leading gateway for the import of grain and animal feed, the export of recycled metal and the movement of goods between Great Britain and the Republic of Ireland.[254]

In 2021, the city port was given a further boost when it was selected as one of eight areas in the country to become a freeport. This means that it will be subject to different tax, customs and planning rules to the rest of the country. For example, Jebel Ali Freeport in Dubai pays almost no tax and duties aren't applied to imports and exports. While not as extreme as this, the Liverpool regional freeport will benefit from reduced tax rates, simplified customs procedures and tariff-free imports.[255] One of the first positive consequences of the scheme occurred in February 2024 when it was announced that, on one of the freeport's three tax sites at Widnes, a massive logistics facility was to be developed, creating 500 full-time positions. It is also hoped that, when fully operational, the three sites could create more than 14,000 skilled jobs and generate £850m of Gross Value Added to the region.[256]

There are increasing grounds for optimism regarding the future of Liverpool as a port.

In early 2023, property advisor Frank Knight analysed 41 British ports based on 13 criteria in terms of their potential for logistics, investment and future development. The port of Liverpool topped the table. The report looked at capacity, connectivity and overall site investment, as well as import and export growth potential.[257]

IS THE BRAMLEY-MOORE STADIUM A POTENTIAL THREAT TO THE DOCKLAND HERITAGE OR A NEW FUTURE?

IN JULY 2021, Liverpool lost its UNESCO World Heritage status. This was affected by several planning decisions. These included the Liverpool Waters project and the new Everton stadium at Bramley-Moore Dock.[258]

Of the new stadium, UNESCO commented that 'it would have a completely unacceptable major adverse impact on the authenticity, integrity and outstanding universal value of a WHS'.[259]

However, when Liverpool City Council approved the stadium on 23 February 2021, it did so in the belief that the city's UNESCO status would not be threatened by it. A council report in 2017 even felt that the stadium could help protect this status. The report said a stadium development could actually help preserve the remaining historic features at the dock and that Everton FC would be consulting planners and Historic England right from the start of the design process.

The report added: 'Early ideas are for the stadium development itself to provide heritage interpretation and viewing facilities of the historic dock fabric/system which is currently not accessible to the public.

This will also create non-matchday visitor experience in this location, attracting additional footfall and spend in the area throughout the year, all of which will help further support a sense of place and the protection/conservation of Liverpool's heritage.'[260]

The report stated that the stadium could create up to 15,000 jobs and offer an annual

£1.3bn boost to the local economy, as well as opening up the historic North Docks, which are currently out of view, to the public.[261]

However, the stadium was opposed by Historic England, the government body tasked with the protection of historical heritage. Its spokesman said:

'We consider that the proposal to infill the dock … would result in substantial harm to the significance of the Grade II Listed Bramley-Moore Dock and cause harm to the World Heritage site. Due to the impact of the proposals, we regrettably think that this application should be determined by the secretary of state and will ask for it to be called in for his determination.'[262]

It must be said that on Friday, 26 March 2021, the secretary of state for housing, communities and local government, Robert Jenrick, did give approval to the building of the stadium.[263] One would assume that Historic England now supports the stadium. Certainly, it was less vociferous than UNESCO in opposing the scheme and commended the club for engaging the public and its stakeholders.[264]

The city's reaction to the loss of World Heritage status was divided. Probably the dominant feeling was one of defiance. This was articulated in an analysis article by BBC Radio Merseyside's political correspondent, Claire Hamilton, in 2021:

'Many people argue that tourists visiting the Pier Head, St George's Plateau or Penny Lane are not coming because Liverpool is a designated World Heritage site. They probably don't even realise it is. They're coming for The Beatles, the football, food and the history, but that history will remain.'[265]

Liverpool's civic leaders were predictably hostile to the UNESCO decision. The city mayor, Joanne Anderson, said it was incomprehensible that UNESCO would rather see Bramley-Moore dock as a derelict wasteland than as a gleaming new stadium that would attract hundreds of thousands of visitors to the city. She was adamant that the stadium was not a project that the council could pull: 'We don't want to lose the site, but does anyone book a holiday thinking I'm going to Liverpool for the World Heritage status? Or for going to see the fantastic buildings like St George's Hall and everything else we've got?'[266]

Steve Rotherham, Liverpool city region mayor, said of the UNESCO decision: 'It was a retrograde step that does not reflect the reality of what is happening on the ground ... a decision taken on the other side of the world by people who do not appear to understand the renaissance that has taken place in recent years.'[267]

Michael Parkinson, a professor at Liverpool University, believed that the evidence used by UNESCO to reach its decision was questionable and its judgment was unbalanced in not recognising the need of the city to develop. He stated that the evidence UNESCO considered only recognised threats in the northern end of the city, which was precisely the part of the city which had missed out during the city's renaissance over the past 20 years. He was confident that the city would continue to thrive as a world-class heritage city.[268] He also felt that a lack of investment and regeneration in north Liverpool 'was a stain on the city's conscience'.[269]

However, there was also a worry that the ability of the city to protect its heritage had been diminished.

Jayne Casey, who was co-creative director of Liverpool's capital of culture in 2008, said that the announcement was a depressing landmark in the city's otherwise proud cultural history. She said that the UNESCO title had bestowed international prestige on the city, but it also accelerated a development boom that suffocated artistic life in the city.[270] Dr David Jeffery, a lecturer of British politics at the University of Liverpool, said he believed the decision would

Image of the Bramley Moore Dock site in the 1830s

John Bramley Moore

John Newton – author of Amazing Grace

*William Gladstone – a beneficiary of the
Slave Compensation Act*

Slaves being transported to America

Carving of manacled boy slaves clutching money bags in entrance of St Martin's Bank, Liverpool

Toussaint L'Ouverture – leader of the 1791 Haitian slave revolt

The princes landing stage at Liverpool in the late 19th century

The abolition of slavery in the British empire being announced

not have a 'serious impact' on the city's tourism industry.

'I do hope this serves as a warning to the council to stop approving ugly buildings, though,' he said.[271]

In the Liverpool Report of January 2023, there was concern voiced over protecting the city's heritage into the future:

'Where UNESCO'S withdrawal of its awarded World Heritage status derived largely from the Liverpool Waters and Everton stadium waterfront projects, there is now both significantly less protection for the historical environment and less restriction on the scope, scale and character of future planning developments. Despite the ongoing commitment of Liverpool City Council and related parties to heritage conservation and regeneration in the docklands, Liverpool still has 22 listed buildings or conservation areas on HE's Heritage at Risk Register [2021], including Stanley Dock, recorded as "improving significantly" but still in "very bad condition", and Duke Street, both proximate to the waterfront.'[272]

One development at Liverpool Waters which could support the case for the withdrawal of UNESCO world heritage status started in early 2024. It is the building of a 31-storey tower block with 278 new apartments at the Prince's Dock. This is part of the wider Liverpool Waters scheme.[273] More skyscrapers to be built in the same area were announced in March 2024, this time including the building of 1,200 apartments. The plan has caused some concerns for local businesses. *Carnaval* owner Dom Hope-Smith said: 'If we wish to invest to expand, we're doing so at a massive risk and totally in the dark.'[274]

But the Liverpool report also voiced areas for possible optimism:

'There appears to be a high degree of local investment and communal identity in the historic docks, likely a legacy of the city's earlier campaign for UNESCO status, with institutions of local higher education, such as the University of Liverpool, local heritage societies and tourist tours and retailers making use of the waterside facilities. Liverpool City Council's tall buildings policy does refer to community and heritage interests in relation to the selection of appropriate sites for high-rise constructions, namely HE and the Merseyside Civic Society.'[275]

The city council has since addressed the fears about the protection of Liverpool's future conservation status, announcing in October 2023 that it had created a tall buildings supplementary planning document to shape future development. The paper contains six guiding principles, including that future development integrates with the existing fabric of the city's historic waterfront. This will include not only the Pier Head area but also everything between the International Garden Festival site and the Liverpool Waters area, including the new Everton football stadium site.[276]

Laura Pye, the director of National Museums Liverpool, also questions UNESCO's claim that the city's heritage is in a worse state than it was ten years ago. She argues that between 2003 and 2023 the city has invested £740m into heritage assets and only 2.5 per cent of its historic buildings are in serious disrepair, compared with 13 per cent in 2000. She also claims that UNESCO has overlooked the National Museums Liverpool Waterfront Transformation project, which aims to revitalise the waterfront in sympathy with the architectural heritage of the area along the lines of the Albert Dock conservation.[277]

Keith York, an associate at Civic Engineers, has argued that the city will continue to thrive despite its loss of World Heritage status:'There is no doubt that crowds of people will continue to visit Liverpool and the wider city region because of its unrivalled heritage and its historic architecture. But contemporary developments such as Liverpool One, the Museum of Liverpool and Liverpool

Waters have also become significant and necessary parts of Liverpool's modern story, ensuring that the city remains an attractive prospect for those choosing to live, work and invest here.

'Of course, in cities like Liverpool, where strength of heritage is a key driving force for decision making, new plans and developments must also be tempered with appropriateness and contextual consideration. While UNESCO status prompted such considerations, it also placed too many limitations on an environment where plenty of other checks and balances are already in place.

'The future development of Liverpool needs to continue to be assertive and confident. People will still come to Liverpool and see the city and its famous waterfront for themselves, something which many UNESCO panel members have failed to do even once since the conferring of the city's status back in 2004.

'... Now, without the limitations of UNESCO, there is an opportunity to better plan how major infrastructure is interlinked throughout the city region, ensuring, for example, that Liverpool has a strong focus upon active travel combined with public transport use.

'Liverpool will continue to grow and adapt whilst protecting its history for all the world to admire and those who see the removal of the UNESCO title as a disappointment in terms of the city's prospects would be wise to reframe this news as an opportunity for Liverpool to progress sensitively and appropriately for its 21st century needs.' [278]

In the future, the protection of the waterfront by a council plan, involving the Dutch architecture firm West 8, will knit together future developments to ensure both conservation and regeneration. However, *Liverpool Echo* regeneration reporter Dan Haygarth believes the council needs to ensure that in future it builds a diversity of buildings, not just a mismatch of residential high rises.[279]

The Liverpool Waters scheme pre-dated the new Everton stadium and, as early as 2012, it was seen as endangering Liverpool's UNESCO status. The scheme included the building of offices, shops and restaurants. In 2012, a team of UNESCO inspectors visiting the city said that the scheme would 'cause serious loss of historical authenticity'.[280] The reasons given for this conclusion were that it would cause 'a serious deterioration of [Liverpool's] architectural and town planning coherence, a serious loss of historical authenticity and an important loss of cultural significance'.[281] However, the people of Liverpool seem to be overwhelmingly in favour of the plan. In April 2023, admittedly in a consultation exercise carried out by Peel Holdings, the masterminds of the scheme, most of those residents consulted gave their approval to the plan.[282] The total value of the scheme is £5bn and it is one of the largest regeneration schemes in Europe. It covers 60 hectares and spans 2.3km of the city's waterfront.[283] A relevant aspect of the updated scheme for Everton's new stadium is a planned riverside walk of 2.3km from the Pier Head to Bramley-Moore.[284] This would be part of a new Central Park which, at 4.7 acres, would be the largest green space in the city centre and is currently the city's largest brownfield site. The park will comprise shelters, canopies and water gardens, areas of fitness and sports, green spaces to support wildlife, pedestrianised areas, a cathedral-style bridge, vehicle and bicycle routes, and rooftop gardens with alfresco dining.[285] The first linkage point for the walk was completed in June 2024, with the opening of a new pedestrianised bridge at Liverpool Waters connecting Prince's Dock with Central Dock and the new Isle of Man ferry terminal. The project has cost £340,000 and is part of the vision to eventually open access along the entire Liverpool waterfront from Aigburth to Bramley-Moore Dock. As part of the bridge's refurbishment, the historic lock gates have been preserved.[286]

In July 2024, the Central Park scheme received a huge boost when Rachel Reeves, in her first speech as chancellor, referenced the 2,350 new houses within the scheme as one of the most important priority house-building schemes for the new Labour government. The plan received another boost when the city council received a £55m pledge for the plan from Homes England. The plan was submitted by developer Peel Holdings to the city council on 15 July 2024. At the time of writing, the plan was still subject to Treasury approval, but the chancellor's speech gave grounds for optimism.[287]

In the summer of 2024, the world's first floating sauna will open at Prince's Dock and in March 2024, the signature technology business E-Sign was planning to open its third global office on the third floor of No 8 Prince's Dock. Both projects have been supported by Liverpool Waters and complement the newly opened food, drink and entertainment centre, *Dockside*.[288]

The project was also given a major boost in June 2024 with the opening of the much-delayed new Isle of Man ferry terminal. The terminal building, which features more than 274 tonnes of steelwork, can accommodate up to 1,000 passengers and 1,145m of vehicle lanes. The project has been significantly funded by the Manx government, with the original projection of £38m rising to £70m.[289]

Liverpool Waters, together with the new stadium, could regenerate other previously declining parts of the city like the Ten Streets area. An article in the *Liverpool Echo* stated that both developments could move the social city centre northwards, with local businesses likely to benefit. The lack of public transport means that it is quite difficult to get there from the city centre and the planned new station would make a huge difference.[290] Both Liverpool Waters and the Ten Streets area are included as key areas in a new regeneration organisation, set up with national government backing, called the Locally Led Urban Development Corporation. The local panel setting this up sees Liverpool as having the potential to be the first area in the country to use this regeneration model.[291]

The 2012 UNESCO statement would give a lie to the widespread view that the stadium was the main cause of Liverpool losing its UNESCO status. It would also be fair to say that the club has gone to great lengths to preserve the historic heritage of the site. The stadium architect, Dan Meis, has incorporated a design and features, such as the external brickwork, to give the appearance, as Chris Beesley described it in the *Liverpool Echo,* that 'it grew out of the dock'.[292] It is designed to emulate traditional dockside warehouses and it would have screened the World Heritage site from a wastewater treatment plant on its northern side.[293]

The club have also restored and renovated the Grade II Listed hydraulic tower and engine room, which is the only above-ground original structure remaining at the site. The repairs have been done in consultation with the council and Heritage Project Management. This entailed ensuring that all repairs be done within the framework of the original brickwork to maintain conservation standards. Emily Watson, assistant section manager at Laing O'Rourke, explained: 'We have had close relationships throughout and they have carried out inspections throughout the process, too. There have also been listed building conditions that we've had to sign off and go through just to make sure that everyone was happy with what we were doing to the grade two listed structure.'[294] The tower, which will even feature the original renovated air raid siren, will form an integral feature of the fanzone at the new stadium.[295] It is planned to incorporate within it an exhibition or cultural centre. It will be open both on matchdays and non-matchdays. Its brick design will also be complemented by the brick-faced panels which will form the stadium exterior.[296] New York-based architect Meis says the brick design has been created to look at home in a dockland setting. It was also a nod to the architecture of the old Goodison Park.[297]

Another feature to be retained are the grade two listed dock walls which separate the site from the nearby Regent Road. The club have recorded more than 400 heritage assets at the site, most of which will be incorporated back into the historic footprint of the stadium. These include the railway tracks, capstans, mooring bollards and cobbles, which will be featured in the new fan plaza. They have worked with bodies such as KM Heritage, Historic England and Liverpool city planning to maintain heritage aspects at the site. The work has been helped by a £15m grant from the Liverpool City Region Combined Authority.[298]

John McGovern, the senior design manager at the site, has explained the level of detail used to preserve the historic integrity of the site:

'One example of the level of detail involved is that they have undertaken a detailed survey of the Regent Road boundary wall, in 3m sections, to record conditions, the works necessary and proposed treatments. That included analysing the mortar in the walls to determine the granularity, the colouring and the materials in it. We found that there is coal ash in the mortar and you can't replicate that these days, so we have an alternative proposal that has been developed to replicate the original mortar.

'Such attention to detail is necessary, including the justification required to gain permission from the authorities for entrances 'cut' into the Grade II Listed boundary wall, in order to accommodate the influx of more than 52,000 supporters via the only accessible route.[299]

The club have also ensured that the giant steel doors which will greet all fans on arrival will blend into the boundary wall by having the original elements of the wall reinstated around them. Tom Stove, contracts manager for the locally based gate manufacturer, commented:

'When the framework is positioned centrally to the cutout, we will basically fill in the existing stone down the sides and across the top, so you won't see any of the top beam.

'All the original blocks we removed have been numbered, especially the coping stones, so they will all be going back in their original position to blend in.

'It's going to be a unique feature that you won't find in a stadium anywhere else in the world.'[300]

One interesting conservation feature is that the dock walls under the stadium have been preserved so that, in the unlikely event of the site reverting to a dock, it could. The maintenance of the adjacent water channel has also ensured that the site is interconnected to the other docks.[301]

It is also worth emphasising the positive environmental footprint the stadium is going to have. There is a target of reusing 95 per cent of all materials on site, providing for car charging points, parking for bicycles and a shuttle bus to the city centre. It is also hoped to improve the local rail infrastructure.[302]

At this stage, we cannot be sure of the long-term economic impact of the stadium and the Liverpool Waters project on north Liverpool. However, we do know it has been an area in long term decline which has not greatly benefitted from the wider regeneration of the city, dating back to the reopening of the Albert Dock and the Garden Festival in the early 1980s.

Everton FC themselves are, obviously, optimistic about this. In the short term, they claim that two thirds of the site workers are from the local area. In addition, 150 jobs have been created within a 30-mile boundary, with further employment opportunities coming from the supply chain. A total of 55 apprenticeships have been created via an ongoing transfer partnership with John Moores University, enabling more students to be actively involved in the project. Overall, Everton FC estimate that the stadium will contribute £1.3m to the UK economy and create thousands of extra jobs, as well as bringing 1.4m visitors to the city. They also envisage the project having a regenerative effect on the adjacent Ten Streets development.[303]

In January 2023, it was estimated that 69 per cent of the stadium workforce were from the local area, with more than 100 apprentices working on or contributing to the new stadium. The social value is estimated to be £208m.[304]

Local businesses are slightly more circumspect. *Sans* Chinese Café chef Lin hopes that the project ushers in a new era for the area where her sales have slumped after the closure of the docks. Riccardo Borfido, who runs *Caffe Riccardo*, hopes it will bring greater visibility to the area and inspire more food and drink venues to be set up. Liam Kelly, the chief executive of Make CIC, which supports creative start-ups across Merseyside, believes that many new businesses will be set up, but that some of the existing businesses, such as a local metal recycling plant, may be adversely affected. He also thinks that the available land and warehouses won't recreate the same fan experience currently enjoyed by the streets around Goodison Park such as County Road.[305]

Michael Parkinson, a professor at Liverpool University, sees a lot of potential in the stadium to regenerate the area: 'Bramley-Moore isn't necessarily a football stadium, it's an economic lever. It's more than a football stadium. It's something much more fundamental to the next two decades of the city, because that's where the action is going to be.'[306]

Liverpool city region mayor Steve Rotherham believes Bramley-Moore Dock is one of the most significant regeneration projects in the region in the last decade. He sees it as important in creating thousands of new local jobs, as well as offering training and apprenticeship opportunities. He also expects that thousands of new visitors will be attracted and that the development will encourage the launch of programmes to tackle health and social inequalities.[307]

He even thinks it could have a similar impact on Liverpool's regeneration to that of the Albert Dock in the 1980s. During the saga over Everton FC's ownership, Rotherham suggested that, if the project were ever endangered by uncertainty over the club's ownership, there was a case for the Liverpool City region local authority stepping in to support the project with central government support.[308]

In November 2023, Rotherham also talked about the possible revival of the mothballed tram system to service the new Everton stadium and Anfield. The old plans were shelved in 2011 after fighting between the local authorities. However, he believes there is more opportunity to revive the plans today as a new devolution deal in 2015 gave the Liverpool city region greater control over transport. There is also a growing belief that a

Labour government will be more sympathetic to the plans.[309]

One definite transportation consequence of the new stadium is the plan to improve capacity at Sandhills railway station, currently the nearest to Bramley-Moore. The plans were first put forward in 2022 after funding was awarded by the department of transport as part of the City Region Sustainable Settlements project. The Liverpool City Region Combined Authority is working with the club to develop a fan management zone at the station. This would allow fans to queue at the station and be let on to the platform as space becomes available. An additional entrance and footbridge are to be built.[310] Another tangible transport system already in place is the £320m already invested by the council in highways infrastructure around the stadium, including a permanent segregated cycle lane, which runs in front of the stadium as part of a lane stretching from the city centre to Bootle.[311]

There is also huge potential for the stadium to benefit the community more than on the intermittent use for matchdays. Neil Joyce, of the CLV group, which advises owners how best to unlock incremental value among their fanbases, cites the Tottenham Hotspur Stadium as an example of how a club can tailor multimedia events to the specific needs of the fans, which can be facilitated due to digital technology. He emphasises that this will be more than just putting on pop concerts.[312]

It is worth noting that football clubs always exaggerate the economic benefits of new stadia. However, football journalist Jonathan Liew has cited the example of the new Wembley as having a 15 per cent increase in local property values. He also feels that Everton have a proven track record of community involvement. He feels that the long term impact is impossible to guess but that 'if *they* can't pull it off, it's hard to see who else can'.[313]

As early as April 2021, Liverpool City Council agreed to the proposal to build a new hotel on Regent Road opposite the new stadium.[314]

In November 2023, more than 12 months before the possible completion of the stadium, there were some signs of new investment in the area. One of their planning proposals to the council that month was the plan to change the use of a tyre storage depot into a Bierkeller and the new home of the *Hot Wok* takeaway, which is currently situated opposite Goodison Park. This building will be called the Bluehouse and will have seven serviced apartments.

Another part of north Liverpool affected by the new stadium is the site of the old stadium at Goodison Park. The club are determined to leave a substantial proportion of the land for community use, as their term 'the Goodison Park Legacy' project indicates. One hundred and seven thousand square feet are earmarked for community use. A further 63,000sq ft are intended to house a six-storey care home, with a further 63,000sq ft set for offices and 8,000 for retail use.[315]

One aspect of community use will be 173 residential units and the local community will be encouraged to continually identify with the club through the preservation of the historic entrance gates on the south-west side and by keeping memorial plaques to former fans and the historic Dixie Dean statue.[316]

The club have already invested over £10m in buildings and facilities in the area as part of the Everton in the Community project. Some of this could be expanded at the stadium site, including the Everton Free School. There could also be a new facility for adults and potentially a new community children's centre. Environmentalism will be emphasised, with green space built in; for example, the Goodison centre circle will remain as a reminder of Everton's footballing legacy. The club are also keen to encourage local enterprise with a potential youth enterprise zone to encourage business start-ups. There will also be accommodation and care facilities for a range of people, including intensive social care for people with dementia and other illnesses.[317]

The need to regenerate the northern end of the city is encapsulated by this quote from journalist Jonathan Liew:

'It's about two miles from Albert Dock to Bramley-Moore Dock, two places that share a postcode but may as well be on different planets. To the south, a long snake of tour buses spits out its latest clutch of foreign tourists on to the waterfront, into the Tate Gallery and The Beatles Museum and the swish bars and restaurants. To the north, a bare notice warns pedestrians away from a barren patch of disused wasteland next to a sewage treatment plant. Liverpool's Northern Docks lies in an area ranked in the top 0.5 per cent most deprived wards in Britain and, as with much of the surrounding area, it's impossible to escape the sense of loss and decay, the bones of a more gilded age.

'Perhaps it feels strangely appropriate, then, that this is the spot that Everton have chosen to build their new dreamscape, a 52,000-seater stadium that they hope will lay their own crumbling ghosts to rest.' [318]

The northern end of Liverpool's dockland has been neglected for many years and has largely missed out on the tourist boom inspired by the Albert Dock and Garden Festival developments in the 1980s. It is this book's conviction that the new Everton stadium and the other proposed developments can have a similarly transformative effect on this part of the city.

The new stadium has brought to light the city's historic links with slavery, but the final chapter examines historic links between the city's football clubs and slavery and the abolition movement.

EVERTON FC'S HISTORIC LINKS TO SLAVERY

FOOTBALL HISTORICALLY has extensive links with slavery. Many of Everton's founders had links with the slave trade, according to historian David Kennedy. They were early patrons of the club who were recruited to enhance the public profile of the club.[319]

It was inevitable that the club would have some historical links given how fundamental slavery and the products of slavery were to the growth of the port in the 18th and 19th centuries. One of the main products of that trade – cotton – was not only fundamental to Liverpool's trade in the 19th century but it was also crucial to the growth of the east Lancashire and Manchester cotton mills, many of whose wealthy owners played a role in providing investment in the early professionalisation of football.

Therefore, Everton is not unique in having slavery links; for example, both the major Manchester clubs have badges depicting ships which transported cotton from American slave plantations to Manchester in the early 19th century. These three-masted ships travelled the seven seas, picking up cargo and depositing it. Until the end of 1865, when slavery was abolished in the USA, that cargo was often produced by slave labour. Sometimes, the cargo *was* the slave labour.

Simon Hattenstone wrote in *The Guardian* that the ships had nothing to do with football and everything to do with the business from which Manchester made its money. The product of slavery became so subtly embedded in Manchester's culture that it was celebrated in the Manchester United and City badges without the clubs even realising it.[320]

This *Guardian* article and its claims about Manchester's links to slavery have created a great amount of controversy in Manchester. Manchester United historian Iain McCartney at least acknowledges the ships' links with slavery but believes it is irrelevant to modern day football:

'I don't think there is anyone who supports either club who ever considered the badge as a link to slavery and refused to buy or wear anything with it on. Neither will any player have refused to sign for one or other because of the badge and its links to slavery.'[321]

Others have voiced even more opposition to the article and questioned its whole premise. Graham Stringer, MP for Blackley, said: 'Manchester had nothing to do with the slave trade. People from the city at the time of the US Civil War in 1861 were protesting against slavery ... I don't think there is any evidence that the ship on the Manchester coat of arms is anything to do with slavery.'[322]

However, at least one Manchester City fan wants the club to drop the ship from its badge. Lester Holloway, editor of the London-based African-Caribbean newspaper *The Voice*, feels embarrassed to wear his club's shirt because of the badge:

'The presence of that ship on badges worn by City and United remains an embarrassment; they must be removed. We wouldn't accept Aston Villa having an image of a child in a chimney as its emblem. Well, black lives matter and so it is time Manchester clubs reckoned with history and decommissioned their ships.'[323]

The deputy leader of Manchester Council, Luthfur Rahman, declined to criticise the clubs in retaining their badges but instead highlighted the work of the council in commemorating the city's links with slavery:

'Like many cities, Manchester's past is a complex mix of stories, lives and voices and we're in the middle of a long term project that began in 2020 to highlight and reflect on aspects of the city's past, including the city's black history and connections to the slave trade.'[324]

Several prominent companies that sponsor British football also have historic links to slavery. As part of its 'Proud to Pitch In' campaign, pub chain Greene King pays cash grants to local sports groups throughout the UK. The company has also been shirt sponsors for several prominent clubs, such as Ipswich Town. However, its original founder in 1799, Benjamin Greene, had slaves working on his sugar plantations in the West Indies and criticised abolition, even though it would have awarded him nearly £500,000 in today's money. To be fair, in 2020, Greene King chief executive Nick Mackenzie said the company was planning to offer financial reparations.[325]

Barclays Bank, which was the title sponsor of the Premier League from 2001 to 2016 and continues to be the league's banking partner, was originally founded by David and Alexander Barclay, who made their money through the financing and insuring of slave ships.[326] The bank also historically acquired many banks that laundered slave money – including, ironically, Heywood's Bank in Liverpool, which was founded by slave traders Arthur and Benjamin Heywood.[327]

There was a diversity of investors in the slave trade, many of whom subsequently received compensation from the British government after abolition. Kris Manjapra documents recipients from a wide variety of backgrounds 'from widows in York to clergymen in the Midlands, attorneys in Durham to glass manufacturers in Bristol'.[328]

Football historians David and Peter Kennedy also found that, although the main beneficiaries from the slavery emancipation fund were major slave owners, the largest numbers of owners were middle class people who owned a few slaves. These were the class of people who invested in and governed Victorian sports organisations.[329]

The first professional football clubs began to emerge in the late 19th century in the cotton mill towns of east Lancashire. Teams like Blackburn Rovers, Blackburn Olympic, Burnley, Accrington Stanley and Darwen were all financed by mill owners whose companies would have been trading in the pre-US Civil War days when the cotton would have been produced by slaves. Some of the cotton mills of this area were set up after the owners had received generous financial compensation for their slave estates. One of them was William Fielden, who was a key figure in setting up the Blackburn cotton industry and whose father had received two massive payments for slave-owning estates in Jamaica. Another cotton mill owner from Blackburn, James Hornby, was able to claim almost £31,300 in 1838 after being appointed auditor for John Tarleton in Liverpool, whose slave-owning company had gone bust. Hornby went on to acquire land at Raikes Hall in Blackpool which was the site of the original Blackpool FC ground.[330] An interesting 19th century cotton fortune was also created by the Hill-Wood family in Glossop in North Derbyshire.[331] In 1897, the backing of Samuel Hill-Wood enabled Glossop to briefly enter the Football League. Glossop remains the smallest town ever to have had a Football League club. By 1919, their Football League place was taken by South Shields. After being elected as MP for the town, Hill-Wood lost interest in the club, but not in football; in 1929, he joined the board of Arsenal, where his son would eventually serve as chairman for 20 years from 1962.[332]

Liverpool's historic role as Britain's largest slaving port make the links between football and slavery in the city inevitable. If Everton do commemorate the new ground's historic links to slavery, they will be acting in line with the moral views of most of the Everton board rebels who voted in 1892 to form their own Everton Football Club in opposition to the chairman

John Houlding and his allies. My first book, *Everton: The Fans Born Not Manufactured*, clearly intimated that the forces propelling the split were moral and party political rather than religious. Specifically, they were motivated by their support of the temperance movement and their Liberal party politics. [333]

Historian David Kennedy has also shown how many of the Liberal leaders of Liverpool in the early and mid-19th century were prominent in the movement to abolish slavery. They had suffered electorally because of the city's reliance on the slave trade and the latter cotton trade created by the slave economy of the southern states of the USA. However, by the late 19th century, using the temperance campaign to draw attention to the perceived social and moral condition of the city's working class population, the Liberals were able to successfully break the dominance of the Tories over the city's electoral politics. Kennedy has also suggested that the temperance movement was particularly strong in the Everton district, which aided the rebels in the split of the football club board.[334] Earlier in the 19th century, it was a flood of Liberal MPs entering the House of Commons after the passing of the 1832 Reform Act which led to a huge rise of urban MPs, who voted for the 1833 Slavery Abolition Act.[335]

However, Kennedy has also shown that a slightly earlier generation of Everton patrons had rather different views on the issue. In the very early years of the club, after its inception in 1878, the club were keen to invite local businessmen to support what was then a minor sports organisation. The businessmen, in turn, were keen to support the club as a means of promoting their status and forwarding their civic ambitions. It was a time of the gradual extension of the franchise to the working class, so the potential mass support of the club was an obvious attraction. On their part, the club committee were keen to use the early patrons as a means of impressing on other footballing bodies that Everton were the premier club in Liverpool.[336] Somewhat ironically, one of the driving forces in recruiting these patrons was future Liverpool FC chairman John Houlding. He himself had indirect links to slavery, being connected by marriage to the Milliken-Napier family who owned extensive sugar plantations on the Caribbean island of St Kitts. Here, the sporadic slave rebellions were particularly harshly dealt with through hanging or burning.[337]

One of the club's earliest patrons was a local shipping magnate called Robert Galloway. His company – Moran, Galloway and Co – plied their trade with South America, in particular Peru, which produced a particularly valuable cargo in the 19th century in the form of the calcified bird manure guano, which was used as a fertiliser. Before the Peruvian abolition of slavery in 1854, guano mining was carried out exclusively by African slaves. Even after abolition, it was mined either by kidnapped Pacific islanders or by Chinese coolie labour who were transported to Peru in their thousands and experienced such horrendous conditions that almost half of them died through suicide, exhaustion or mistreatment. Lung damage was guaranteed through their work due to breathing in guano dust, which was a long-term death sentence. There were also numerous accidents involving falling piles of guano.[338]

Not only did Galloway profit from slavery and, later, coerced labour, but in 1874 he was accused of supplying weapons in one of his ships to Peru's dictator-in-waiting. As a result of weapons incident, questions were raised in parliament and he was forced to resign from the Mersey Docks and Harbour Board. He later became a Conservative councillor for the Everton district, where he began his connection to the football club.[339]

Another early patron was Donald MacIver, who had his own shipping line, D&C MacIver, and was a co-founder of the Cunard Line with

Samuel Cunard. In the 1860, during the US Civil War, he had been a prominent supporter of the Confederate slave states. He also used Cunard personnel to crew Confederate ships built at Birkenhead's Cammell Laird. The company also had a markedly racist attitude to the few black passengers it carried across the Atlantic. One was the African-American abolitionist, Frederick Douglass. In 1847, Douglass was denied access to first-class passage aboard the Cunard liner *Cambria* on its voyage from Liverpool to Boston. Douglass was given a steerage cabin and instructed to take his meals alone. He was also told not to enter the saloon areas of the ship.[340] The public outrage caused by the incident eventually led to Cunard Line owner Samuel Cunard issuing a public apology.[341]

Another patron was the city coroner, Clarke Aspinall. Although he wasn't directly connected to slavery, his family wealth was derived from it. His South Carolina mother owned a sugar plantation in Jamaica. His grandfather owned a Liverpool shipping company that made 113 slave voyages between 1785 and 1807 from Nigeria to the Americas. Clarke Aspinall's uncle, James Aspinall, was involved in one of the most horrific acts of barbarity in the history of the Atlantic slave trade when, in 1781, the slave ship *Zong*, of which he was a co-owner, threw overboard 138 slaves due to the boat running low on water. This incident played a crucial role in the future abolition of slavery. Clarke Aspinall appeared to take pride in his forefathers when he offered a full-size portrait of his grandfather, a slave trader and former Liverpool mayor, to the town hall.[342]

Another co-owner of the *Zong* was William Gregson, who resided in the Everton district and was the third most prolific slave trader, with a total of 152 slave voyages. His villa was called Everton House and had a private well. To this day, the district's Gregson Street is named after him.[343]

The Everton district in the late 18th and 19th centuries was a suburban area where many profiteers of the slave industry chose to live. Gregson's son, John, owned property in both Everton and West Derby. He went on to become another mayor of Liverpool with involvement in the slave trade. He seemed to be more civic-minded than his father, as he became the first subscriber for a scheme to set up Sunday schools for poor children. The supreme contrast between this scheme and the horrendous treatment of his slaves seems to have been lost on most of his contemporaries.[344]

Ken Rogers's research on the world's first iron church, St George's in Everton, has found evidence that five young black slaves were working as servants in the district. He also suggests that there is some evidence that the founder of the church, James Atherton, was also involved in the slave trade.[345]

Although there is no evidence that John Bramley-Moore was involved in Everton FC, his

Brazilian links were echoed by some of the early club patrons such as the Earl of Harrowby. He was a Liverpool MP who, like Robert Bramley-Moore before him was closely associated with the Liverpool Brazilian Association, many of whose members were continuing their involvement in slavery after abolition.[346]

John Bramley-Moore's links with slavery are also shared by the man who created the St Domingo estate which later gave its name to two roads built nearby – St Domingo Vale and St Domingo Grove. Between these roads in Everton was later built the St Domingo's Church, which set up Everton Football Club in the first place. The house was close to Prince Rupert's Tower, which is still the club emblem today.[347]

In 1878, Everton Football Club were formed and known as St Domingo's Football Club. The club were named after the methodist church where the Reverend Ben Swift created a football team for the winter.[348]

The man who built the estate was George Campbell, who was involved in 25 known slave voyages between 1750 and 1756. The estate was named St Domingo in reference to his capturing of a French prize ship off the island of St Domingo in the West Indies.[349]

Today, a Google Maps search for an island called St Domingo in the Caribbean draws a blank. So, where exactly is this mythical island of St Domingo? Some 19th century texts do refer to such an island. For example, James Barskett wrote a whole history on the island of St Domingo in 1818. However, his description of the island should leave nobody in any doubt that he is describing the island of Hispaniola, named by Christopher Colombus when he discovered it in 1492:

'Between Porto Rico on the east, and Jamaica and Cuba on the west ... the island of St Domingo.'

Later, he explains that the island is, indeed, Hispaniola:

'It was originally called Hayti, by the natives, and afterwards Hispaniola, in honour of the country which sent out the squadron under Colombus.'[350]

The *Encyclopaedia Britannica* has also confirmed that, during colonial times, the island was commonly called Santa Domingo.[351]

Slavery first began on the island in 1501 when King Ferdinand and Queen Isabella of Spain allowed the importation of slaves from Africa in the belief that they would be harder workers than the native Taino population. Four hundred thousand Tainos died in the first two decades after the landing of Colombus due to enslavement and exposure to European diseases. By 1574, it was estimated that 12,000 African slaves were on the island.[352] The slave trade in Hispaniola was the oldest in the Americas, 116 years before slaves arrived in the American colonies. Santa Domingo city was also the oldest permanent European urban settlement in the Americas. It boasted the first paved roads, military fort, cathedral, convent and university built in the New World.[353] In 1502, its governor, Nicholas Ovando, transferred its major institutions to the west bank and developed a checkerboard street layout that became a reference for almost all town planners of the New World.[354]

The city layout is so well preserved that, in 1990, it was approved as a UNESCO World Heritage site. It seems hugely ironic that the capital city of the island which gave the name to the church which founded Everton FC continues to enjoy UNESCO World Heritage status, but the building of the club's new stadium was the critical factor in Liverpool losing this status. After French piratical settlements on the western part of the island in the 17th century, the western third of the island was ceded by the Spanish to the French under the 1697 Treaty of Ryswick. It would be called Saint-Domingue.[355]

The western side of the island quickly began to overshadow the Spanish eastern side, both in terms of wealth and population. It was known as the 'Pearl of the Antilles'.[356]

It was a particularly wealthy colony. By 1789, it was producing 40 per cent of the world's sugar and 60 per cent of the world's coffee. It accounted for 40 per cent of France's foreign trade, contributing more than any other French colony.[357] This wealth was based on a slave economy whereby slaves made up 90 per cent of the population.[358]

The greatest and most successful slave rebellion in the world took place in Saint-Domingue. The rebellion began in 1792 and ended in 1804 with the setting up of the independent republic of Haiti after the failed attempt by Napoleon to retake the island. He initially succeeded in taking virtually the whole of the island and seizing the rebellion leader, Touissant-Louverture. Although he was taken to France, where he died a year later, news that slavery was to be reinstated led to another rebellion, which was aided by the English and was eventually successful.[359]

This effective revolution was the only slave uprising that led to the founding of a state free from slavery and ruled by non-whites and former captives. The historian Franklin W. Knight describes it as 'the most thorough case of revolutionary change anywhere in the modern world'.[360]

The uprising was the first major defeat for the Napoleonic army and the whole affair was one that Napoleon would bitterly regret. He later believed that he should have allowed the slaves a degree of self-government, as would have been the case with an internal provincial dispute.[361]

Fearing the influence of a society of slaves that had successfully revolted against their owners, both the United States and the European powers refused to recognise Haiti. US policy to Haiti was to fluctuate. Initially, it was influenced by the fact that many of its leaders were slave owners themselves. This led them to provide aid to put down the revolt. Although they eventually supplied aid to the rebels, they didn't officially recognise the state until 1862 under the presidency of Abraham Lincoln, who was abolishing slavery. The president at the time of the rebellion, Thomas Jefferson, was in a particular dilemma. He was a strong supporter of the ideals of the French revolution, but he was also a Virginia slave owner. Consequently, he gave limited aid to suppress the revolt. It took the Federalist administration of John Adams to change policy and aid the revolt through fear of losing trade with the colony.[362]

Paradoxically for Jefferson, some of the ideals of the French Revolution included the abolition of slavery and these had inspired the rebels. The governor of the island said that: 'The blacks all share an idea that struck them spontaneously; that the white slaves kill their masters and now they govern themselves and regain possession of their land.' These fears even led to some of the slave owners contemplating independence from France. This eventually led, in 1790, to the French National Assembly exempting the colonies from the constitution. When the slaves rebelled in 1791, the National Assembly rescinded the rights of freed slaves.[363]

France demanded a high price for the compensation to slave owners and Haiti, saddled with this enormous debt, became one of the poorest countries in the Americas. The French were able to claim enormous compensation from Haiti as its price for its liberty because their warships surrounded the island. Jefferson worked to isolate Haiti diplomatically and to strangle it economically. They were to suffer even more in 1825 when the French warships of Charles X surrounded the island and Haiti was told that it would have to pay 150m francs to retain its independence. This was ten times the sum that the USA paid France for the Louisiana Purchase which doubled the size of the country. To pay, the young state took out loans which weren't repaid for 122 years. University of Virginia scholar Marlene Daut has described it as 'the greatest heist in history'.[364]

Haiti continues to be an impoverished and politically unstable country to this day. In March 2024, the government announced a state of emergency when armed gangs stormed two major prisons, freeing thousands of inmates. This happened during the attempt of a prominent gang leader to remove prime minister Ariel Henry from power. The prime minister – whose immediate predecessor had been assassinated – was trying to win support for a United Nations-backed security force to stabilise the country. However, his mission wasn't a success. After he was prevented from returning to the country, he resigned in March 2024, leaving the island in the unstable situation of being controlled by rival gangs.[365]

Paradoxically, the eastern part of the island, which had briefly been under the control of the French from 1795 to 1808, eventually, after being restored to Spanish control, became the Dominican Republic, and gradually became one of the largest economies of Central America and the Caribbean.[366] It thrived because of the booming sugar cane industry, which brought in tens of thousands of Haitians to work in the fields. Their towns were known as bateyes and remain poor Haitian communities to this day. Their life is often grim and they can live in fear due to incidents such as the Parsley massacre in 1937 when the military slaughtered thousands of Haitians near the border on the orders of President Trujillo.[367]

Before becoming the Dominican Republic, the Spanish colony of Santa Domingo had previously abolished slavery in 1822.[368]

Politically, the country was almost as unstable as its western neighbour, with a series of dictators interspersed by the American occupation from 1916 to 1924. This period culminated with the particularly repressive regime of President Trujillo from 1930 to 1961. In 1963, the first democratically elected president, Juan Bosch, came to power on a moderately reformist manifesto. However, the USA, fearing the development of a communist regime, reoccupied the island from 1965 to 1966. There followed a series of mainly conservative-inclined democratic governments until 2010 when the more leftist PLD were elected and became the dominant force in the country. Since the 1980s, the country has become one of the Caribbean's most popular tourist destinations. By the end of the 1990s, it had one of the highest economic growth rates in the world. This was further boosted by the signing of the United States-Dominican Republic free trade agreement in 2005.[369]

The island of Hispaniola and Everton Football Club are, therefore, inextricably linked. The links with slavery from some of the early patrons of the club also show the club's historic connections with the trade.

CONCLUSION

IT SEEMS that slavery has major historic connections with Everton Football Club and continues to be associated with the club through the siting of its new stadium at Bramley-Moore Dock. This is not that surprising in a city that owes its development and expansion as a port to the slave trade. The club, it would appear, are determined not to forget this legacy with the promise to include a commemoration in the new stadium development. This is particularly appropriate in a city which currently has no monument commemorating slavery. The intention to not name the stadium after John Bramley-Moore is also a clear desire to not in any way celebrate the link. I believe this is the right policy and I firmly hope that these historic links are recognised and not celebrated. The club need to avoid the process of the maritimisation of slavery which the historian Jessica Moody has identified as dislodging narratives of slavery in Liverpool's history and focusing on other more comforting aspects of the port's history. This has arguably happened at the site of the old Goree warehouse, named after the slave departure island off Senegal in West Africa and where slaves were arguably bought and sold in Liverpool. In the 1950s, the warehouse was knocked down and then, in the 1960s, replaced by the new Wilberforce House – named after the abolitionist William Wilberforce.[370] There could be a danger of the process identified by Moody happening at the new stadium, with the emphasis on the conservation of the dock's historical heritage features. It would also seem appropriate, as recommended by historians David and Peter Kennedy, that the club also recognises the slave connections of some of the earliest patrons of the club.[371] Hopefully, the commemoration inside the listed pumping station will create a fitting historic legacy in a stadium that is built in architectural sympathy with the broader history of the Liverpool docks. It is also to be hoped that UNESCO eventually reviews its short-sighted decision to withdraw World Heritage status from the city of Liverpool. There are some grounds for hope here, as the original decision was a split vote, with 13 in favour and five against with two ballot papers declared invalid.[372] It also must be said that when the M&S Arena opened in 2008 next to the Albert Dock, it didn't lead to any re-examination of Liverpool's UNESCO status. Lord Heseltine even wrote to UNESCO arguing in relation to the building of the new Everton stadium that 'the heritage will be largely enhanced and restored by the project'.[373]

The club couldn't have done more to preserve the heritage aspects of the stadium and, hopefully, this will enhance the experience of visiting it, in contrast to the soulless experience of visiting so many of our new stadia.

NOTES

1. 'Sport: Everton FC reveals final Dan Meis designs'; *CLADmag*
2. 'Goodison Park'; Wikipedia
3. 'Everton announce stadium blueprint'; BBC News, 22 January 2001
4. Chris Beesley – 'Bill Kenwright decision not to build Everton stadium with retractable roof and pitch explained'; *Liverpool Echo*, 5 April 2024
5. D. Kennedy – 'Football stadium relocation and the commodification of football – the case of Everton supporters and their adoption of the language of commerce'; *Soccer and Society* volume 13 No 3, May 2012
6. Jamie Jackson – 'Liverpool and Everton "must" share new ground, council says'; *The Guardian*, 7 June 2009
7. Chris Bascombe – 'Liverpool unveil Anfield's new main stand as Jurgen Klopp urges fans:

"Be as loud as you can'"; *The Independent*, 9 September 2016

8. Hamish Champ – 'Everton FC to launch new stadium consultation'; *Building News*, 25 October 2018

9. Op. cit.

10. Phil Kirkbride – 'Everton win major public support for new Bramley-Moore Dock stadium as consultation results revealed'; *Liverpool Echo*, 13 November 2019

11. Stephen Chapman – 'Everton stadium campaign praised by academics and marketers'; Prolific North, 19 September 2019

12. Phil Kirkbride – 'Everton's consultation over the new stadium at Bramley-Moore Dock wins award'; 22 November 2019

13. 'Public consultation for new Everton stadium wins national planning award for engagement'; peoplesproject.co.uk, 9 September 2020

14. Andy Hunter – 'Everton's plans for £300m new stadium approved by Liverpool City Council'; *The Guardian*, 2 April 2017

15. Simon Goodley – 'The football club, the billionaire – and the bills: Everton's race to build its new home'; *The Guardian*, 13 November 2022

16. 'Liverpool stripped of UNESCO World Heritage status'; BBC News, 21 July 2021

17. Chris Beesley – 'Everton new stadium "structurally complete" as historic milestone reached'; *Liverpool Echo*, 24 February 2024

18. Simon Goodley – 'The football club, the billionaire – and the bills: Everton's race to build its new home'; *The Guardian*, 13 November 2022

19. Paul the ESK – 'Bramley-Moore Stadium, financing options and costs'; *Toffee Web*, 20 April 2022

20. Dave Powell – 'Everton stadium naming rights latest as talks held and double deal expected'; *Liverpool Echo*, 29 December 2022

21. Paul the ESK – 'Bramley-Moore Stadium, financing options and costs'; *Toffee Web*, 20 April 2022

22. Parth Jhaveri – 'Everton new stadium cost increases by 50 per cent as MSP Sports Capital provide £100m loan'; princerupertstower.com, 6 June 2023

23. Paul Wheelock – 'MSP Sports Capital withdraw from investment talks into Everton, claims report'; *Liverpool Echo,* 23 August 2023

24. Neil Hodgson – 'Ray of light for cash-strapped Everton as stadium loan lands'; The Business Desk.com, 14 September 2023

25. Alan Myers – 'Everton takeover, regulatory process to allow 777 Partners to take ownership well under way and progressing'; Sky Sports, 20 September 2023

26. Dave Powell – 'The potential 36bn reason 777 Partners will want to get Everton takeover done'; *Liverpool Echo,* 9 November 2023

27. Callum O'Connell – 'Journalist claims 777 only want Everton to add value to their investments'; *Goodison News,* 10 October 2023

28. Calvin – '777 message to Evertonians an encouraging start amidst underlying concerns'; *Royal Blue Mersey,* 7 October 2023

29. Dave Powell – '777 Partners funding to Everton could tip £100m before takeover is even approved'; *Liverpool Echo,* 18 November 2023

30. Dave Powell – 'Former Everton CEO makes claim should 777 Partners fail to seal takeover'; *Liverpool Echo,* 3 December 2023

31. Patrick Boyland – 'Everton's 777 takeover delay is hurting everyone – it's time for a decision'; *The Athletic*, 16 February 2024

32. Dave Powell – '777 Partners have already made stance clear on Everton points deduction'; *Liverpool Echo*, 17 November 2023

33. Simon Mullock – 'Now £500m takeover hits rocks'; *Sunday Express*, 19 November 2023

34. Will Unwin – 'Everton deducted ten points by Premier League and face compensation bill'; *The Guardian*, 17 November 2023

35. Matt Slater – 'Everton takeover: 777's latest legal scrape must surely mark the end'; *The Athletic*, 5 May 2024

36. Op. cit.

37. Chris Beesley – 'Everton takeover: shareholders release damning statement slamming Farhad Moshiri and 777 Partners'; *Liverpool Echo*, 6 May 2024

38. Joe Thomas – 'Everton takeover: the $600m fraud claims against 777 Partners and what they could mean for the club'; *Liverpool Echo*, 8 May 2024

39. Joe Thomas – 'Everton give clarity on "alternative scenarios" as 777 Partners takeover deadline set'; *Liverpool Echo*, 14 May 2024

40. Patrick Boyland et al – 'How the crisis gripping 777 Partners is affecting the clubs in their portfolio'; *The Athletic*, 16 May 2024

41. Dave Powell – 'Everton takeover: 777 Partners have assets seized after court order'; *Liverpool Echo*, 16 May 2024

42. Matt Woosnam – 'Crystal Palace co-owner John Textor "I want to be involved in an English club that wins championships"'; *The Athletic*, 26 May 2024

43. Op. cit.

44. Matt Slater – 'Everton's 777 takeover has fallen through; so what happens next?'; *The Athletic*, 1 June 2024

45. Joe Thomas and Dave Powell – 'Everton takeover: Andy Bell and George Downing plan among rival proposals for future of club'; *Liverpool Echo*, 7 June 2024

46. Joe Thomas – 'Who are Andy Bell and George Downing? Wealthy Everton supporters trying to take over club'; *Liverpool Echo*, 7 June 2024

47. Paul Joyce – 'Tenth-richest man in world behind bid for Everton'; *The Times*, 8 June 2024

48. George Overhill – 'Everton takeover development as buyer suddenly withdraws from talks with Moshiri'; *Goodison News*, 8 June 2024

49. Shamoon Hafez & Nizaar Kinsella – 'Roma owner Friedkin interested in Everton takeover'; BBC Sport, 8 June 2024

50. Shamoon Hafez – 'Consortium with Saudi royal makes 400m Everton bid'; BBC Sport, 10 June 2024

51. Shamoon Hafez – 'Friedkin Group agrees deal for Everton takeover'; BBC Sport, 14 June 2024

52. Danny Wright – 'Farhad Moshiri agrees deal in principle for Everton as Premier League test update emerges'; *Goodison News*, 15 June 2024

53. Shamoon Hafez – 'Friedkin Group granted exclusivity in Everton takeover talks'; BBC Sport, 21 June 2024

54. Joe Thomas – 'Everton takeover: key questions answered with crucial days ahead for Dan Friedkin Group'; *Liverpool Echo*, 21 June 2024

55. Dave Powell – 'Everton takeover: Dan Friedkin deal takes step forward as major move confirmed'; *Liverpool Echo*, 25 June 2024

56. Chris Beesley – 'Everton takeover: new stadium gives Dan Friedkin huge advantage after Roma plan collapses'; *Liverpool Echo*, 1 July 2024

57. Dave Powell – 'Why Friedkin Group pulled out of Everton takeover and what happens next'; *Liverpool Echo*, 19 July 2024

58. David Ornstein – 'Crystal Palace shareholder John Textor granted exclusivity in Everton takeover talks'; *The Athletic*, 15 August 2024

59. Dave Powell – 'What Friedkin Group will bring to Everton is clear as silence speaks volumes in takeover twist'; *Liverpool Echo*, 21 September 2024

60. Shamoon Hafez – 'What does "momentous" Friedkin takeover mean for Everton?'; BBC Sport, 23 September 2024

61. Petra Kendall Raynor – 'Exclusive: Everton to acknowledge Bramley-Moore Dock's history of slavery at the new stadium site'; *Liverpool World*, 20 August 2021

62. Op. cit.

63. Joe Mulhern – 'Everton's new Bramley-Moore stadium is a stark reminder of Liverpool's historic entanglement with slavery in Brazil'; LSE Latin America and Caribbean blog, 24 February 2021

64. Petra Kendall Raynor – 'Exclusive: Everton to acknowledge Bramley-Moore Dock's history of slavery at the new stadium site'; *Liverpool World*, 20 August 2021

65. 'Speech of J. Bramley-Moore Esq. on Dock Extension addressed to the Liverpool Town Council'; January 1846 (J. Mawdsley)

66. Mike Royden – 'The History of Bramley-Moore Dock'; Everton Heritage Society, 30 August 2018

67. 'Bramley-Moore, John (1800-1886); *Liverpool Footprints*

68. Joe Mulhern – 'Everton's new Bramley-Moore stadium is a stark reminder of Liverpool's historic entanglement with slavery in Brazil'; LSE Latin America and Caribbean blog, 24 February 2021

69. Sarah Brown – 'Brazil's heart-breaking site of two million enslaved Africans'; BBC Travel, 15 February 2024

70. Joe Mulhern – 'Everton's new Bramley-Moore stadium is a stark reminder of Liverpool's historic entanglement with slavery in Brazil'; LSE Latin America and Caribbean blog, 24 February 2021

71. Joe Mulhern – 'Everton's new Bramley-Moore stadium is a stark reminder of Liverpool's

historic entanglement with slavery in Brazil';
LSE Latin America and Caribbean blog, 24
February 2021

72. Joe Mulhern – 'Everton's new Bramley-Moore
stadium is a stark reminder of Liverpool's
historic entanglement with slavery in Brazil';
LSE Latin America and Caribbean blog, 24
February 2021

73. Op. cit.

74. Mike Royden – 'The History of Bramley-Moore
Dock'; Everton Heritage Society, 30 August 2018

75. 'Bramley-Moore, John (1800-1886)'; *Liverpool
Footprints*

76. Joe Mulhern – 'Everton's new Bramley-Moore
stadium is a stark reminder of Liverpool's
historic entanglement with slavery in Brazil',
LSE Latin America and Caribbean blog, 24
February 2021

77. 'Bramley-Moore, John (1800-1886)'; *Liverpool
Footprints*

78. Dominic Moffitt – 'History of Merseyside's first
slave ship'; *Liverpool Echo*, 27 October 2021

79. Simon Hughes – 'John Bramley-Moore, slavery
and the site of Everton's new stadium'; *The
Athletic*, 26 October 2022

80. Mark Chapman – 'Everton's Bramley-Moore stadium and the uncomfortable truth'; *The Athletic Football Podcast*, 26 October 2022

81. Petra Kendall-Raynor – 'Everton to acknowledge Bramley-Moore dock's history of slavery at the new stadium site'; *Liverpool World,* 20 August 2020

82. 'A brief history of Liverpool'; Liverpool History localwiki.org

83. Steven Horton – 'Mike Royden's local history pages'; 2000

84. Gomer Williams – *History of the Liverpool Privateers*; Cambridge, 1897

85. Andrew Lees – *Liverpool the Hurricane Port*; Mainstream Publishing, 2011

86. *The Norris Papers*; Picton Library, Liverpool, 1846

87. Lee Grimsditch – 'All of Liverpool's 43 docks and how they got their names'; *Liverpool Echo*, 14 March 2020

88. 'A short history of Liverpool'; *The Monro*

89. Wendy Northway – 'Life in the Liverpool docks'; lancashiremcs.org, 14 March 2018

90. Lawrence Westgaph – 'The sinister history behind Liverpool's buildings and monuments'; *Independent Liverpool,* 6 July 2020

91. 'A brief history of Liverpool'; Liverpool History localwiki.org

92. Tony Lane – *Liverpool: City of the Sea*; Liverpool University Press, 1997

93. 'History of Liverpool Docks'; *Northern Daily Times*, 5 June 1855

94. Ken Pye – *Liverpool: Bloody British History*; The History Press, 2012

95. Liz Stewart – 'Uncovering the history of the Canning Graving Docks'; National Museums Liverpool, 2023

96. Gomer Williams – *History of the Liverpool Privateers*; Cambridge, 1897

97. F.E. Sanderson – Liverpool and the slave trade: a guide to sources'; hslc.org.uk

98. 'Liverpool and the transatlantic slave trade'; Information Sheet Three, Archives Centre, Maritime Museum, National Museums Liverpool

99. 'About the museum'; International Slavery Museum Liverpool, National Museums Liverpool

100. Claire Shaw – 'Liverpool's Slave Trade Legacy'; *History Today* volume 70, 3 March 2020

101. Lawrence Westgaph – 'The sinister history behind Liverpool's buildings and monuments'; *Independent Liverpool,* 6 July 2020

102. 'About the museum'; International Slavery Museum Liverpool, National Museums Liverpool

103. Maya Wolfe-Robinson – 'Slavery Museum to be expanded in ten-year Liverpool waterfront project'; *The Guardian,* 28 January 2021

104. Patrick Edrich – 'Liverpool reckons with legacy as "capital of transatlantic slave trade"'; *Liverpool Echo,* 21 August 2023

105. 'Watt Papers'; Picton Library, Liverpool

106. 'Liverpool and the transatlantic slave trade'; Information Sheet Three, Archives Centre, Maritime Museum, National Museums Liverpool

107. 'Leyland Papers'; Picton Library, Liverpool

108. 'Liverpool and the Northwest'; Historic England

109. 'Liverpool and the transatlantic slave trade'; Information Sheet Three, Archives Centre, Maritime Museum, National Museums Liverpool

110. Gomer Williams – *History of the Liverpool Privateers*; Cambridge, 1897

111. 'Liverpool and the Northwest'; Historic England

112. Sanchez Manning – 'Britain's colonial shame: Slave owners receive huge payouts after abolition'; National African American Reparations Commission, 7 October 2021

113. Patrick Daly – 'Family of former PM William Gladstone to apologise for links to the slave trade'; standard.co.uk, 20 August 2023

114. Denis O'Brien – 'Caribbean needs our cash to defeat legacy of slavery'; *The Times*, 20 December 2023

115. David Olusoga – 'The history of British slave ownership has been buried: now its scale can be revealed'; *The Guardian*, 12 July 2015

116. Paul Coslett – 'Penny Lane'; 15 February 2007

117. 'Penny Lane: Museum finds "no evidence"' of slavery link'; BBC News, 19 June 2020

118. 'Liverpool and the Northwest'; Historic England

119. Lawrence Westgaph – 'The sinister history behind Liverpool's buildings and monuments'; *Independent Liverpool*, 6 July 2020

120. 'Liverpool and the Northwest'; Historic England

121. Lisa Rand – 'Liverpool University accepts slavery roots as links revealed'; *Liverpool Echo,* 21 August 2020

122. Emilia Bona – 'Liverpool's shameful history and why we should never forget'; *Liverpool Echo,* 14 June 2020

123. BBC Home – 'Liverpool identifies first streets for slavery plaques'; BBC News, 24 August 2020

124. Lawrence Goldman – 'Remembering slavery: The City of Liverpool gets it right'; History Reclaimed, 21 March 2023

125. Molly Cottrill – 'Controversial colonial landmarks across Liverpool'; University of Liverpool, 27 October 2021

126. 'Black Lives Matter: Liverpool "not doing enough" over slavery links'; BBC News, 8 June 2020

127. 'Liverpool school renames houses over slave trade links'; BBC News, 24 June 2022

128. 'William Gladstone; Liverpool students rename hall after anti-racism activist'; BBC News, 28 April 2021

129. Gomer Williams – *History of the Liverpool Privateers*; Cambridge, 1897

130. Chantelle Lunt – 'Liverpool's historical links to slavery is something everyone should learn about'; *The Black Curriculum*, 22 September 2021

131. 'Edward Colston statue pulled out of Bristol harbour'; BBC News, 11 June 2020

132. Steven Morris – 'Bristol's Colston Hall to drop the name of slave trader after protests'; *The Guardian*, 26 April 2017

133. Tom Saunders – 'Bristol University to keep names of 'slavery buildings'; *The Times*, 29 November 2023

134. Deborah Anderson – '62 Glasgow street names and areas with links to slave trade'; *Glasgow Times*, 29 March 2022

135. Christine Whyte – 'Boot the Wellington: the growing resistance to Glasgow's colonial monuments'; *Counterfire*, 9 June 2020

136. Lorraine – 'George Square and the slavery debate'; The Archivist History Blog, 24 June 2020

137. 'Podcast: Birmingham's shameful links to slavery uncovered by academic'; Aston University, 6 October 2021

138. 'Old Glasgow Club' – meeting minutes, 13 January 2011

139. Katie Dickinson – 'Newcastle's historic links to the slave trade as two street names to be reviewed'; *Chronicle Live*, 19 June 2020

140. Jonathan Morris – 'City square to lose slave trader name'; BBC News, 8 November 2023

141. Emine Saner – 'Renamed and shamed: taking on Britain's slave trade past, from Colston Hall to Penny Lane'; *The Guardian*, 29 April 2017

142. 'A new memorial for the victims of the transatlantic slave trade'; london.gov.uk

143. Gomer Williams – *History of the Liverpool Privateers*; Cambridge, 1897

144. Andrew Lees – *Liverpool the Hurricane Port*; Mainstream Publishing, 2011

145. Gomer Williams – *History of the Liverpool Privateers*; Cambridge, 1897

146. F.E. Sanderson – 'Liverpool and the slave trade: a guide to sources'; hslc.org.uk

147. 'John Newton in Liverpool from slaver to customs official'; bygoneliverpool.wordpress.com, 29 March 2021

148. Gomer Williams – *History of the Liverpool Privateers*; Cambridge, 1897

149. 'John Newton in Liverpool from slaver to customs official'; bygoneliverpool.wordpress. com, 29 March 2021

150. F.E. Sanderson – 'Liverpool and the slave trade: a guide to sources'; hslc.org.uk

151. 'History of Liverpool Docks'; *Northern Daily Times,* 5 June 1855

152. Lawrence Westgaph – 'The sinister history behind Liverpool's buildings and monuments'; *Independent Liverpool,* 6 July 2020

153. Alex Robinson – 'Rushton, slavery and Liverpool'; edwardrushton.org.uk

154. Andrew Lees – *Liverpool the Hurricane Port,* Mainstream Publishing, 2011

155. Dr Jim Powell – 'Cotton, Liverpool and the American Civil War'; University of Liverpool, October 2018

156. 'Speech of J. Bramley-Moore Esq. on Dock Extension addressed to the Liverpool Town Council'; January 1846 (J. Mawdsley)

157. 'History of Liverpool Docks'; *Northern Daily Times,* 5 June 1855

158. Jesse Hartley; Wikipedia

159. John Hinchliffe & Tim Darmody – 'Liverpool Docklands Conservation or Construction'; TIICH Bulletin No 91, first quarter 2021

160. Ken McCarron & Adrian Jarvis – 'Give a dock a good name?'; Merseyside Port Folios, 1992

161. 'Speech of J. Bramley-Moore Esq. on Dock Extension addressed to the Liverpool Town Council'; January 1846 (J. Mawdsley)

162. Mike Royden – 'The History of Bramley-Moore Dock'; Everton Heritage Society, 30 August 2018

163. Mark Chapman – 'Everton's Bramley-Moore Stadium and the uncomfortable truth'; *The Athletic Football Podcast*, 26 October 2022

164. 'Liverpool and emigration in the 19th and 20th centuries'; Information Sheet 64 Archives Centre, Maritime Museum, liverpoolmuseums.org.uk

165. Paul Milner – 'Liverpool: An Essential Emigration Port'; bifhsgo.ca, 2022

166. Ken Pye – *Liverpool: Bloody British History*; The History Press, 2012

167. Chris Beesley – 'Shane Macgowan spoke of his love for Everton and cheeky Anfield memories'; *Liverpool Echo*, 30 November 2023

168. Tony Lane – *Liverpool: City of the Sea*, Liverpool University Press, 1997

169. Andrew Lees – *Liverpool the Hurricane Port*, Mainstream Publishing, 2011

170. Tony Lane – *Liverpool: City of the Sea*, Liverpool University Press, 1997

171. Hippolyte Tain – *Notes on England*, Henry Holt & Co, 1874

172. Lee Grimsditch – 'All of Liverpool's 43 docks and how they got their names'; *Liverpool Echo*, 14 March 2020

173. Tony Lane – *Liverpool: City of the Sea*, Liverpool University Press, 1997

174. Op. cit.

175. 'The Mersey docks and harbour company history'; fundinguniverse.com

176. 'The Mersey Docks 1949'; old-liverpool.co.uk

177. 'Liverpool Firsts'; Liverpool Historical Society

178. 'Cunard & Liverpool mark 175 years of passenger shipping'; cruise-liverpool.com, 26 May 2015

179. Tony Lane – *Liverpool: City of the Sea*, Liverpool University Press, 1997

180. John Shepherd – *Liverpool's Last Ocean Liners: The Golden Age*; Tempus, 2009

181. Ken Longbottom – *Liverpool and the Mersey volume one: Gladstone Dock and the Great Liners*; Silver Link Publishing Ltd, 1995

182. 'The Lusitania disaster'; Newspaper pictorials: World War One Rotogravures, 1914-1919, Library of Congress

183. '*RMS Mauretania*'; greatoceanliners.com

184. Ken Pye – *Liverpool: Bloody British History*; The History Press, 2012

185. 'The great transatlantic liners'; Information sheet eight, Archives Centre, Maritime Museum, liverpoolmuseums.org.uk

186. John Shepherd – *Liverpool's Last Ocean Liners: The Golden Age*; The History Press, 2009

187. Op. cit.

188. Adrian Jarvis – 'The Port of Liverpool and the shipowners, c1910-38'; The Northern Mariner XII, No 2, April 2002

189. John Shepherd – *Liverpool's Last Ocean Liners: The Golden Age*; The History Press, 2009

190. G. Gladden – 'Post Second World War transatlantic travel for business and pleasure: Cunard and its airline passengers'; Journal of Transport History 41, Liverpool John Moores University

191. John Shepherd – *Liverpool's Last Ocean Liners: The Golden Age*; Tempus, 2009

192. 'Liverpool cruise liner terminal building begins'; BBC News, 22 March 2012

193. Ken Pye – *Liverpool: Bloody British History*; The History Press, 2012

194. Adrian Jarvis – 'The Port of Liverpool and the shipowners, c1910-38'; The Northern Mariner XII, No 2, April 2002

195. 'The battle of the Atlantic'; National Museums Liverpool

196. Ken Longbottom – *Liverpool and the Mersey volume one: Gladstone Dock and the Great Liners*; Silver Link Publishing Ltd, 1995

197. Ken Pye – *Liverpool: Bloody British History*; The History Press, 2012

198. 'The Spirit of the Blitz'; Merseyside Maritime Museum, 10 July 2003-5 December 2004

199. 'Liverpool'; McGill School of Computer Science Wiki

200. Bill Hunter – *They Knew Why They Fought*; London, 1994

201. Tony Lane – *Liverpool: City of the Sea*; Liverpool University Press, 1997

202. 'A look at the Bramley-Moore Dock'; *Belfast Telegraph*, 23 March 2017

203. Henry Overman & Alan Winters – 'North and South'; Centrepiece cep.lse.ac.uk, winter 2004

204. Op. cit.

205. 'The fall and rise of the Liverpool docks'; *Liverpool Echo*, 25 November 2015

206. Bob Waterhouse – *Liverpool Football Club Ruined My Life: 60 Years of Supporting Everton*; Pitch Publishing, 2024

207. Tony Lane – *Liverpool: City of the Sea*; Liverpool University Press, 1997

208. Simon Parker – 'The leaving of Liverpool: managed decline and the enduring legacy of Thatcherism's urban policy'; LSE blog, 17 January 2019

209. Op. cit.

210. 'London Docklands Development Corporation (Area and Constitution) Order 1980'; Hansard, 1 July 1981

211. Miss Smyth – 'The regeneration of the London docklands'; hastingsinternational.com, 21 February 2023

212. Michael Collins – 'Legacy of the docks'; *The Guardian*, 5 August 2009

213. 'The Regeneration project'; Cardiff Harbour Authority

214. Debra Kamin – 'At the Domino Sugar Refinery, a Glass Egg in a Brick Shell'; *New York Times*, 12 February 2023

215. 'Urban Regeneration'; bilbaoport.eus

216. Ron Jones – *The Albert Dock Liverpool*; RJ Associates Ltd, 2004

217. Molly Cottrill – Controversial colonial landmarks across Liverpool'; University of Liverpool, 27 October 2021

218. Ron Jones – *The Albert Dock Liverpool*; RJ Associates Ltd, 2004

219. 'Historic facts 1860-1970'; Albert Dock Company, 2 October 2008

220. OP. Cit.

221. 'Royal Albert Dock Liverpool'; albertdock.com

222. Andrew Lees – *Liverpool the Hurricane Port*; Mainstream Publishing, 2011

223. Jess Molyneux – 'Liverpool's "sugar girls" and lost factory workers loved'; *Liverpool Echo*, 18 April 2024

224. The Rt Hon the Lord Heseltine and Sir Terry Leahy – 'Rebalancing Britain: Policy or Slogan? Liverpool City Region'; assets.publishing. service.gov.uk, October 2011

225. 'Why is Liverpool one of the most visited cities in the UK?'; One Touch Property Investment

226. Liam Thorp – 'Heseltine: Liverpool work is my biggest career achievement'; *Liverpool Echo,* 17 July 2023

227. Paul Coslett – 'International Garden Festival'; BBC Liverpool, 1 May 2009

228. Op. cit.

229. 'Liverpool Festival Gardens'; visitliverpool.com

230. Merlin Fulcher – 'Festival Gardens, Liverpool'; *Architects Journal,* 26 June 2023

231. Helen Carter – 'Liverpool's Garden Festival back in bloom after 27 years'; *The Guardian,* 12 June 2011

232. 'Milestone development for historic Festival Gardens site'; Liverpool City Council, 23 June 2023

233. Dan Haygarth – 'The regeneration projects which could transform Merseyside'; *Liverpool Echo,* 23 December 2023

234. Julia Hatmaker – 'Liverpool opens 24-acre park by Festival Gardens'; *Place Northwest,* 7 August 2023

235. 'The great transatlantic liners'; Information sheet eight, National Museums Liverpool

236. Tony McDonough – 'Liverpool seeks private cruise terminal backer'; *Liverpool Business News,* 3 December 2022

237. David Humphreys – 'Liverpool Council to confirm it's ending management of cruise terminal'; *Liverpool Echo,* 12 December 2023

238. Dan Haygarth – 'The regeneration projects which could transform Merseyside'; *Liverpool Echo,* 23 December, 2023

239. 'Liverpool cruise port to double operations with £25m plan featuring new pontoon'; *Liverpool Echo,* 3 April 2024

240. Dan Haygarth – 'The regeneration projects which could transform Merseyside'; *Liverpool Echo,* 23 December 2023

241. Liam Thorp – 'Starmer "interested" in tidal power amid Mersey link plans'; *Liverpool Echo,* 12 January 2024

242. Liam Thorp – 'Multi-billion-pound vision for the River Mersey revealed'; *Liverpool Echo,* 7 March 2024

243. Liam Thorp – 'Video shows how multi-billion-pound Mersey tidal project would look above and below water'; *Liverpool Echo,* 19 March 2024

244. 'Tobacco Warehouse'; tobaccowarehouse.co.uk

245. The Rt Hon the Lord Heseltine and Sir Terry Leahy – 'Rebalancing Britain: Policy or Slogan? Liverpool City Region'; assets.publishing. service.gov.uk, October 2011

246. John Hinchliffe & Tim Darmody – 'Liverpool Docklands Conservation or Construction'; TIICH Bulletin No 91, first quarter 2021

247. 'Welcome to the Titanic Hotel'; titanichotelliverpool.com

248. Molly Doolan – 'Titanic Hotel Liverpool opens in the heart of historic docklands'; sleepermagazine.com, 9 July 2014

249. Natasha Young – 'First UK theatre with revolving auditorium planned for Liverpool's Ten Streets'; *YM Liverpool*, 2 February 2017

250. 'Ten Streets Liverpool'; tenstreetsliverpool. co.uk, 6 October 2017

251. 'England's Liverpool: Port City, Architectural marvel'; odysseytraveller.com, 24 September 2021

252. 'Sea freight tonnage arriving at Liverpool port in the United Kingdom between 2000 and 2020'; statista.com, 2023

253. Port technology international team – 'Port of Liverpool sets a number of records across its terminals'; globaltrademag.com, April 2022

254. Phillip Adnett – 'Port of Liverpool: the rich history of trade in the Merseyside docks'; Institute of Export, 4 July 2023

255. Tom Arnold – 'Liverpool City Region's freeport is now open, but what exactly is it?'; University of Liverpool, 12 January 2023

256. David Humphreys – '500 new jobs to be created at city region freeport'; *Liverpool Echo*, 14 February 2024

257. Ian Hughes – 'Port of Liverpool ranked as UK's top port for port-centric logistics potential'; Invest Liverpool, 19 January 2023

258. 'Liverpool stripped of UNESCO World Heritage status'; *Liverpool Echo*, 21 July 2021

259. Tony McDonough – 'Everton stadium "completely unacceptable" says UNESCO'; *Liverpool Business News*, 16 February 2021

260. Alistair Hughes – 'Could new Everton stadium affect Liverpool's World Heritage status?'; *Liverpool Echo*, 27 March 2017

261. Tony McDonough – 'Everton stadium "completely unacceptable" says UNESCO'; *Liverpool Business News*, 16 February 2021

262. 'Liverpool: Conservation group opposes stadium as expected'; Mecree, 22 February 2023

263. Sam Carroll – 'Everton new stadium receives government decision'; *Liverpool Echo*, 26 March 2021

264. Tony McDonough – 'Everton stadium "completely unacceptable" says UNESCO'; *Liverpool Business News,* 16 February 2021

265. Claire Hamilton – 'Analysis'; BBC Radio Merseyside, 21 July 2021

266. Tom Houghton – 'Liverpool north docks regeneration "not a project we can pull" as city faces losing UNESCO title'; *Business Live*, 25 June 2021

267. Josh Halliday – 'UNESCO strips Liverpool of its World Heritage status'; *The Guardian*, 21 July 2021

268. Michael Parkinson – 'I've been chronicling Liverpool's renaissance for 40 years – here's why the city's UNESCO status should not have been removed'; *The Conversation*, 21 July 2021

269. Dan Haygarth – 'How Liverpool's Northern docks are preparing for Everton's arrival and £500m stadium'; *Liverpool Echo*, 4 June 2022

270. Josh Halliday – 'UNESCO strips Liverpool of its World Heritage status'; *The Guardian*, 21 July 2021

271. Clare Hamilton – 'Analysis'; BBC Radio Merseyside, 21 July 2021

272. 'Liverpool Docks'; Liverpool Report, January 2023

273. Dan Haygarth – 'Work begins to build 278 flats in huge tower on waterfront'; *Liverpool Echo*, 11 January 2024

274. Liam Thorp – 'Business owners fear over skyscraper plans'; *Liverpool Echo*, 18 March 2024

275. 'Liverpool Docks'; Liverpool Report, January 2023

276. Dan Haygarth – 'Six demands made in new vision for Liverpool's world famous waterfront'; *Liverpool Echo*, 20 October 2023

277. Laura Pye – 'A city that needs no labels'; National Museums Liverpool, 3 July 2023

278. Keith York – 'Liverpool can thrive without UNESCO world heritage status'; Infrastructure Intelligence, 28 July 2021

279. Dan Haygarth – 'Liverpool must be watchful when changing its defining image'; *Liverpool Echo*, 28 April 2024

280. 'Liverpool Waters project would damage the city: UNESCO'; *Liverpool Echo*, 24 January 2012

281. Op. cit.

282. 'Residents and community "excited" by the regeneration at Liverpool Waters'; Liverpool Waters, 4 August 2023

283. 'An ambitious 30-year vision to completely transform the city's northern docks'; Peel L&P, June 2022

284. 'Residents and community "excited" by the regeneration at Liverpool Waters'; Liverpool Waters, 4 August 2023

285. Ahroob Jabbar – 'Liverpool Waterfront Regeneration'; City Rise, 25 October 2022

286. 'New bridge opens access along Liverpool waterfront'; explore-liverpool.com, 14 June 2024

287. Pat Hurst – 'New plans for Liverpool waterfront regeneration submitted by developers'; *The Independent,* 15 July 2024

288. 'This is Liverpool Waters'; liverpoolwaters. co.uk

289. Dan Haygarth – 'Date when new Isle of Man terminal will open for passengers'; *Liverpool Echo*, 9 January 2024

290. Remy Greasley – 'Liverpool's hidden oasis set to be next best part of city'; *Liverpool Echo,* 9 September 2023

291. Liam Thorp – 'Nine Liverpool areas to form new "zone" at heart of city's future'; *Liverpool Echo*, 22 March 2024

292. Chris Beesley – 'Dan Meis shares Goodison Park feature that new Everton stadium will retain'; *Liverpool Echo*, 19 August 2023

293. Martin Sloman – 'What price heritage?'; *Liverpolitan*, 1 July 2023

294. Chris Beesley – 'Everton to get another tower as "jaw-dropping" new stadium feature takes shape'; *Liverpool Echo*, 4 December 2023

295. Adam Jones – 'Everton's plans to combat World Heritage concerns at proposed Bramley-Moore Dock stadium'; *Liverpool Echo*, 19 March 2020

296. Chris Beesley – 'Everton work on new-look tower to provide "jaw-dropping entrance" to new stadium'; *Liverpool Echo*, 21 March 2023

297. Zak Garner-Purkis – 'Everton reveals new stadium design'; *Construction News*, 26 July 2019

298. Chris Beesley – 'Everton to get another tower as "jaw-dropping" new stadium feature takes shape'; *Liverpool Echo*, 4 December 2023

299. Everton FC – 'Everton stadium's nod to the past'; 18 October 2022

300. Chris Beesley – '"You won't find anywhere else in the world" … Work begins on unique feature at new Everton stadium'; *Liverpool Echo*, 30 November 2023

301. 'About the project'; evertonstadium.com

302. Jonathan Edwards – 'Everton FC: The people's project creating a sustainable sports stadium for future generations'; Rider Levett Bucknall

303. 'Everton stadium puts premium on social value'; Everton FC, 25 October 2022

304. Chris Beesley – 'Everton new stadium; what is planned as Michael Jones pledge made'; *Liverpool Echo*, 1 January 2024

305. Dan Haygarth – 'How Liverpool's Northern Docks are preparing for Everton's arrival and £500m stadium'; *Liverpool Echo*, 4 July 2022

306. Op. cit.

307. Ian Herbert & Simon Hart – 'A parlous financial state, 132 days since a home win at Goodison Park … but down by Bramley-Moore Dock there's still hope Everton won't sink'; *Daily Mail*, 6 October 2023

308. Joe Thomas – 'Everton new stadium plans at Bramley-Moore Dock hailed as "most

significant in a decade'"; *Liverpool Echo,* 23 April 2022

309. 'Everton and Liverpool stadium update as tram plan back on the agenda'; *Liverpool Echo,* 9 November 2023

310. Paddy Edrich – 'Major work on north Liverpool station ahead of Everton FC move'; *Liverpool Echo,* 28 December 2023

311. 'Views sought on a parking zone for Everton FC's new stadium'; Liverpool City Council, 1 December 2022

312. Dave Powell – 'Everton told new stadium can have unexpected benefit with new plans'; *Liverpool Echo,* 27 October 2022

313. Jonathan Liew – 'Everton's new ground poses a fundamental question: can football stadiums serve the public good?'; *The Independent,* 26 July 2019

314. Neil Hodgson – 'Plans approved for hotel opposite site of Everton's proposed new stadium'; *The Business Desk,* 6 April 2021

315. Ahroob Jabbar – 'Liverpool Waterfront Regeneration'; City Rise, 25 October 2022

316. Rob Hakiman – 'Liverpool council approves demolition of Everton's Goodison Park stadium'; New Civil Engineer, 4 May 2022

317. 'Everton submits outline planning application for Goodison Park legacy project'; Everton Football Club, 8 April 2020

318. Jonathan Liew – 'Everton's new ground poses a fundamental question: can football stadiums serve the public good?'; *The Independent*, 26 July 2019

319. David Kennedy – 'Merseyside football and the slave trade'; *Soccer & Society* volume 24, 12 January 2023

320. Simon Hattenstone – 'Abandon ship: does this symbol of slavery shame both Manchester clubs?'; *The Guardian*, 19 April 2023

321. Adam Shergold – 'Man United historian says woke brigade are making a mountain out of a molehill over the "slavery links" of three-mast ship on the club badge and says there's no need to change it'; *Mail Online*, 20 April 2023

322. Op. cit.

323. Lester Holloway – 'I'm a Man City fan. Despite the backlash, it's time to sink these ships'; *The Guardian*, 21 April 2023

324. John Scheerhout – 'City and United won't be changing their badges following claims they "celebrate slavery"'; *Manchester Evening News*, 21 April 2023

325. Jasper Jolly – 'Barclays, HSBC, Lloyds among UK banks that had links to slavery'; *The Guardian,* 18 June 2020

326. 'Slave trade and the British economy'; BBC Bitesize

327. Ndindu – 'Barclay's Bank and Liverpool FC are all beneficiaries of slave trade'; Kenya Talk, 6 February 2021

328. Kris Manjapra – 'When will Britain face up to its crimes against humanity?'; *The Guardian,* 29 May 2018

329. David Kennedy & Peter Kennedy – 'Merseyside football's earliest patrons and the slave trade connection'; Harm & Evidence Research Collaborative, The Open University, 15 December 2023

330. Dominic Moffitt – 'Every Lancashire slave owner and how much compensation they received from the abolition'; Lancs.live, 21 June 2020

331. 'Milltown, Glossop, Derbyshire'; Oxford Archaeology North, April 2007

332. 'Gone and forgotten: Glossop FC'; theballisround.co.uk

333. Bob Waterhouse – *Everton: The Fans: Born, Not Manufactured*; Blue Horizon, 2022

334. David Kennedy – 'The Division of Everton Football Club into Hostile Factions: The Development of Professional Football Organisation on Merseyside, 1878-1914'; University of Leeds School of History, 1 January 2023

335. Dominic Moffitt – 'Every Lancashire slave owner and how much compensation they received from the abolition'; Lancs.live, 21 June 2020

336. David Kennedy & Peter Kennedy – 'Merseyside football's earliest patrons and the slave trade connection'; Harm and Evidence Research Collaborative, The Open University, 15 December 2023

337. Op. cit.

338. Brigit Katz – 'Remains of 19th-century Chinese labourers found at a pyramid in Peru'; *Smithsonian Magazine*, 29 August 2017

339. David Kennedy & Peter Kennedy – 'Merseyside football's earliest patrons and the slave trade connection'; Harm and Evidence Research Collaborative, The Open University, 15 December 2023

340. Op. Cit.

341. 'Debate in the House of Lords'; *Douglass Monthly*, September 1860

342. David Kennedy & Peter Kennedy – 'Merseyside football's earliest patrons and the slave trade connection'; Harm and Evidence Research Collaborative, The Open University, 15 December 2023

343. 'William Gregson (slave trader)'; Wikipedia

344. 'The Gregson Syndicate'; visitlancaster.or.uk, February 2021

345. Ken Rogers – *St George's Servants or Slaves? The Lost Tribe of Everton & Scottie Road*; Trinity Mirror Sport Media, 2010

346. David Kennedy & Peter Kennedy – 'Merseyside football's earliest patrons and the slave trade connection'; Harm and Evidence Research Collaborative, The Open University, 15 December 2023

347. 'The Origins of St Domingo'; efcstatto.com, 15 September 2016

348. 'The Origins of St Domingo'; efcstatto.com 15 September 2016

349. 'Historic Liverpool Dwellings: St Domingo House'; The Football Voice, 16 September 2022

350. James Barskett – *History of the Island of St Domingo From Its First Discovery by Colombus*; Kessinger Publishing, 1818

351. 'Hispaniola Island, West Indies'; *Encyclopaedia Britannica*, 22 November 2023

352. 'The island of Hispaniola is founded'; African American Registry, 12 June 1992

353. Lebawit Lily Girma – 'Santo Domingo; the city that kept slavery silent'; BBC Travel, 18 November 2020

354. 'Colonial City of Santo Domingo'; UNESCO World Heritage Convention

355. Anthony Stevens-Acevedo – 'The Santo Domingo slave revolt of 1521 and the slave laws of 1522: black slavery and black resistance in the early colonial Americas'; Dominican Studies Institute, 2019

356. 'The early transatlantic slave trade'; Lowcountry Digital History Initiative, 4 October 2018

357. 'Hispaniola Island, West Indies'; *Encyclopaedia Britannica*, 22 November 2023

358. 'The island of Hispaniola is founded'; African American Registry, 12 June 1992

359. David Patrick Geggus – 'The British occupation of Saint-Domingue 1793-98';

Department of History, York University,
November 1978

360. Franklin W. Knight – 'The Haitian Revolution';
The American Historical Review, February 2000

361. Fondation Napoleon – 'Napoleon, the dark
side'; Napoleon.org, 14 April 2021

362. 'The United States and the Haitian Revolution,
1791-1804'; Office of the Historian,
history. state.gov

363. 'Slavery and the Haitian Revolution: Liberte,
egalite, fraternite'; revolution.chnm.org

364. Greg Rosalsky – '"The Greatest heist in
history"; how Haiti was forced to pay
reparations for freedom'; Planet Money, 5
October 2021

365. Evens Sanon, Pierre-Richard Luxama,
Maroosha Muzaffar – 'Haiti declares state of
emergency as thousands of inmates escape after
armed gangs storm prison'; *The Independent*, 4
March 2024

366. 'The island of Hispaniola is founded'; African
American Registry, 12 June 1992

367. 'A brief history of Hispaniola'; CNN

368. Anne Eller – 'Emancipation in Santa
Domingo'; islandluminous.fiu.edu

369. 'Dominican Republic'; Britannica

370. J. Moody – 'Liverpool's local tints: drowning memory and "maritimising" slavery in a seaport city'; University of Bristol, 2016

371. David Kennedy & Peter Kennedy – 'Merseyside football's earliest patrons and the slave trade connection'; Harm and Evidence Research Collaborative, The Open University, 15 December 2023

372. Livia Gershon – 'Liverpool loses its UNESCO World Heritage status'; *Smithsonian Magazine,* 22 July 2021

373. 'Liverpool will thrive without UNESCO says Lord Heseltine'; *Liverpool Business News,* 7 July 2021

TERROR BIRDS

JASON RUBIS

SEVERED PRESS
HOBART TASMANIA

TERROR BIRDS

PROLOGUE: SOUTH TEXAS, PLIOCENE

There was one egg left.

One had been broken shortly after it was laid, the victim of a savage fight between its parents. The big male *Titanis* had decided that a full belly suited it better than fatherhood; the mother had eventually sent him packing, but not before a misplaced step had reduced the precious egg to a gooey smear of pulverized shell and yolk.

A scavenger had made off with the second egg. After a month of vigilance, the mother's own empty belly had finally gotten the best of her and she had abandoned the nest to hunt. Normally her mate would have stood guard while she was gone, or else done the hunting himself and brought her meat. Since she had chased him off, those were no longer options.

The hunt hadn't taken long; within an hour, the female had tracked down a heavy, tapir-like mammal and brought it down with a single blow of her massive beak. Her hunger temporarily sated, she had returned to the nest just in time to see the thief: a ground-dwelling bird not unlike the *Titanis*, but considerably smaller and more agile, its short upper limbs equipped with grasping claws. There were a number of creatures like it in the *Titanis* nesting grounds, always on the lookout for a quick meal. This one had been caught feasting, yolk smeared around its beak.

The mother crouched and screamed with fury, a hoarse, guttural noise that shook the hot, heavy air. At that moment she looked remarkably like the gigantic carnosaurs that were her remote—and long extinct-cousins. She did not understand the rage that gripped her at the sight of her smaller cousin eating her egg; had no idea why the large, heavy ovoids she had delivered with such pain should be protected. An instant later she charged, her clawed feet kicking up a storm of dust as she went after the thief.

The smaller avian squawked and tore off with a bounding stride, abandoning its ill-gotten meal with no hesitation. It turned a glance back at the mother, its staring eyes almost comically fearful.

The chase ended quickly. The egg-thief was nimbler and marginally more intelligent than the *Titanis*, but the larger bird moved with far greater speed, and had the advantage of surprise. A moment later the scavenger was seized up shrieking in the mother's beak, its hollow bones crunching as its body was scissored neatly in two. Then the mother's head bobbed up and down with lethal speed, beating the creature's remains into the ground.

Its anger at last spent, the female plodded back to the nest.

One egg left.

The mother gathered up a portion of the twigs and dried grass that made up the nest in its blood-smeared beak, and carefully covered the egg. She moved with a delicacy that belied the savage rage that had taken her only moments before. Slowly, she positioned itself over the egg and sank back down to see out the rest of her vigil. She had no concept of regret or promises, but deep in her tiny brain a spark burned, which a human being would have taken for steely resolve: no matter what danger threatened her, she would not move from this nest, not until her last precious egg hatched.

**

Then the world seemed to break apart.

Only a few yards away from her nest, *something* shimmered and twisted in the air, like the ripples on a pond's surface when broken by a stone.

The mother hissed deep in her throat, the feathers atop her head rising. It was perhaps the first time in her life that the mother *Titanis* had felt fear. She was, after all, the chief predator of this new land, which her forefathers had penetrated from the south. Over eight feet tall, and weighing well over three hundred pounds, she was given a wide berth by the knife-toothed cats and dire wolves that roamed these plains. Mammoths ran trumpeting from her. Giant sloths-usually slow-moving and indifferent, but savage when roused to anger, kept well away from her. She could be killed, but only with great effort and at great cost to her assailant.

But *this*—this was like nothing she had ever encountered.

When it reached full size, it was about a quarter of her size, a shining gash in the air itself, hanging scant inches above the stony ground. Looking into the aperture made the mother shake her head and shriek in frustration; looking into the thing *hurt*. Wind kicked up around her, but it was a strange wind; she could hear it, but though it seemed to howl about her head, she couldn't *feel* it, and the grass around her remained still. Odors floated out of the rift, sickening smells like nothing she had ever encountered.

Finally she put fear aside and clambered to her feet, breaking her resolve to not leave her nest. She faced the hole in the air head on, head bowed and stumpy wings extended, screaming at it with a ferocity that would have routed the fiercest predator.

The hole did not move, or react in any way.

Enraged, the mother kicked at the ground before it, sending a shower of stones and twigs at the hole. This was the final signal sent to the most formidable enemies before she attacked.

The hole did not respond, but the debris the mother had kicked up hung in the air, each separate pebble and scrap of bark rotating slowly, as though being considered by some cold intelligence.

Then, just as the mother was about to charge, the hole *swallowed itself*. The stones were sucked inside, and the rift's shining edges imploded, the whole thing shrinking to a glowing, puckered mass in the air before simply dissolving into nothing.

The strange enemy was gone.

The mother took a few hesitant steps backward, watching for any sign of the shining thing's return. After a few moments she returned to the nest, shaken but triumphant.

For the moment, at least, she had won.

ONE: VANDER, SOUTH TEXAS, PRESENT DAY

Alex Drummond suddenly realized that Dr. Bruckner had finally stopped talking. He had been standing in Bruckner's doorway for nearly an hour, sweating freely in the mid-day Texas sun, dropping in and out of consciousness as Bruckner talked on and on. Actually, *yammered* might be a better word. Like a lot of academics, the guy clearly loved the sound of his own voice and had a regard for his own research that bordered on the obsessive. As his voice barked on and on, the topic swerved gradually from the assistant position Alex had come to apply for to the finer points of his theory of wormhole dilation and its possible relevance to cryptozoology. Admittedly, this was a topic Alex found almost as fascinating as Bruckner himself; he read Bruckner's blog religiously, and devoured his books almost as soon as they were published. When he learned the man himself had come to Vander to teach a course on Pseudoscience and the Paranormal, he had quickly changed plans to attend a larger school up north. And when he'd gotten word that Bruckner was looking for an assistant, he applied immediately. He hadn't thought twice about driving the twenty miles outside campus to Bruckner's home, simply because that suited the professor better than meeting at his office. He went gladly, excited as hell as he drove through the flat south Texas countryside.

But when the topic of Bruckner's chatter turned to the bitter humiliation he was forced to put up with every day as Vander's "cow-town college" professors laughed at him behind his back and (Bruckner believed) blocked him for tenure, Alex's mind began wandering.

Then, at some point, the harangue had stopped. Bruckner lifted a finger in a "hold that thought" gesture, as though Alex were the one who had been talking on and on. He looked over his shoulder into the interior of his tiny house.

"Did you hear that?" he asked, his voice hushed.

"Hear what?" In fact, now that Alex thought of it, it seemed to him that he had…not heard something, exactly, so much as *felt* it. Like the sudden shifts in air pressure on airplanes that always made his ears pop. Strange, but not something he would have remembered, had Bruckner not mentioned it.

"Aw hell, it went off! Come on! Hurry!" With that, he ran into the house, his tennis shoes pounding on the worn carpeting. Alex watched him disappear, wondering now how badly he really wanted to work for the famous Dr. Thaddeus Bruckner. Even though Bruckner had all but ordered him to follow, Alex couldn't help but consider the possibility of just running back to his car and disappearing. His dorm room wasn't exactly a prince's suite, but it *was* air-conditioned. He could lay low and hope Bruckner forgot about him—which he had a feeling was probably a good possibility. Very likely Bruckner had completely forgotten about him even now. The urgent matter that had sent him scampering back into the house was probably nothing more than his microwave signaling his lunch was done.

In the end, curiosity won out. If he left now, he would never get another chance to see the Great Man's house. He stepped through the door, cautiously shutting it behind him.

Bruckner's house didn't surprise him at all; the place was a hoarder's paradise of fossils, framed prints of paintings by well-known paleontological artists, crates of canned food and soda from the local discount store, no fewer than three computers, all of which looked as though someone had smashed them in a fury with a ball-peen hammer, and books—more books than Alex had ever seen in one place, outside the University library. The books covered the unpainted wooden shelves built into every available wall, and stood in towering stacks on the floor. Alex recognized zoological texts, well-known and obscure works on paleontology and theoretical physics in several languages, and every cryptozoology-related book he had ever heard of—as well as many he hadn't. The rest of Bruckner's library was comprised of a crazy mish-mash of mystery and horror paperbacks, comic book collections and cookbooks.

"Where *are* you?" Bruckner's voice bellowed, coming from somewhere ahead. Alex started, realizing he hadn't been forgotten after all. "Get over here, this is incredible!"

Alex maneuvered his way between the stacks of books into a smaller space beyond the living room (more books, more junk, a small windowless bathroom), then into the kitchen (the stove and table covered with canned goods, computer equipment and still more books), where a sliding door stood open. Alex hurried through it into the back yard, then pulled up short.

Dr. Bruckner's house was located on the outskirts of Vander, which itself was fairly remote; no one would have heard of it were it not for the university. His nearest neighbors had to be miles away—yet Bruckner had erected a high wooden fence around the back yard, creating an enclosure about twenty feet wide. But Alex had seen the fence while driving up to the house. What really startled him was the machine set up in the middle of the brownish stretch of grass.

At least, he *assumed* it was a machine—of some sort, anyway. Two metallic pylons stood upright with about ten feet of ground between them. A crazy tangle of wires connected either pillar to a boxy structure covered with buttons, switches and dials. Bruckner stood before the pillars, twirling something between thumb and forefinger and grinning maniacally.

The moment he saw Alex he strode forward, thrusting the something into Alex's face. "What is that? Huh? What the hell's that?" He sounded delighted rather than confrontational, but Alex found himself stepping backward nonetheless. Bruckner wasn't a particularly big man—in fact, he verged on scrawny, with a little pot belly to go with the bony limbs. The faded Hawaiian shirt didn't help make him any more impressive. But the dark eyes staring out of the thin, bearded face didn't seem to know any of that; they had all the raging confidence and swagger of a beanstalk giant.

"Uhhm, a feather?" Alex guessed. That was certainly what it *looked* like: a broad, rather bedraggled feather, a dark blue, almost black, that lightened to a pale metallic sheen along the edges. It was about as long as Bruckner's bony forearm, which certainly qualified as odd…but apart from that, for all that Alex could see, it was nothing special.

"That's *right*, Sonny Jim," Bruckner cried, brandishing the feather like a pirate's cutlass. "But what *kind* of feather? What kind of birdie did this sucker come from, hah? You're the one studying to be a scientist. Go ahead. Put Daddy and Mommy's money to use for a change. Take a shot."

"A peacock, maybe?" Alex murmured, beginning to regret his decision to want to work for this maniac. "Some of the farmers out here have them."

Bruckner nodded. "Not a terrible guess, given the dearth of other information. You're right about the farmers—I've heard those peacocks of theirs croaking like toads in hell, generally when I'm trying to sleep. But no. You're fixated on the length, and the way it shines. Think: you've seen peacock tail feathers before, I assume. Does this really *look* like one?"

"Not really," Alex conceded. It was true; peacock feathers all had those round shapes in them, like eyes. Bruckner's prize didn't. Also, peacock feathers were kind of thin and wispy, with spaces between the individual filaments; the filaments on this feather were packed tight, making it look almost like a knife.

"Then what could it have come from?" Bruckner asked. "Better yet, where is the bird now? This didn't come from some tiny widdle chickadee flitting about the pussy willows. This came from a *big* bird, all due apologies to Mr. Spinney. And look at these!"

Tossing the feather aside as though it now meant nothing to him, Bruckner squatted down and ran his finger through the dry grass before the two pillars, gathering up a number of stones and bits of random debris. He stood up, arranging them on his palm like a miser counting his gold.

"What's this?" he asked again, his eyes gleaming at Alex. "What's this stuff, hah?"

Alex leaned forward, examining the handful of garbage. To him, that was exactly what it looked like: garbage. But Bruckner was right; he *was* supposed to be a scientist in training, even if the chief inspiration behind his career choice had been *Doctor Who* and his collection of cryptozoology paperbacks. He didn't know much, but he knew scientists carefully considered available evidence; they didn't just shrug their shoulders and ignore it because they couldn't immediately identify it.

Hesitating, he reached for one of the bits of trash on Bruckner's palm: a chunk of some dark, fibrous material.

"Good, good," Bruckner murmured approvingly. "Your instincts are sound. What is that?"

"It looks like tree bark," Alex said, squinting at the object. He wished he knew more about local trees so he could impress Bruckner, but trees had never especially interested him. "But really old and dry…"

"Dry because it's probably been dead for quite some time. Most likely fell off a dead tree and got carried along by the wind. Not unlike the feather. It's possible the wind carried it over my fence and into my humble enclosure, but now what about these?"

He offered Alex one of the stones in his palm. Picking it up, Alex was surprised by how heavy it was, even though it was not much bigger than a small chicken's egg.

"It's not impossible a googie like that got pitched over my fence, assuming a high enough wind. They do get some nasty storms here. But there hasn't been one recently, and I can tell you for certain-sure this wasn't here in the yard before you arrived. I check regularly for new foreign objects. That'll be your job, once you start."

Alex blinked. "You mean, I got it? I'm your assistant?" He was pleased, though not entirely sure he should be.

"I don't see any other candidates hanging around crying in their beer," Bruckner said coolly. "This is going to be an amazing summer for you. Going to do fantastic things for your career eventually, in ways that won't become apparent to you for years yet. You're welcome, by the way."

"So…I mean, that's great, but…we still don't know where the feather and this stuff came from."

"Ah!" Bruckner grinned, lifting a finger. "Very good. Your question shows an ability to focus. Eyes on the prize, and all that. But you're overlooking the one factor that would have made these artifacts' provenance obvious from the beginning." He slowly lowered his finger, pointing at the humming box wired to the pillars.

"That?" Alex stared at the box. He couldn't make head or tail of it. "Alright, I give up. What is it?"

Bruckner's grin widened until he looked the father of all mad scientists. "It's a time machine."

TWO

"Babe. Babe? Hey, Babe…Babe."

A delicate shudder moved over Camila Flores' twenty-year-old body. Behind her mirrored shades, her eyes squeezed tightly shut, and the gentlest of wrinkles formed on her brow—which worried her, because she'd been getting those wrinkles since she and Diego had started dating, and Tia Josette had told her they were murder on your face, eventually.

Diego's voice had been droning in her ear for what must have been fifteen minutes. She could just keep on ignoring him; act like the warmth of the sun had lulled her to sleep. She could make it look entirely plausible; she loved to fall asleep while sunbathing. But Diego would know better; he wouldn't stop, and the small amount of time she had allotted to relaxation this morning would be eaten up, leaving her with a headache.

"Babe? Babe. Honey. Babe. Babe."

Finally Camila gave in. Removing her shades, she turned her head on the towel, trying not to glare. "What? What is it, *babe?*"

A few feet away, on his towel—the one imprinted with the symbol of his beloved Knicks—Diego moved his smartphone from his ear to his shining, hairless chest. *"I could die for a cream soda,"* he mouthed.

Smiling stiffly, Camila stood up and shuffled over to the cooler, wincing at the heat of the poolside concrete on her bare feet. Christ, it was hot today; she half expected to smell her feet start cooking up like burgers on the burning concrete beside the pool. Which was gross.

She flipped open the cooler's lid and stared morosely down into the few bottles floating in the melted water. Three bottles of water, a Corona, and three bottles of the special cream soda Diego insisted on ordering by the case from some deli in New York. She picked a bottle out, watching it drip. She wished Diego would find more sensible things to spend his money on, but the soda *was* good, though she preferred it over ice. Otherwise it was too damned sweet. She considered indulging in a bottle now, but after frowning down at her belly—soft rather than plump, but nowhere near as flat as it should have been-she decided against it. Then she turned back to her boyfriend, who was now chattering animatedly into his phone. He had finally gotten through to whatever "client" he had been trying to call, no doubt being as persistent with call-backs as he had with his summons to Camila.

Diego wasn't from Texas; everything about him screamed *Nuevo* York. His short black hair was gelled into spikes and he liked bling; lots more gold than guys usually wore in Texas, which had gotten him into some trouble with the locals early on. Of course, he had also had trouble back home—of a kind he never specified, though he liked to hint it was the kind of trouble spelled M-O-B—which was the whole reason he had transferred down to Vander. He had family in town, a couple of cousins he rarely saw, but whom his family back in Brooklyn were convinced could keep him on the straight and narrow. *Not so much,* Camila thought ruefully.

"That's right, my friend," Diego said, taking the bottle from Camila with a wink and a quick air-kiss. "You just leave the details to me. This is going to be one party you'll never forget. I'm-a hook you up Manhattan-style, *jefe.*"

As Camila lay back down on her towel, Diego finished up his call with a few more pleasantries, then clicked off and laughed out loud, punching air with his fist and kicking his feet with delight. It reminded Camila of why she had started dating him in the first place. All her friends told her that he was just a wannabe-player with nothing going on. He refused to get a real job, insisting he was a "promoter," something nobody in Vander had ever heard of.

But he had *something*—a spark, a liveliness that none of the local guys had. The stories he told Camila about New York, and his promises to take her there someday always seemed a little too over-the-top...but she had been in Vander all her life, and she was starting to think a little over-the-top might make up for a whole lot of same-old same-old.

"What is it?" she asked finally.

"Score, babe! Total score. This rich kid over in Richter Heights wants a serious party for his twentieth, and your boy is going to give it to him!"

Camila was impressed in spite of herself. Richter Heights was serious money, at least by Vander standards. "How'd he even know to call you?"

"Somebody picked up one of the business cards I left in a nightclub. That cowboy place. See babe, I *told* you those cards were gonna pay off!"

"So how much's he gonna pay you?" *And when's he gonna pay you?* This was the key question; rent was coming due soon, and Camila had promised her mother she wouldn't ask for money this month. Her own job at the Pet Safari would cover it, but there wouldn't be much left for little things like food and the textbooks she'd need for the business course she had signed up for. A decent paycheck from Diego would help an awful lot right about now.

Diego waved the question away. "That's for later, babe. We're in the early stages of this shit right now. I gotta come up with a concept for this little *soiree*, you know? Something really nutzoid." He twisted off the top on his bottle and took a long swig. "Shit, that's good. Best in the City." There wasn't much doubt he meant City with a capital "C."

But you're not in *the City anymore*, Camila wanted to tell him. But they'd had arguments about that subject before, and they had all ended with makeup sex after days of fighting.

Sighing, she shut her eyes again. She had work in another couple of hours, and when Diego got another "client" it could mean weeks of sleepless nights, working on fliers and doing "reconnaissance" in expensive clubs where they had to pay their own cover. She needed to sleep while she could, and hope payday would come early.

THREE

The mother *Titanis* was getting hungry again.

More than a week had passed since she had stood down the shimmering rift in the air, but the incident was as fresh in her memory as though it had occurred the previous day. She had spent the intervening days in a state of nervousness unlike anything she had ever experienced. Apex predators typically don't get nervous, but the mother bird had slept almost as little as she'd eaten recently; the slightest noise or change in air pressure was enough to make her lift her huge head, glaring in every direction. The safety of her egg was a large part of her worry, but there was more to it than that; something about the shining thing was *wrong*, like the scent of disease on a prey-animal. It was dangerous in a way she could not understand, but knew enough to fear.

She had more to worry about than the rift in the air, however. Two more egg thieves had been lurking about the area, attracted by her nervousness. Irregular behavior, they knew, might signal illness. And illness might precede weakness or slower reflexes. The little avians moved stiffly under the scanty shade of a bush, watching the *Titanis* with beady, cautious eyes. If their instincts were correct, eventually it would be an easy matter, working in tandem, to rob her nest of its single remaining egg. After that, if their luck held, they might make a real feast of the mother's body. Her meat would be tough and ropy, but the egg-thieves were not fussy.

All they had to do was wait.

FOUR

"What you tryin' to do there, Alex, twist the damned dial off? *Slowly*, kiddo, put some finesse into it. How you ever gonna make love to a woman?"

Alex had grown up with three uncles and an older brother; this was by no means the first time he suffered teasing of this kind. Even so, he could feel his face turning red as he turned the dial on Bruckner's "time machine." The two pylons made a series of low, whining noises that made his head ache. They seemed to be disturbing the local wildlife as well; crows were circling the yard, occasionally swooping down uncomfortably close to Alex's head. A couple of them were dive-bombing Bruckner as well, but he seemed completely unaware of them. He squatted directly in front of the pillars, chin in hand, bitching under his breath.

"Damnation," he muttered. "Come on. You did it before, *come on*."

Alex knew Bruckner wasn't speaking to him. He had already become acquainted with his new boss' tendency to speak to his machine. He had become acquainted with a *lot* of Bruckner's eccentricities and ideas over the last week; often they were the same thing.

"You know what wormholes are?" That conversation had taken place on Alex's first day. They had been eating at a sandwich place in town. Skinny as Bruckner was, he liked to eat; that day he had been macking down on a Rueben that looked about as thick as his head. Though Alex hadn't yet heard so much as a mention of what his salary would be, Bruckner was never stingy about picking up the tab; since signing on as the cryptozoologist's assistant, his food budget had gone down to practically nothing.

"Sure, they're supposed to be like tunnels in time and space. One end opens up in one point in time-space, and the other point opens up somewhere else. Supposedly you could go through a wormhole from one time to another."

"Right, but no *supposed to* about it, kiddo," Bruckner said, wiping Russian dressing from his beard. "Nothing theoretical about them for the streamers to sneer at, wormholes are *real*. Anytime you got streamers juicing up their careers writing papers about something, there's *something* there. Always keep that in mind, Sonny Jim."

"Streamers" was Bruckner's catch-all term for mainstream scientists, the people he claimed lived to humiliate him while simultaneously stealing his ideas.

"Okay, but I thought wormholes were like, really small. Like microscopic. That's why we can't use them for time-travel outside of science fiction."

"Exactly right," Bruckner nodded. "But they can get bigger, under very special circumstances. Atmospheric pressure, for example. Electricity in the air. Or special kinds of pressure created by tectonic shifting, sometimes vast distances underground. If you really look at the classic cryptozoological cases, really *study* them, you'll see they often occur during circumstances like those. Lightning storms, areas with strong magnetic activity. Perfectly conducive to creating wormhole dilation."

Alex knew all this, of course, having read Bruckner's three major books: *Monsters in the Mist, Creatures from the Void* and *Hell's Bestiary*. "Wormhole dilation" was central to their author's thesis that cryptids were simply prehistoric creatures fallen temporarily out of their own time period. But Alex found Bruckner's in-person rants fascinating. Bruckner either believed completely in his own genius or was convinced everyone else in the world was an idiot. Quite possibly both.

"Your so-called 'Bigfoot?' Nothing but some poor *gigantipithecus* that accidentally walked through a dilated wormhole. Yeti? Same thing, just further east. Loch Ness monster? 'Ohh, it can't exist! There's not enough room in the lake to sustain a breeding population!' Wormhole."

"But why Texas?" Alex asked. "Why *Vander*? This isn't one of the big cryptid hotspots, like Northern California or some lake in Scotland." He knew by now that egging Bruckner on was a potential disaster. His boss had been getting loud, and some of the good old boys in the deli had been nudging each other and grinning in his direction. But Alex couldn't resist. He was genuinely interested in this stuff. *Which is probably the reason I'm still a virgin*, he thought ruefully.

"So?" Bruckner demanded. "Maybe it'll *become* one. Maybe a few months from now, Vander, Texas will be known as the Loch Ness of the sagebrush circuit. Hell, we've already got some archaeological findings suggesting a race of highly-evolved reptilian entities may have once flourished in these parts. Of course, that's a whole 'nother story.

"Either-or, I have reason to believe that that whole area behind my house is a potential hotspot for wormhole dilation. That's the whole reason I moved down here to Cowboy Land." Suddenly his voice dropped to a perfect imitation of a typical Vanderite: "It weren't for the food, buddy, I tell you what."

Bruckner took a long swig of his sweet tea until the last drops rattled in his straw. "Now let's get going. We got work to do. And go get one of those take-out boxes for the rest of your sandwich. People are starving in India, kiddo."

That had been Alex's first-hand introduction to Bruckner's world. Most of his work since then had been writing up his incomprehensible notes, ordering pizza for lunch, and, as now, endlessly fiddling with the machine.

"Darn it, Alex, I said be careful!"

"Sorry." Alex gave the dial another, slower twist. He understood the basic principle of the machine: according to Bruckner, it was able to manipulate different kinds of "ambient pressure" in the immediate area in order to "pierce the quantum foam" and "goose" wormholes into dilating. The pylons worked to sort of "catch" the wormholes and hold them steady as they began growing. The problem was that it was, at this stage, virtually impossible to predict the optimum time for beginning the process. The machine had an "automatic" mode that kept moving from one end of the ambient spectrum to the other—but Bruckner claimed hands-on manipulation of the dial was more effective, even though the machine had succeeded in doing its magic while in automatic, on the day of Alex's arrival. Bruckner swore that, had he not been distracted by Alex ringing the doorbell, he would have witnessed a genuine wormhole opening, with debris swirling in on a wind from another age.

"Hey, Dr. Bruckner?"

"Straw's cheaper."

"Huh?"

"Don't worry about it." Bruckner remained squatting before the pillars, rubbing his hands and squinting like a baseball umpire. "What's on your mind, kiddo?"

"If we do get a wormhole to open, what then? I mean…"

Bruckner sighed, keeping his eyes on the space between the pillars. "Didn't I already explain this to you? We're *not* going to step through the wormhole, if that's what you're worried about. We'd almost certainly never come back, no matter where and when the other end opened up. Nor are we trying to bag a live megatherium or a carnosaur, delightful as that prospect might be. Our goal is to prove the wormhole *will* open, as an observable phenomenon we can make happen anytime we want, *capiche*? I can then release that information through the correct channels—making certain first that the correct proprietary considerations are in effect…"

"You mean making sure you establish ownership," Alex said drily.

Bruckner chuckled. "See? One week in my employ and you're already smarter. Yes, Sonny Jim, I will make sure I 'own' the phenomenon, crass as that sounds to your pink young ears. Believe me, if you were in my shoes, you would do the same. Nothing like having years of your work stolen to keep you on your toes."

"Well…how'd you invent the machine? To begin with, I mean. People have been trying to come up with something like this since forever, but they never even managed to formulate the most basic equations."

He was expecting another rant from Bruckner on his own genius, but it didn't come. Instead, Bruckner, looking down at his hands, said, "I didn't invent it. I mean," he went on, laughing, "I'm a pretty smart guy, but I'm not *that* smart."

"Really?" The idea of Bruckner admitting he was not quite the most brilliant scientist in the world was a little startling.

"A colleague of mine, overseas. Name's Dieter Wolfschmidt. You won't have heard of him, his usual field is theoretical physics. Breathes air far more rarefied than what you and I snort up. He and I made a deal a while back. He's what you call a silent partner in my little adventure here. He backs me—how do you think we've been eating so good?"

"He's rich, then?"

"No, but works for a university that's apparently got more money than common sense. He's one of these geniuses when it comes to getting grants. Grant after grant after…I dunno how he does it. But you know how Europeans are. Charm the stripe off a skunk's *tuchis*."

Before Alex could ask him another question, Bruckner said, "Come on. Let's give it one more try, and then we'll go back to automatic for a while."

Alex sighed. It wasn't like standing around twisting dials was the hardest work in the world, but he knew what would follow was a couple hours of him taking down Bruckner's notes on the day's work, struggling to keep up as the scientist hemmed and hawed and mumbled. How Bruckner got an entire spiral-bound notebook out of what could have been easily summarized as "Tried again; failed" was beyond him.

Well, he thought, *I guess it beats going home and bagging groceries for the summer.*

At that moment, the blinking lights covering the machine stopped blinking. The grinding, headachey sound it had been making came to an abrupt halt. Alex and Bruckner traded stares.

"God *dammit!*" Bruckner cried, flailing gracelessly back into a standing position.

"What happened?" Alex asked, staring guiltily down at the array of dials. "Is it broken?" What he meant was, "Did *I* break it?"

Without answering, Bruckner stormed into the house. Loud shouts of rage ensued from within; some minutes later he emerged from the front door, dragging a second boxy object.

"Gimme a hand here, will ya?"

Alex hurried over and between them they managed to set up the box.

"So what's wrong?" Alex asked, wiping sweat from his brow. *Next time we order lunch*, he thought, *I definitely have to stick with salad...*

"They turned my power off," Bruckner said, kneeling before the smaller machine and beginning to unplug its dangling cables from a series of surge protectors that trailed from inside the house.

"They...you mean the city?"

Bruckner was busily attaching the cables from the smaller device to the surge protectors. "I don't mean the heavenly choirs, kiddo. They finally caught up with me. See, enterprises like this require power—electrical power—and power costs money."

"But you said your friend..."

"He's not sending me *that* much. He's a little naïve when it comes to factoring utility costs into the monthly checks."

"Yeah, but...so what? I mean, the machine was working..."

"Alex," Bruckner said, glaring up at him. "I wasn't *paying* for the power. I was tapping it out of the city's lines. An old trick I learned back in the 70s."

"You stole power?'"

"I prefer to think of it as 'liberating' power. We liberated a lot of stuff in the 70s."

"But that's not...legal!"

Bruckner gave him what was no doubt intended as a wolfish grin, then flung a switch on the boxy object. It began powering up with a hitching, grinding noise. "You are correct, sir. It is *not*, in fact, legal. But I'll simply call up the power company and tell them I had no idea *how* it is that my power wasn't being correctly metered. No doubt it was a bunch of kids from the university playing tricks. And I'll demand my power be restored. After all, I'm not just a faculty member at the university. I'm a published author. A noted expert in the cryptozoology field. They wouldn't *dare* fuck with me."

"But they..."

"Bureaucrats," Bruckner snorted, waving away Alex's concern. "Never overestimate them, my young friend. In the meantime, we've got this nifty portable generator to provide for at least part of our needs."

Alex frowned at him. "Did you 'liberate' that, too?"

"Shaddap. Please go back to turning dials." Bruckner shaded his eyes and stared up at the sky. Clouds were beginning to gather there. "Just for a while more, yet. Looks like we've got some rain coming."

FIVE

When Camila was nine years old she and her sisters had a hamster named Panchito. They made a hobby of overfeeding Panchito until he resembled a furry tennis ball with quizzical little black eyes. Despite her mother's grim predictions, Panchito lived to a ripe old age and never bit any of the girls. He preferred to bask in their attention, happily eating everything set before him or stuffing it in his little hamster cheeks until his head looked positively ready to pop. Young Camila thought Panchito was the cutest, fattest little thing she had ever seen.

When she met Diego's new client, she thought Panchito might have a contender in the world of fattest...cutest, maybe not so much. Kirby Van Zandt was very nearly as round as her old pet, and the excessive neatness of his outfit—white polo shirt, white shorts, white tennis shoes, all expensive—seemed cute at first, as did his crew cut, pug nose, and plump lips. Just the sight of him as he greeted them at the front door of his family's house brought out the same urges in her to cuddle and feed that Panchito always had.

The problem was that Kirby was also a creep. That became evident almost immediately, the moment his beady little eyes locked on her. "Well, my, my, *my*," he whispered, giving himself a tour of Camila's body from her hairline to her freshly painted toenails. From the way he said it Camila could tell he thought of himself as deathlessly clever and charming.

Luckily for her, Diego stepped in immediately, seizing Kirby's hand and pumping it. "Kirby! Homes, how you doin'? I'm Diego, of course...Diego Mercado."

"And who's *that*?" Kirby demanded, poking his spherical head past Diego's back far enough to renew his grinning inspection of Camila's body. Camila was beginning to wish she had worn something slightly more conservative; maybe a suit of plate armor.

"Aww, that's my lady Camila. She's just here for, you know, moral support and shit. So how about we sit down and talk about your par-*tay*? Because I'm telling you, we are gonna blow the roof off this thang!"

Diego managed to lead Kirby back into the living room, talking constantly—Camila recognized the technique. He was trying to dazzle Kirby with bullshit, keeping his mind off little things like his fee—or his girlfriend. He shot Camila a brief grimace over his shoulder and mouthed the words *I'm sorry, babe.*

Sighing, Camila turned around and took a look at the house. It was exactly what she would have expected from Richter Heights; the ceilings were so high she wouldn't have been surprised to see birds flitting around. The décor was all sleek and ultramodern, but the area around the couch and TV was littered with pizza boxes, carryout containers and numberless empty energy drink and soda cans. There were streaks on the wall that looked like someone, angry or bored, had taken to flinging slices of pizza at it. The white leather couch bore so many colorful stains it could have been an arts project. Two pimply teenage boys sat side by side playing a video game. One gave Camila a quick, vaguely interested look before going back to his joystick. The TV showed a jungle landscape from whose trees jerkily-moving zombies regularly emerged to be mowed down by an invisible machine gun. The game quickly threatened to give Camila a headache.

Diego had told her the house belonged to Kirby's parents, who traveled almost perpetually. Camila couldn't help but imagine her mother's response to the house—and to what Kirby had done to it. *She'd be horrified. She'd be filling a bucket right now, trying to mop the walls.*

"Can you get me Pud?" Kirby's voice demanded, somewhere behind her. When he wasn't keeping it all low and would-be sexy, it was shrill, with a grating edge that suggested it was perpetually hovering on the edge of a tantrum. "I like their last album."

"Pud? Aw, hell man, you know I could, I got Justin Slade on speed-dial. But those guys are so last century, dude! You leave the music to me…"

"How about Wanger?" It wasn't clear from Kirby's tone whether he had actually heard Diego.

"Naw, naw, I'm tellin' you, I'm-a hook you up with some *real* music."

"To tell you the truth, the music is a secondary concern. I want girls."

"Girls?" Diego laughed loudly, in a way Camila didn't entirely like. "Girls? *Course* we're gonna get you some ladies, homie. Place'll be *crawlin'* with PYTs."

"For what?" Camila heard herself asking. She turned around to confront Diego, who was sitting with Kirby on another, less dilapidated couch. Diego gave her the faintest shake of his head, and a pleading expression to go with it. Camila could practically hear him: *Please, babe, I got this; this could be so good for us; don't ruin it.*

Camila didn't like it, but she bit back the question. Unfortunately, she had once again attracted Kirby's attention.

"For what?" he leered. "For *companionship*, what do you think?"

One of the guys on the couch—the one who couldn't be bothered to look up at Camila earlier—now lifted his head, like an animal that had just scented meat. His pimply face cracked into a smile that was, if anything, even creepier than Kirby's. He didn't say anything, but Camila could read his meaning easily: *Companionship. I know what* that *means.*

Diego was chattering and trying to laugh it all off, but Camila had had enough. She walked out of the room, heading for the front door and the car. About half an hour later—much longer than Camila liked—Diego joined her. He started up the car and pulled out of the Van Zandt's driveway. His face was thoughtful rather than angry, but it was as though he were alone in the car. Camila didn't like that.

After a while, Camila couldn't take it any longer. "So you're a pimp, now?"

"Huh? No, baby, come on. It's not like that."

"Come on, nothin. You heard that little bastard." She made a face and essayed a fairly solid impression of Kirby's whine: "'*Compaanionship.*' What you think he meant by that? And his little bitch too. Who were those guys, anyway?"

Diego shrugged. "His friends. You know, his buds."

Camila snorted. "They probably don't even know his name. He just keeps them around because nobody else will put up with him. They hang out with him because he has a better gaming system than they do and they're too cheap to either buy their own or go to an arcade."

They drove in silence for a while. "Babe, be reasonable," he said. "This is gonna make us so much money. Kirby's just clueless. He's like a kid wanting a big car he don't even know how to drive."

"And that's fine, but Diego, I don't like it when you suck up to guys like that. Promising him everything. You don't know all those big-ass bands."

"Right, but he don't need to know that, see? I'll get him some up-and-comer band who'll work for nothing. I'll just talk 'em up a little so he thinks they're the next big thing. He thinks he's like a patron of the arts, the band get exposure…everybody's happy."

Camila shut her eyes, pulling her shades down. "And you won't be bringing no skanky hoes to the party?"

"Baby, you know better than that." She could hear the renewed confidence in his voice; he thought he had won, that he had worn her out. Well, let him think that. She could hear him making plans in his head as well, and had no doubt some of those plans involved getting girls for Kirby's party—of one variety or another.

But she was making plans as well; plans that involved her watching Diego very carefully.

As he started chattering on about "next steps" and "people to talk to," Camila eased down in her seat, watching the flat, dried-out landscape zoom by. She frowned up at the sky. It was considerably darker than it had been at their arrival at the Van Zandts', the billowing clouds lit up occasionally by little flashes of lightning.

A storm was coming.

SIX

A storm was coming.

The egg-thieves could sense it. The winds had turned cool and blew with increasing force, carrying drops of cold rain that made the avians wince and sharply shake their heads, hissing in irritation. The mother *Titanis* did not seem to notice. She lay as she had for the past week, neck extended along the dusty ground, completely motionless. She could sense the thieves' presence and kept her eyes on the shrubbery where they hid, but so long as they kept a respectful distance, she would ignore them.

She could feel the egg beneath her quiver as the life inside it began its struggle. Soon it would break free of its prison. The mother would feed the fledgling—after satisfying her own fierce hunger-and provide basic lessons in hunting, but it would soon be strong enough to take on any predators foolish enough to attack it—predators far larger than the little egg-thieves.

Thunder boomed in the blackened sky, and then the rain came, slowly at first, then with increasing fury. The mother lifted her head and squawked in irritation at the clouds, then thrust her head under one stubby wing. It provided little real protection from the sluicing rain, but at least it kept it out of her eyes. Her slick feathers kept the water from soaking her through.

As the storm continued, she became aware of a strange unease. The shining thing had faded from her memory days ago, but now she found herself remembering it. Something in the air--wet and cold as it was— seemed to the mother to echo the day when she'd faced the shining thing down, a sickening sense of *wrongness*.

Then pain: a ripping in the side of her throat that sent hot blood to mix with the cold rain. Shrieking, the mother scrambled to her feet, just in time to see one of the egg-thieves fleeing back to its hiding-place. The creature had taken advantage of the bad weather to venture out and attack her. Its sharp-edged beak had missed any major arteries; still, it had sliced deep, and was painful enough to awaken the mother's rage.

Even so, she did not attack. The downpour made it all but impossible to focus on the thieves, and though her tiny brain had no concept of strategy, she was not without cunning; she could sense the thieves were trying to enrage her enough so that she would leave her nest. The storm and their own hunger had emboldened them. They would have preferred rich yolk over a live fledgling, but the baby, in its weakened state, would be perfectly acceptable to them. The mother couldn't chance leaving the nest for a direct attack. Hissing deep in her throat, she settled herself again, ignoring the pain in her throat.

At that moment another jolt of pain—this time in her thigh—made her scream again. The second egg-thief had circled around her nest while she watched the shrub, and attacked her from the rear.

She rose to a crouching position and lashed out with her heavy beak. It slammed into the sodden earth with easily enough power to crush the egg-thief's skull, but the little avian had already darted out of reach.

The mother tried again to lower herself back onto the nest, but incredibly, rather than keep its distance, the thief made a quick dart at the egg. It had to retreat before the mother caught it in her ravening beak, but it had succeeded in its attempt to enrage her past the point of caution. As it ran through the pouring rain, the mother tore off after it, screaming like a fury, her massive body lit by occasional flashes of lightning.

It was a short chase; the mother ran the thief down within minutes, seizing up its small body and tilting its head back, jerking as she swallowed it whole. The impromptu meal was satisfying, even more so the pleasure of dispensing of an enemy, however small. But when the mother turned back to her nest, the satisfaction immediately evaporated.

She saw the second egg-thief, illumined by a quick flash of lightning, using its beak and clawed hands to push the remaining egg out of the wet, disheveled mess of the nest. It started at the mother's thunderous shriek, then snatched up the egg in its claws and scampered off through the storm.

The mother was nearly insane with rage. Nothing mattered to her now; not the storm, not the sickening feeling that by now completely filled the air, speaking of some fundamental upset in the world, some bizarre transformation ready to birth itself. She had no reason to care about the eggs, nothing but a sharp instinct that told her the eggs were *hers* and not to be trifled with. All she cared about was crushing the thief under her huge clawed feet.

She should have caught the thief. The egg was far too large for it to carry easily and though its tiny mind was less sensitive than the mother's to the weird change in the air, it still felt it. Between the strangeness and the storm, whose fury had not abated, it was running blind, stumbling over the muddy ground, its only objective to get to some quiet place where it could devour its prize in peace. It could hear the mother's feet pounding behind it, only a couple of feet away now. The thief *should* have felt her beak close around its bony body and end its life with barely any effort at all.

But that was the moment when the shining thing opened in front of it, tearing reality open like a piece of rotten cloth.

SEVEN

"Alex!" Bruckner cried from the back door. "Dammit Alex, get in here! Don't *touch* that thing! You wanna *die*?"

Alex whipped his t-shirt at the machine again and again, trying to put out the flames that were licking over the dials and knobs and blinking lights that covered its surface. He would have happily obeyed his boss' order; the rain had started falling in earnest, hard enough to put out the flames on its own.

But it *wasn't* putting the flames out, that was the problem. They hissed and crackled, but instead of extinguishing, they changed color, from dull orange to a bright whitish-blue, and crawled like fiery worms over the machine's surface.

Alex Drummond had never thought of himself as a hero, certainly not as a martyr for science. If Bruckner valued his life above the machine—that he apparently *did* came rather as a pleasant surprise—so did he.

The problem was, it was his fault the machine was on fire. Kinda-sorta. Maybe. Once Bruckner had hooked up the generator, everything seemed to be going swimmingly. The humming noise had started again and Alex had started twisting the dials again. Bruckner had gone back in the house for something, and that was the moment when the knob stuck.

So far as Alex could tell, there was no reason it should have stuck. It just did, and no matter how much force he put on it, it didn't turn. Irritated, Alex tried turning harder, which only succeeded in making his fingers slip on the knob. The edges of it hurt his fingers. This caused more pain than real damage, but it was enough to push Alex over the edge.

Normally Alex wasn't one to lose his temper, but occasionally it did happen. It happened now. It had been a long day of listening to Bruckner's yapping and standing in the heat turning dials. He cried out and kicked the machine with one tennis-shoed foot. It rocked a little, the lights blinking erratically, but it didn't tip over. That convinced something in the hindmost part of Alex's brain that kicking it one more time for good measure would a) do no harm and b) feel really fucking good. So he did. That second time, it fell over onto its side, making an unpleasant shrieking noise. If machines could throw tantrums like a two-year-old, Alex thought, that's what it would sound like.

That was when God or whoever was in charge of these things decided to have some real fun. It happened in an eyeblink, just as the storm hit hard; something white and hot seemed to burst in the air between Alex and the machine. It took him a minute to realize that it had just been struck by lightning.

Then came the flames, and the sickening noise, even worse than the tantrum sound. That was when Alex had torn off his tatty *They Might Be Giants* t-shirt and, in the interest of guilt and responsibility, tried to put the flames out. By the time Bruckner came out and grabbed his arm, he still hadn't succeeded, though his shirt was now blackened and foul-smelling.

Bruckner pulled him away from the machine, back towards the house. This time he made no resistance; he was too busy staring open-mouthed at the flame-edged circular hole that was slowly opening up between the pylons.

Apparently Bruckner saw it too; they stood side by side in the doorway, watching it. To the end of his life, Alex remembered the noise Bruckner made then; it was simultaneously the most joyous and scariest sound he had ever heard. It was only a bit like the laughter it was no doubt supposed to be.

"Houston?" Bruckner howled. "We have wormhole! Repeat, *we have wormhole!*"

EIGHT

The mother *Titanis* shrieked in rage at the shining thing. The anger she felt now was far worse than what she'd felt when the egg-thieves had dared attack her.

The thing was much as she remembered it; circular, with shimmering, silvered edges that kept peeling back, getting wider and wider. The round edges of the thing framed a dark, greenish landscape, but the mother's eyes were too weak to perceive details, nor did she care about them. Even her stolen egg took second place in her attention now. Shrieking at the top of her lungs, she ran with furious speed, determined to fight the shining thing with all the strength she possessed.

Along the way, she tripped on the egg-thief, which was running directly before her. Raging, frantically flapping her rudimentary wings, she tried to regain her balance, only to lose her footing on a wide stretch of slick mud. She went down hard on her side. Meanwhile, the egg-thief had managed to scramble back to its feet. The terrifying shining thing was directly before it, the mother *Titanis* directly behind it. The egg it held stubbornly to its breast.

It did the only thing it could do. Closing its eyes, it kept running. There was a moment of burning brightness, as though it had walked directly into a white fire. But there was no heat or pain as such, though the *discomfort* it felt was somehow far worse. So much worse that when the brightness ended, it fell to the ground, senseless.

The mother, for her part, tried to renew her attack on the shining thing, but the shining thing was shrinking now, growing steadily smaller with the speed of a dry leaf burning. A moment later it was a tiny, shining thing, as though a star had dropped from the sky and now shined a few feet above the ground. Then it was gone entirely, and for the second time, the mother threw her head back and screamed her loss and rage to an uncaring sky.

NINE

"What the *hell* is *that*?" Alex struggled to remain upright. He felt seriously like fainting.

Bruckner moved slowly to the left, keeping his eyes locked on those of the creature that had just come shambling and screaming through the wormhole into his yard. He seemed to be trying to guide it away from the pillars, as though afraid it might somehow open up a new wormhole and escape through it.

The thing's head only came up to his waist, but he didn't like the idea of getting close to it. More than anything, it resembled a small, bipedal dinosaur, but covered in feathers, and with a bird's beak rather than a snout full of gnashing teeth. It high-stepped away from Bruckner, hissing at him. It had stumpy forelimbs that seemed undecided as to whether they wanted to be wings or arms. They ended in clawed almost-hands that were grasping what looked for all the world like a huge egg, like the emu eggs sold at high-end yuppie supermarkets.

"What is it? What *is* it? It's a *verkakte* miracle, kiddo, that's what it is! Now go get my shotgun."

Alex balked. "You're gonna kill it?"

"Not if I can help it. But I don't like the way he's looking at me. I imagine he feels the same way. So I'm asking you to go put in for a little life insurance policy for me. A dead miracle is still a miracle."

"How do you know it's a he?"

Bruckner gave Alex a look. Standing in a crouch, his hair soaked with the last of the storm and his eyes glaring, he didn't look remarkably less formidable than the creature. "Alex…" he said warningly.

"Okay, okay…" It wasn't as though Alex wanted to stick around out here. As he ran back into the house, Bruckner called, "See if you can get something we can use to catch it, while you're in there. I got a dog crate somewhere, but we need something to overpower it first."

"Okay," Alex replied. After a momentary pause, frozen in the kitchen, he called, "Something to overpower it…like what?"

"Oh, just get some salt to put on its tail," Bruckner said blithely. Then: "For God's sake, kid, *improvise*!"

Alex nodded. He went for the shotgun first, because he knew where Bruckner kept it; in a cabinet in his bedroom. He grabbed a box of shells for good measure. The search for dino-bird capturing equipment didn't yield results immediately, but eventually he returned to the yard with a heavy wool blanket over one arm.

When he got back outside the rain had stopped and Bruckner was continuing his dance with the creature. He had gotten it away from the pillars, but if anything it seemed even more hostile, hissing at Bruckner with its crest upraised. Whether because its trip through the wormhole had affected its temper or simply because it suspected Bruckner was trying to steal the egg, it was not happy.

"Ohh, you're a beauty, aren't you?" Bruckner murmured. "What are you, exactly? Like an *oviraptor*, but clearly an avian. You're probably not even on the fossil record, are you? Christ on a crutch, Heuvelmanns would *shit*!"

The last word came out in an enthusiastic, very Bruckner-like shout, and the dino-bird finally freaked out for real, dropping the egg and charging the strange human who insisted on making noises at it.

The creature was between Bruckner and his house's back door, so he was forced to run along the wall. Miraculously, he managed to keep his footing on the rain-soaked grass. The creature's head lashed out again and again, snapping and shrieking. Once it managed to close its beak on Bruckner's flapping shirt-tail. Fortunately, Bruckner was faster than he looked, and stronger; without breaking his stride, he reached behind himself and tore his shirt free. By then he had nearly reached the door.

"Alex!" he screamed. "*Blanket!*"

Alex dropped the shotgun and threw the blanket at the bird creature. Unfortunately, he hadn't properly unfolded it; it hit its target, startling it enough to make it back up, but it then fell heavily to the ground.

Now it was Alex's turn to run. Unlike Bruckner, he panicked, zig-zagging furiously around the yard. He nearly tripped over the toppled machine, just managing to avoid the bird-thing's slashing beak in the process. He tore back in the direction he'd come from, only to pull up short when Bruckner screamed at him.

"The egg! *Watch the egg!*"

His momentary confusion cost him his balance and he flopped face-forward onto the muddy grass. Then something shrieked in triumph and landed on the small of his back with small but surprisingly heavy clawed feet.

Alex could see the bird-thing in his mind's eye, crouched on his back with its rudimentary wings spread, ready to tear his back open. Squeezing his eyes shut, he waited for the end.

Killed by a prehistoric monster. Okay, a small one, but still. And Dad said I wasn't doing anything with my life...

At that moment, something squished in the mud before his nose. Overhead, a loud *crack* sounded, like a bat connecting with a heavy softball, and the bird-thing's weight toppled off his back with a drunken cawing noise. Opening his eyes, Alex saw Bruckner directly before him, breathing hard and holding his shotgun by the barrel.

"Seriously?" he demanded shrilly, shaking the gun. "You didn't *load* it?"

"I forgot," Alex said, wincing as he got to his feet.

Bruckner was looking over the prone bird-creature. "Meh. Just as well. At least now we got a fifty-fifty chance our little birdy is still alive. Always looks good when the specimen is alive; the Nobel people like that. Remember that, kiddo."

Nodding, Alex reached behind himself and pressed his back, as though prepared to crack it. His hands came back bloody and for an extremely unpleasant moment he thought he was going to faint or puke. Or both. "Oh my god…"

"Let me see," Bruckner said gruffly, turning him around. "Ahh, it'll be okay by the time you're married. We'll put some mercurochrome on those bad boys, you'll be good as new."

"Bad boys?" Alex quavered. "*How* bad, exactly?"

"Look kiddo, pretty Polly over there was getting ready to take your kidneys out. So which do you want? A little mercurochrome or peeing into a bag the rest of your life?"

Alex sighed. "Fine. So what do we do with it?"

"First thing we do is get him wrapped up in that blanket you so thoughtfully forgot to open up. I clocked him pretty good, but I don't want to take any chances. Otherwise both of us will be doing the pee-bag boogie well into our senescence. Senescences. Sess…you know what I mean. Then we'll get him into that dog crate and…well, I'll let you know when I figure the next part out."

"So I guess this proves your theories are right, huh?" Alex said, retrieving the blanket.

"Well, it's a pretty damn good start," Bruckner said, taking it from him and shaking it open. He laid it over the bird and began rolling it up in the blanket, like the world's most ungainly burrito. "I'd like to see one of the streamers explain this guy away as swamp gas or a misidentified heron. Because you *know* they're gonna try that shit."

"Right, but I don't…"

"Watch where you're going!" Bruckner screamed. Startled, Alex looked down and saw his foot about to descend upon the bird-thing's egg.

"I'm sorry! Jesus!"

"Jesus my eye! C'mon, Alex, are you *trying* to destroy the scientific discovery of the age?" Bruckner demanded, reaching down to retrieve the egg. He dusted it off lovingly. A moment later, a strange look came over Bruckner's face and he stared down at the egg with a weird, dumbstruck smile, as though it had just spoken to him.

"I felt it move," Bruckner crooned. Alex felt sick.

"You think it's going to hatch?" Alex asked. The idea didn't inspire any smiles in him.

"Not immediately," Bruckner said. "But I'm guessing soon. Come on, let's get our two guests inside and find suitable accommodations. I'm telling you, kiddo," he went on, setting the egg carefully down and moving over to help Alex lift the wrapped-up bird thing. "This is gonna be one hell of a summer."

TEN

Camila stared moodily out the window of the PetPlace shop. The storm of the previous day showed no signs of making an encore, but the weather had continued dark and unpleasant. Nail salons did well in weather like this, but no one in Vander had much use for a fancy pet store...except for a few borderline creepy teenage boys who came in regularly to brag to her about their reptile collections. Apparently they thought girls found chameleons as sexy as muscle cars. Apart from them, the store's main clientele were good old boys coming in to buy gigantic sacks of kibble for their hounds.

Sighing, Camila went back to her magazine. The PetPlace wasn't just empty of customers; Julie and Chris had both called in sick, apparently neither knowing or caring if anyone knew they had started fucking. Ronald simply hadn't bothered to come in at all. Most likely he was sitting at home stoned out of his mind, watching shows about Ancient Aliens on the Discovery Channel. Chad the Manager had the day off. It was just her and the hamsters and cockatiels and bearded dragons. When the phone rang, she was almost glad for a change.

"PetPlace," she said. She was also supposed to state her name and inquire how she might be of assistance to the caller, but to hell with it. It was raining.

"Uhm, hey...I was wondering...uh, do you have any incubation equipment?"'

"Incu...what, you mean for hatching eggs?" Camila was suspicious—or would have been; the question sounded like the lead-in to a phone prank, except she'd never heard one involving incubators...and she had pretty much heard them all. Plus, the guy on the other line didn't sound like a prankster; he sounded young and nervous, as though he were being forced at gunpoint to make the call.

"Right, but not like chicken eggs...I mean, *like* chicken eggs, except, uhm...bigger."

Camila wrinkled her nose. "Like *how* big? You raising ostriches over there?"

"Oh!" The guy seemed startled by the question. "Oh, uh, close...emus."

It's like the girl says in that book by that one English pedo guy, Camila thought. *Curiouser and curiouser.*

"Emus."

"Right. Like ostriches, but…smaller."

"Okay, first of all, an incubator for emu eggs is probably more like farming equipment. We're a *pet* store. There are some places nearby that sell that kind of stuff…"

"Yeah, Smitty's and Agri-All." The guy sounded relieved than disappointed. "I tried them already. Thanks, though."

"Wait! Hold on. Do you *have* emus?"

The guy sounded profoundly disappointed at having his escape thwarted. "Some people raise them for their eggs…you know, and feathers."

"Okay, so is that what you're doing?" Chad would have her ass for quizzing a customer like this, she knew. Well, Chad wasn't here, and she was bored. Teasing shy boys was the most dependable source of entertainment she knew, apart from sex and shopping.

"I…I…my boss is. Raising them."

"Yeah?" Camila demanded, putting on her best sassy Latina voice. "And who's your *jefe*?" *I should've said "Who's your daddy?"* she thought, wanting to giggle. *He would have probably peed himself.*

"He's…uh, Thaddeus Bruckner."

That startled Camila. "Wait. Bruckner like the guy who teaches at the University? Everybody says he's this total weirdo who believes in like the Loch Ness Monster and shit."

"That's the one," the guy said miserably.

"He's your boss? So who are you? His TA or something?"

"No, I'm just…I…look, I really gotta go."

"Tell me your name," Camila demanded, making her voice as cold and threatening as she could manage. "You tell me, or I'll come out there and…"

The poor guy sounded like he was about to have a full-on panic attack. "Alex Drummond, okay? I…"

"Wait! I know you! You were in my English class last semester. You helped my friend Julie with her paper." The minute she said it, Camila winced and wished she hadn't. Julie had basically cock-teased the poor guy into writing her paper for her, then pointedly ignored him one time he tried to talk to her in the Student Union. Camila had disapproved, but not enough to actually say anything to Julie. Trying to call Julie out on bad behavior was an exercise in futility.

"Yeah," Alex said, his voice sounding hollow.

"Okay, so…you actually have emus out there?"

"We have an egg," Alex said shortly. He didn't sound scared or nervous now; he sounded pissed-off and Camila couldn't actually blame him.

"An egg you're gonna hatch?" she said. She knew she was just babbling now, but she couldn't quite help herself.

"That's the idea. Look, thanks for your help. I really just…I gotta go." With that, he hung up.

Camila walked over to the tropical fish section, staring at a swarm of neon tetras.

"Well, that sucked," she told the fish. It had, too. She had just been having some fun and now she had probably ruined the poor guy's day. It would serve her right if he called up the head office and complained about her, got her fired.

Except she knew he wouldn't. She didn't really know Alex Drummond, but she knew guys like him didn't do vengeful things like that. Well, maybe the really creepy ones did…like in that movie she'd seen on Lifetime about the revenge porn guy. But she knew Alex wouldn't do it.

"I should apologize to him," she told a morbidly obese guinea pig shuffling around its cage.

But you can't, she imagined the guinea pig saying. *You don't have his number.*

I could get it from someone. Or I could look it up.

And get busted for stalking, the guinea pig retorted. *Wouldn't that be a genius move? Because face it, you have no interest in this guy; you just feel guilty, and not even about something you did.*

He wouldn't bust me, Camila thought back. But after that she was silent for a long while, standing with her lips pooched out, thoughtfully tapping the glass of the guinea pig's case with one red fingernail.

How about this, though? I can look up Dr. Bruckner's address and leave a nice apology note in an envelope with Alex's name on it. That way I can apologize without looking like a stalker, or even bothering Alex too much.

Your funeral, chica, the guinea pig thought, and irritably turned its back on her.

It took Camila only a couple of minutes to find Dr. Bruckner's address on her smartphone's web browser, and then a few minutes more to write a short, sweet note of apology on PetPlace stationary and fold it into an envelope with ALEX written on it. Should she draw a little smiley heart on it? *No, that's too much.*

By then Ronald came in, still smelling quite strongly of pot.

"Hey, Ronald McDonald! You mind if I take off early?"

Ronald shrugged as he ambled past her. That was good enough for Camila; a few minutes later she was on her way to Bruckner's place to do the right thing and—had she but known—nearly destroy western civilization in the process.

ELEVEN

Alex picked up the science fiction paperback he had been trying to read for the last half an hour, and promptly put it back on the chair's armrest. He took off his glasses and rubbed his eyes, thinking about the large amount of cold pizza, leftover Chinese food and potato salad in Bruckner's refrigerator…then he decided he didn't have the stomach for it.

What he did *not* want to think about was the girl he had just spoken to at PetPlace, but she had destroyed his peace of mind for the next week, at least. As soon as she mentioned Julie Garcia, he knew who she was: tall and brunette, more cute than gorgeous, but seriously good-looking all the same. He had never spoken to her directly before today and he didn't intend to ever again. His experience with Julie had been enough.

A sudden hissing shriek made him nearly jump out of his chair. The bird-thing was out in the back yard, in the dog carrier they had finally managed to find in the spare bedroom Bruckner used as storage space. It was large enough to hold it, allowing it to stalk around the carrier fully upright, giving vent every few minutes to one of those shrieks. Alex preferred not to think about why Bruckner had the carrier in the first place.

Bruckner had offered the thing (which at Alex's suggestion they had dubbed "Thing One") half a dozen eggs from his refrigerator; it had gobbled them up with every sign of pleasure, then polished off a couple of freshly-thawed pork chops that represented all the foodstuffs in the house not meant to be eaten with a plastic fork. Alex's boss had headed into town to buy more food, charging Alex with looking into incubation possibilities for the egg. The egg itself had been wrapped in an old towel and set near one of the radiators. Bruckner confessed he had no idea what kind of temperature would work to hatch it.

"We're gonna have to do this by trial and error, kiddo. But that's par for the course with great scientists, right? Just pretend you're Jonas Salk and everything'll be groovy."

"Right," Alex muttered. "Groovy." Thing One shrieked again and he got up to get himself a coke.

As he was making his way to the kitchen, he heard a car door slam outside the house. *That's weird*, he thought. Was Bruckner back already? He picked his way back through the living room and flung the door open. A dark-haired girl about his age was standing crouched slightly, about to slide an envelope through the mail-drop.

"Oh," she said, straightening up. She looked embarrassed, and a little guilty, like she'd been caught doing something illegal. "I'm sorry, I didn't know anybody was here. I…"

"Camila?" he asked, finally remembering her name. The girl from PetPlace. Julie's friend.

"Yeah." Brushing hair out of her eyes, she handed him the envelope. "I, I just wanted to give you this."

Alex opened the envelope. Inside was a sheet of PetPlace stationary with the words, "Alex – Sorry I gave you a hard time. Hope we're cool. C."

"Oh…that's okay. I mean…it wasn't any big deal." Alex could feel his cheeks heating up. He felt something else as well, a surge of hope that he knew deep down was a really, really bad idea. *You felt the same way when Julie asked you to help her.* That *worked out pretty well, didn't it?*

"Yeah, so…where are the emus?"

"Emus?" For a moment he had no idea what she was talking about. Then he remembered their conversation, and Bruckner's instructions. "For god's sake, try not to give away any more information than you need to. If they want to know what we're incubating, tell 'em I'm raising emus."

"Yeah, I'll bet they're cute, especially the babies. I looked up some pics on the way over, see?" She held up her phone, showing Alex a collage of photos of tall, gawky-looking birds with big, staring eyes.

"Oh, yeah, I…I'm not really supposed to…" Thing One picked that moment to scream again. Alex winced, but Camila had already darted past him, making for the source of the sound.

"Ohmigod, I can hear them! He has them out back, right?"

Alex stood with slumped shoulders. Finally he began folding up the note, then carefully slid it back into its envelope. *I should probably keep this as a souvenir or something. The last time a hot girl gave me anything.*

"Alex," Camila's voice called. "Alex, I don't think this is an emu."

"Yeah," Alex said. Of course, Dr. Bruckner is going to be giving me something. He's going to be giving me six shades of hell for betraying his secret to the outside world. Cause somehow I don't think Camila is real good at keeping secrets. "Yeah, no…it's not."

"I mean, emu eggs are green, usually. Right? Like, real dark green."

"Yeah, like…wait, *what*?"

As Alex ran out of the room, Camila continued. "And what do you have it in this old box for? It should be out with its mom."

As he turned the corner, he saw Camila in the little nook outside Bruckner's bedroom, kneeling over the box containing the egg. She must have seen it before continuing on to the kitchen.

She hadn't seen Thing One yet. There was still hope, if he could just keep her distracted long enough to get her out of the house. It shouldn't be difficult; she was smiling down dreamily at the egg, tracing gentle spirals on its shell with her fingertip.

"Yeah, that's...I mean, it's a new species Bruckner is trying to develop." Alex actually felt proud of himself for a moment before Camila said, "Why? Birds aren't his field, I thought. I thought it was like weird crypto-paranormal stuff."

"He...he...uh..." Thing One began shrieking again in its carrier, as though in resentment that the egg had distracted attention from it.

Camila squealed suddenly, clapping both hands to her mouth with an expression of delight. "Oh my god! It's *hatching*!"

Alex stared at the box. A jagged crack had appeared in the egg's shell, then widened while the egg jerked and rocked on its rounded end. Then a section of the shell fell away from what was clearly a beak— broad and strong-looking, with a wicked hooked edge. It didn't look anything like the beak of the creature that had carried it through the wormhole. The beak opened as widely as it could, and a voice—breathy and feeble, but also much louder than Alex would have expected, exploded into the room.

"*Ra-awwk!*"

"Oh god!" Camila cried, grabbing his arm and tugging at it in unreasoning delight. "It's a *baby*! Oh, it's so *cute*!"

On the back porch, Thing One suddenly went silent—and stayed that way, as though it no longer cared to draw attention to itself. Alex couldn't be sure, but he had a feeling that was a bad sign.

TWELVE

The mother *Titanis* tore a vast chunk of meat from the thigh of the antelope. She threw her head back, letting the flesh work its way inch by inch down her throat. Days after she had lost her last egg, hunger still burned in her belly. Without the nest, there was nothing to keep her from satisfying that hunger whenever she wanted. But there was another reason her territory was littered with bones and darkened with the blood of prey animals of every size.

Time had not diminished the mother's anger. Three times her nest had been robbed, and each time she had been unable to prevent it. She didn't feel her anger the way a human would—it did not change to grief and did not provoke longings for revenge, as such. It burned without reason or any ability to articulate it. The shining thing infuriated her most—not merely for its wrongness now, but because it had swallowed up not merely her egg, but the egg-thief that had stolen it.

She fully expected the shining thing to return. In the meantime, she would strengthen herself with as much meat as she could devour. Screaming with renewed rage, her head jerked downward, her beak hammering the antelope's skull to pulp. When there was nothing left, she lifted her head and once again bellowed her battle-cry.

"Rawwk! *Ra-awwk!*"

THIRTEEN

"Poor little ugly baby," Camila cooed. "He's all naked."

Alex didn't understand her delight with the little monster that had emerged from the egg. Whatever it was, it certainly wasn't the same species as the bird that had brought it over. It stood nearly a foot tall, and looked like a plucked chicken equipped with a wicked hooked beak roughly a quarter of its own body mass. It teetered around like a drunkard, trying to keep its balance. Every now and then it glared at them.

"It's hungry. Can we feed it?"

"It…it eats a special food," Alex said. His ability to lie quickly and fluently was developing steadily; he wasn't certain how happy he was about that. "Designed for baby emus. I'll have to mix up a new batch. Dr. Bruckner wasn't expecting it to hatch today."

He was no paleontologist, but that massive hooked beak didn't look like it was made for birdseed. So far Camila had been willing to go along with the emu story—he had an idea she wasn't real clear about what emus were like-but Alex had a feeling she'd get suspicious if she saw him feeding it ribeye steaks.

Even so, the baby was clearly hungry; its shrieks were getting louder and its movements—now that it was a bit steadier on its feet—more aggressive. It kept its beady eyes fixed on Alex, as though sizing him up as a possible candidate for its first meal. He was keeping his eyes on it as well, though he had an idea that, as with an angry dog, meeting its glance was a bad idea. He didn't trust the little monster not to take a bite out of him if he looked away.

"What are you gonna name it?" Camila asked. Alex risked looking at her and his blood froze—she was aiming her smartphone at the creature, firing off multiple pictures of it.

"I…I don't think Dr. Bruckner wants pictures…" That was a severe understatement. He could already hear his boss ranting and screaming; he was already starting to get a headache.

"Know what I think you should name it? 'Roc.' 'Cause that's what it keeps saying, you know?"

"*Ra-awwk*!" Roc said.

"Plus, wasn't there some kind of legendary bird that was like really big and…"

"Yeah, it was called a roc," Alex said. "From the *Arabian Nights*. But I don't think...*ow!*" He jumped back from the baby, which had taken an experimental peck at his pantleg. Luckily, Alex had never gotten used to the local taste for wearing shorts 24/7; his jeans were the only thing that kept him from a minor flesh wound. But he had a feeling that as Roc grew larger, he was going to need a lot more than denim for protection.

"Anyway, I gotta go. Meeting my boyfriend. Can I come back and see the baby sometime?"

"I..." He had told himself he was going to be firm, tell her that she had to delete the pictures on her phone immediately. But the word *boyfriend* struck with unexpected sharpness and left him standing dumbfounded. He wasn't surprised by it exactly, he just...

"I'll just drop by, okay?" She smiled as she pocketed her phone. "I'm glad I came today. No hard feelings about before, right?"

For a moment Alex wasn't sure what she was talking about. Then she was gone. He stood staring at the doorway, listening to the sound of her car starting and driving off. Then he shouted, wincing and dancing back a few steps as Roc had another go at his leg.

This time his beak cut through the denim and drew blood. The bite wasn't too painful, but it was bleeding freely.

"I sure hope Dr. Bruckner gets back soon," Alex told Roc, glaring as he rubbed his leg. "He'll know what to do, because I sure as hell don't."

FOURTEEN

When Camila got to Diego's place, she found two cars she didn't recognize parked in the driveway. One was a Porsche, one a beat-up looking Subaru, both large enough that they were parked nose-to-ass with the Subaru's bumper sticking out onto the street. Diego's truck was parked on the street facing the building. *That's interesting*, Camila thought. Diego lived on the top floor of a small duplex; the first floor was uninhabited, so he was used to having the driveway to himself. He rarely had visitors; certainly not the kind of visitors who drove Porsches.

When Camila let herself in, she stiffened up immediately; Diego was seated on the threadbare couch, surrounded by three girls. The girls weren't *exactly* giving Diego a three-way lap dance, but they were definitely being more friendly than they needed to be.

During this assault, Diego was talking away to Kirby Van Zandt, who sat perched in a straight-backed kitchen chair, squirming uncomfortably. Diego had picked the chair up from a dumpster—simply because it was free, as Camila recalled—and took a perverse pleasure in telling everyone it was the most uncomfortable seat in the house. Kirby's discomfort seemed to have more to do with the girls, though; his piggy little eyes were focused on their writhings with laser intensity. He didn't even look up when Camila shut the door behind her with pointed force.

"Babe," Diego said, hurriedly struggling to disengage himself from his visitors. "Where were you? We were just talking over some logistics with Kirbs here."

Kirby turned a sickly grin on Camila, one that reminded her of a fat little boy who had just been given the key to a warehouse full of candy. "This's our band," he said dreamily.

Camila turned her attention to the girls, who sat snuggled into one perfumed, skanky mass, looking her up and down with something a little too much like contempt for her liking. All three looked to her like self-conscious "bad" girls, the kind who hung out at rock clubs and wore too much makeup and made a hobby of stealing the boyfriends of girls who had to work at pet stores for a living.

"Band, huh?" she demanded, looking them up and down in her turn.

"Yeah, honey, I told you about these girls, right? They're Fuzzpie."

The girl on the left stood up and extended her hand—the look on her face made it look more like a challenge than friendliness. She was tall and Asian, her blue-streaked black hair piled up on her head and speared through with a chopstick. Her face was pretty, but her features so strong they looked witchy, a quality not relieved by her two-inch blood-red nails. Like her *compadres*, she wore very little; torn cut-offs and a baby-doll tee that showed off swelling boobs Camila decided were fake.

"I'm Gina," she said shortly. "Bass and lead singer. That's Missy," she went on, nodding at a washed-out looking blonde. "Guitar. And that's Dusty, our drummer." Dusty was a tiny redhead with a pixie-cut and a wide, somehow deranged-looking smile.

"What kind of music you guys play?"

"Skronk," Missy said, in a surprisingly deep voice. She sat pulling her bleached-looking hair through her fingers, watching the action with wide, empty eyes.

"What kind of music?"

"Skronk," Gina said. "Actually neo-Skronk. We're bringing it back. Skronk was like a post-punk thing in New York in the late 70s. Arto Lindsay? Lydia Lunch?"

Camila shook her head, then turned to Kirby. "So these are the guys who are going to play your party?"

"Sure," Gina purred, sashaying over to Kirby and fingering his hair. "We'll do mos' anything Kirby-Wirby here likes, won't we Kirby?" Kirby made an unpleasant giggling noise.

"Diego, can I talk to you for a minute?" Camila seized his hand and pulled him into the kitchenette.

"Babe…"

"Shut up!" Camila hissed. "Just. Shut. Up." She jerked her head back at the group in the living room. "Seriously, Diego? Seriously? Where'd you even find these girls?"

"I told you, honey…they're playing the clubs downtown."

"What clubs, Diego? What clubs in Vander book 'neo-Skronk' bands? Last time I checked, the only kind of live music you could see in town was *tejana* and those creepy guys who do George Jones covers."

Diego sighed heavily, his shoulders slumping. Camila watched carefully, recognizing the signs that Diego was ready to tell the truth. "Okay, look. They're not playing anywhere. I found them through their Facebook page."

"Do they even know how to play their instruments?"

"Babe, I'm not 100% sure they *have* instruments. But they're willing to play Kirby's party—get this—for beer. And they'll, you know, flirt with him a little. That's all he wants. You saw how Gina had him eating out of her hand back there. I'm telling you, we'll come out of this so good…"

"I don't care. But if I see those bitches lay their hands on you just one more time…" It took her a moment to actually get it out, but finally she managed it. "That's it. We're done. You hear me?"

"Baby," Diego smiled. "Trust me. Alright?"

FIFTEEN

"*Titanis walleri,*" Bruckner said finally, looking up from the book. "That's gotta be it."

"*Titanis...?*" Alex said, staring out the sliding kitchen door at Roc. Bruckner had been overjoyed when he'd returned home to find the egg hatched, so much so he'd given him the run of the back yard. Roc was considerably steadier on his feet now, and slightly larger looking. A light down covered his naked skin. He ran from side to side, chasing flies and shrieking when he didn't catch them.

"Better known as a 'terror bird,'" Bruckner said, setting the book down on the kitchen table. "What's with you, kiddo, you don't watch the Discovery Channel?"

"Yeah, I do. That's why I thought Terror Birds were only in South America."

"Most of them were, smart guy. *Titanis* was one of the species that migrated north to south Texas. They've also found their fossils over in Florida."

"And they were dangerous, right?" Alex said, glancing at Roc.

"Oh, they were the apex predator back in the day, *bubbi*, apex! Like little pint-sized Tyrannosaurs. They even beat out saber-tooths for a while. I mean, look at that beak on our boy."

Bruckner considered Thing One, who squatted sulking in the dog carrier. "Our friend there must have stolen the egg from a *Titanis* nest and gotten pulled into the wormhole once it opened. Amazing luck."

"Yeah, amazing. Well, how long before he grows up? Roc, I mean. He looks a little bigger than he did yesterday."

"To answer your first question," Bruckner said, digging a hand into a bag of nacho chips, "we can't be sure. I mean, estimating the growth rates of extinct animals is a crapshoot, pretty much. Ostriches and emus mature in about a year, so that'd be a pretty good guess."

"But he looks..."

"I know, I know," Bruckner said through a mouthful of chips. "Bigger than yesterday. Heard you the first time, grasshopper. And you're right. Could be just a normal growth spurt, could be..." He went silent suddenly, chewing industriously and watching Roc's antics through narrowed eyes.

"What?"

Bruckner shook his head. "It could be a side effect of coming through the portal. He might be aging at a slightly accelerated rate."

"But when he's fully grown he'll be a monster. An apex predator, you said."

"Yeah. Well, don't worry, kiddo. I've already set up my grand unveiling."

"Unveil...I thought you said you were going to get in touch with your guys at the university, and..."

"Yeah, yeah. Grow some vision, kid. I only get one shot at this, since *someone* fucked up my machine. So I can't be conservative about it. If I write up my little paper and tell the big boys about it and say, 'Oh please, Dr. Numbnuts, can you validate my incredible, groundbreaking discovery,' it'll be like an open invitation for the streamers to come in and steal my thunder. You'll be seeing documentaries on Roc on TV, and will old Dr. Bruckner's name be on them? No it will not! Because what do streamers do?"

"Lie and steal your work," Alex sighed.

"Bingo. Don't worry about the unveiling, kiddo. Leave that to me. Now get me another bag of chips. Can't be brilliant on an empty stomach."

SIXTEEN

"What's this thing?"

"What thing?" Camila grimaced at her reflection in the mirror. She had woken up to a phone call from Chad asking if she would take an early shift. She couldn't pass up the extra money, but she didn't have much time to get to the store. Chad was incredibly tight-assed about people getting in on time.

"This…Jesus! What is this, like a plucked chicken?"

"Plucked…Diego!" Getting up from her makeup table, she whirled to confront Diego where he lay on her bed, scrolling through the photos on her phone.

"I told you not to go through my phone!" she cried, snatching it from his hands. There was nothing on the phone she was ashamed of, but she had a thing about privacy, ever since her mother had caught a guy she had been dating going through her checkbook. Sometimes she thought if she were less of a stickler for privacy, she might have easily caught Diego sexting with some bitch…at the same time, that wasn't something she was particularly eager to do.

"Okay, sorry," Diego muttered. He always felt sorry, but never quite got that going through her stuff was something he shouldn't do in the first place. "But seriously, what is that thing?"

"It's a baby emu," Camila huffed, scrolling quickly through her pics of Roc to make sure none had been accidentally deleted. "Haven't you ever seen a baby emu before?"

"I ain't never seen an *adult* emu before," Diego admitted. "Or a, what'cha call, geriatric emu. That thing looks like a damned baby dinosaur."

"Well, it isn't. It's a bird, and one of the professors is raising them."

"For real? Why?"

"I don't know, Diego. Feathers…or eggs or some kinda science thing. Look, I just gotta go, or Chad'll be all up my ass." Setting her phone on her dresser, she began digging through a drawer with increasing agitation.

"Jesus, I don't have any clean jeans!"

"Gotcha covered, babe. I put a load in last night."

Camila hesitated before asking, "*And* in the drier?"

"Of course!"

Camila smiled gratefully, clutching briefly at Diego's arm before running for the drier on the second floor. As soon as she was through the door, Diego grabbed her phone and quickly sent himself three of Roc's pictures before replacing it carefully on the dresser.

"Some *Jurassic Park* shit over here," he remarked to himself, before getting back on the bed.

SEVENTEEN

"Wait till I tell you, then turn the juice on," Bruckner said, out in the yard. The pause that followed went on for a small eternity, then: "Okay…nn-nn--*now*!"

Alex snapped the red switch on the surge protector into the "On" position, then sat back on his heels, waiting. Almost immediately Bruckner said, "Shit."

"Still nothing?"

"A little flicker, then it went out. Don't worry, we'll get it."

Alex sighed. They had spent most of the morning trying to get the machine up and running again, without much success. The one consolation was that his boss showed no signs of being seriously pissed at him for breaking it. Of course, he had been so busy with Roc—taking pictures of him from every angle, recording what he ate and what condition it came out in later—that he had had time for little else. There had been phone calls as well, dozens of them, made in Bruckner's office with the door shut. Alex found that a little off-putting.

But the pictures he had let Camila take worried him more. He didn't think Bruckner would be so forgiving.

"Raaw-wk?"

Alex started. The *Titanis* fledgling had stolen up to him while he was lost in thought and now stood outside the patio doors, looking quizzically at him. Roc was now half as tall as Alex himself, his plumage coming in at a slow but steady rate. Bruckner had insisted on giving him the run of the yard. There had been one incident early on where he had gone after Bruckner, but that had been stifled easily enough when Bruckner cracked him on the beak with a wrench.

"He needs exercise," Bruckner had said when Alex had protested. "Once he reaches his full size, we'll have figured out how to sedate him."

Thing One cowered in its carrier, hissing a little. Since Roc had begun roaming the yard, it had showed little interest in leaving the carrier. Now Roc, his interest piqued, stepped into the house, his claws clicking on the faded linoleum. He bent down and gave the hard plastic of the carrier an experimental poke with his massive beak, sending it sliding a few inches. Thing One hissed frantically, and Roc carefully bit a bar of the cage with his beak's hook, applying enough pressure to bend it close to the breaking point.

"Hey! Get away from there!" Alex said, waving his hands at the fledgling. "Go on, *hsst*! Get out!" Roc gave him a quick "Are you crazy?" look, then went back to its efforts to get to Thing One.

Alex got up and got the broom. "You want this?" he shouted, shaking the bristles at Roc. "You want it? Huh?" He felt like an idiot, but Thing One figured only a little less in Dr. Bruckner's plans than Roc himself. If he let it get eaten, his boss would *not* be pleased.

Roc didn't deign to reply until Alex's tentative poking succeeded in brushing the broom's dusty bristles over the side of his face. Then, with a movement so quickly Alex gasped, he seized the broom in his beak and yanked it backward out of Alex's hands. Holding the broom down with one foot, he tore at the bristles, then caught up the shaft in his beak and bit down, snapping it in two with a loud *crack*.

"Shit," Alex breathed, taking a step back. The broomstick was solid wood; he couldn't imagine the strength it would take to simply bite it in two. He imagined his hand in Roc's mouth, or his arm. The bird eyes were fixed on Alex's, and though he tried to look away, he couldn't.

Roc lowered his head, hissing, and took a step towards him. *Oh, Jesus.* He moved backward, one hand groping on the table for something he could use to defend himself.

"Alex!" Bruckner shouted. "Try it now!"

Roc started at Bruckner's voice, then sauntered back out towards the yard, as though he had completely forgotten about Alex.

Relief washed over Alex. "Thank God," he muttered, resisting the urge to cross himself. A strange sensation ran over his body, a shivery feeling of danger barely averted.

I've got to tell Bruckner. Tell him his little science project almost killed me. It's dangerous, and it's only going to get bigger. And I've got to tell him about Camila taking those pictures while I'm at it.

"Alex! C'mon, kiddo, what'cha doin' in there?"

Starting, Alex hurried to the surge protector and flipped the switch. *I've got to just go out there and do it, while he's not preoccupied. Just say 'Dr. Bruckner…'"*

"Yeah!" Bruckner's voice exploded from the yard. Alex caught a glimpse of his boss jumping around punching air. Roc, squawking in agitation, scampered to get out of his way.

"It worked! Back online, motherfucker! Whoo-*hoo*!"

"Ah, crap," Alex muttered. From the dog carrier, Thing One made a low *merp*ing noise, apparently in sympathy.

EIGHTEEN

Kirby Van Zandt's stubby finger stabbed at the image on Diego's phone.

"I want it."

Diego's smile had a slightly sickly appearance, like a man realizing he'd bitten off a little more than he could chew. "Dude, that's great, but I can't like…"

Kirby waddled back to his couch and threw himself down, loudly slurping at the fountain drink he had made Diego drive a mile out of his way to bring him. "So what are you saying? You come in here, show me a picture of a live fucking dinosaur, say 'Take a look at this, dude,' and then you're all like, 'Duh, duh, well, I can't, duh-hh…'"

Diego inhaled, swallowing Kirby's tirade—delivered with rolled eyes and appropriately spastic motions of the shoulders. "Dude, I was just trying to give you an idea of what my concept for the party was all about. The whole prehistoric thing, yeah? Like, I was thinking we could get some sculptures made that look like that little guy? Set 'em up around the stage, see, and then the girls come out in their little fly cavegirl shit, right, and…"

Another slurp, much louder. Turning the conversation to the girls was normally a dependable way to bring Kirby to heel; not tonight, it seemed. "Let's start over. I said that's a *live fucking dinosaur*. What is it about that statement that escapes you?"

"Dude, it's not a dinosaur. It just looks like one. I mean, birds are basically dinosaurs, right? I saw that on the Discovery Channel and shit."

"Yeah? What kind of bird is it, then, 'dude?'"

Diego groped for the word that described the weird little bird. It escaped him, and he could tell his efforts to bring it to mind were being watched with some irritation by Kirby.

"It's an ostrich, man," he said finally. "That's all. Baby fuckin' ostrich."

"Seriously? Do you see the beak on that thing? When's the last time you ever saw an ostrich with a schnozz like that?"

"So it's a freak or something. Its beak is, what'cha call, abnormally large."

"Yeah, and I'm starting to think your bill is abnormally large for what I'm getting. Especially when you start playing games like this."

Diego fell silent, giving himself a break. He was starting to get seriously pissed; he wasn't used to being spoken to like a damned servant. He had had Kirby pegged as a dumb, spoiled rich kid, easily appeased with fast talk and some vague hints of nookie.

Spoiled and rich he undoubtedly was, but he was starting to show another side, tougher and quicker than Diego liked. Both his parents were supposedly hot-shot CEOs; apparently the lardball hadn't fallen far from the rendering plant.

"Look, Kirby. The problem is, I don't own that thing. It belongs to one of the professors over at the university. Camila—my girlfriend, you remember—took some pics of it."

Kirby blinked at him like a placid toad. "Okay. So go buy it from the professor. I'll pay whatever he asks."

"I don't think it's that easy, dude. He…"

"If he doesn't want to sell, you'll have to acquire it some other way, okay? I don't care how. This is now your top priority. It replaces the party. The party is canceled. Just. Get. It."

"Why?"

Slurp. Slurp-slurp. "Say what, now?"

"Why do you want it so bad? Seriously, man, people are going to see it at the party, they're going to talk. It's going to go all over the internet before you even run out of booze. Okay? If I 'acquire' that thing for you the cops will be on you like flies on shit. Pardon my French."

More blinking. More slurping. "So?"

And then Diego understood. He had played his cards totally wrong. By trying to get Kirby to accept No for an answer, he had sealed his own fate. It was easy to imagine Kirby's Mom or Dad in the boardroom, staring down some peon who dared to tell them no, they couldn't hire a leprechaun for their next meeting. It wasn't the impossibility they cared about, it was an inferior saying no.

He could walk away. Losing the fee Van Zandt had promised wouldn't break him, he'd just have to start over. But it would take him months or even longer to find another pig this fat. Bottom line, he needed the money.

So he was going to have to get the damned ostrich. Whatever it took.

NINETEEN

The mother lay still, her head resting on the ground. She ignored the small insects buzzing about the smears of half-dried blood on her beak, set on remaining absolutely motionless. She had begun this regimen waiting for the return of the shining thing. Now she had something else to worry about.

The male *Titanis*, her former mate, had returned.

He was cautious enough to keep to the outskirts of the clearing, circling it again and again. Periodically he would disappear—probably to hunt-only to return hours later. The scent of blood that hung around the female, combined with her motionlessness, suggested she was dead, but some other sense told him she was very much alive...and dangerous. In fact, he had used a similar ploy himself to lure unwary rivals, many times. He simply didn't remember it.

The female watched him through the almost opaque membranes that served her eyes as second lids. Had she been human, she might have wondered what it was that brought her old mate back to her. The one thing that certainly had *not* motivated him was lust. Mating season was well over. More likely it was the dim memory of an easy meal of the eggs he himself had fathered that brought him back. Or the fact that the female had stayed put in one location may have attracted him. Females did not, as a rule, establish their own territories. It would have established her as a rival, just as if she were another male.

And today she had yet another problem. The male had company—a younger male, not quite as tall, with a startling red crest, stalking along behind him at a discreet distance. It wasn't unheard of for subordinate males to follow alphas, hoping to profit from their hunts. The younger male looked strong, but even if he were a weakling with a broken leg, two males were far worse than one.

But it didn't matter. She wasn't going to leave the clearing until the shining thing returned.

And if she were able to lure one of the males near enough to her to rip it to death, so much the better.

TWENTY

"PetPlace," Camila said into the receiver. Chad was watching her, so, rolling her eyes, she added, "This is Camila, how can I help you?"

"Camila? Hey...this is Alex. From Dr. Bruckner's?"

"Oh, hey!" Camila glanced carefully back at Chad, who, satisfied the customer's needs were being adequately met, had gone back to inspecting the tanks of tropical fish.

"Yeah, hey. Listen, I need to ask you a favor...'

"Sure."

"Those pictures you took...of the fledgling."

"Roc."

"Roc, yeah. Can you delete them from your phone?"

"Aw, why?"

"It's just...my boss. Dr. Bruckner. He gets weird about stuff like that, and the fledge—Roc, is supposed to be part of a...kind of secret experiment. I mean, he'd go ballistic..."

"Hey," Camila said, smiling. Alex was speaking in a breathless rush, coming perilously close to breaking down into babble. "It's okay. I'm sorry, I should have asked before I took them. He was just so cute, y'know?" *Should I say, 'Like you?' No...that wouldn't be cool...I've tortured this poor guy enough.*

Alex exhaled in relief. "Thanks so much, I really appreciate that."

"But I can still come by to see him some time, can't I?" Camila picked up a pen and doodled a baby bird on the PetPlace message pad in front of her. The baby bird had a huge beak like Roc and was emerging from an egg, the top half of which he wore like a hat. She drew a speech balloon next to it with the words "I want Mama Camila!" inside.

"I...let me talk to Dr. Bruckner about that first. I'm pretty sure it'd be okay, but..."

"Okay, sure."

"Oh, and...can you maybe like...delete the pictures now?"

Camila smiled. "Yeah, I'll do it right now. Don't worry, they'll be gone in like two seconds."

"Thanks so much! Seriously..."

Camila glanced up and saw Chad making his way back up the aisle, tapping on the glass tanks. "Okay, gotta go. Call me and let me know about visit rights, okay?"

Alex was in the middle of another feverish flood of thank-yous when Camila hung up.

"Who was that?" Chad asked.

"Prank call. Some kid wanted to know if we had titmice."

Chad snorted. "Assholes. I'm going to be over in Reptiles."

"Kay," Camila said, picking up her iphone. She fully intended to delete the pictures of Roc, but she was immediately distracted by something on the phone's front page, where her recent calls and emails were summarized:

Last sent Yesterday:

5 pics from Gallery to DiegoLuv.

A ball of ice suddenly materialized in the pit of Camila's belly. A moment later it burst into flame. She hadn't sent Diego any damned pics from her damned Gallery. Not yesterday, certainly.

It would have been easy to overlook. Diego had helped himself to Camila's phone and sent himself pics she had taken before; usually from vacations and day-trips to Six Flags or whatever. She had done the same thing to his phone, for that matter. But Diego's "job" as Kirby's party-planner and the fact that Roc was some crazy professor's science project put a whole different spin on things.

"Hey Chad?"

"Hey what?"

"Can I take off early?" She scribbled a quick, not very recognizable photo of a leering Diego on the message pad. He had devil-horns and a tiny goatee, and was saying "Ha ha I fooled Camila, I am so smart!"

Chad grimaced. "Ugh. Andrew called in sick and I really need you here. I mean, is it an emergency?"

"No," Camila said, continuing her doodling. She added a second picture of Diego, this one crying torrents of tears with the words "Waaah I am so sorry Camila!"

"I was just gonna do something, but I can take care of it later, it ain't no thang." She drew a picture of herself next to the weeping Diego, with devil horns and smoke coming out of her ears. "I am going to beat your butt!"

"Ain't no thang," she muttered.

TWENTY-ONE

Dr. Thaddeus Bruckner sat relaxed in his favorite easy-chair, digging his hand into a large bowl of corn chips as he reached for the TV remote. The day was over. Alex had headed home to his dorm and both Thing One and Roc—as Alex insisted on calling it—were safely locked in for the night.

Roc was worrying him a little. He had loudly tut-tutted Alex's concerns—which were plentiful, as always—but the truth was, the young *Titanis* had grown far faster, and far *bigger* than he had expected. One small consolation was that he seemed to have imprinted himself on Bruckner. He followed him around the back yard like a gigantic chicken, his head weaving curiously as he took in everything Bruckner did. He didn't exactly eat from his hand, but stood by politely, neatly snatching from air the increasingly large and expensive cuts of meat Bruckner fed him—as a fledgling would from its mother, Bruckner thought. He deferred to him, never making a threatening move. But Bruckner had been forced to relieve Alex of feeding duty—Roc was already eyeing him much as he did the jack rabbits that sometimes got into the back yard. He couldn't put the kid in that kind of danger. And if Roc ever got out…

It wouldn't be good.

It was high time for the "grand unveiling," but Bruckner's calls to his old mentor had gone unanswered, which pissed him off no end. He had called in every single colleague, confidante and frenemy he had in the scientific world—which frankly weren't many. Wolfschmidt had been no help, but he hadn't expected him to be. He'd even made a cagey cold call to the Smithsonian. No reaction. Zilch. Their loss, ultimately, but he *needed* the bastards, dammit. He couldn't just drive Roc into downtown Dallas chained down on a flatbed truck like an avian *Mighty Joe Young*. He needed to launch his discovery properly, with the legitimacy only a university or scientific institution could provide.

He might have to go to the papers. But not Texas newspapers, god forbid. He needed time to plan…but he also needed to get Roc out of his yard.

Ah well. Bruckner reclined his chair and flicked on *Chasin' the Squatch*, the latest in a series of moronic "cryptozoology" programs currently running. The show featured a pack of twenty-something morons who made the Three Stooges look like brain surgeons. They stumbled around any forest they could find, essaying what they called "tree knocks," and hooting, gibbering noises they apparently thought approximated a sasquatch's calls. Bruckner kept a notepad handy, jotting down choice quotes and his own acerbic commentary, but tonight, as on most nights, the sheer stupidity he witnessed damn near caused him to drive his pen through the paper.

"Idiots," he growled, in an ecstasy of indignation. "That is *not* sasquatch scat, you boob, it's *clearly* black bear scat! Have you *ever* been in a forest before? *Idiots!*"

The doorbell rang.

Bruckner started and turned off the TV, remaining still in his chair like any hunted animal. A moment later the doorbell rang again, and then again. *Bing-bong, bing-bong.*

Bruckner almost never got visitors, unless one counted Alex, and he *never* got them at night. This wasn't some simpleton in overalls come to read his gas meter. And the insistent ringing of the bell wasn't a good sign.

Then again, maybe some local yokel had ordered a pizza and the delivery boy had taken too big a bump of coke and got his silly ass lost. The thought of pizza got Bruckner out of his chair and over to the door. *If this really is a matter of a lost pizza, I could offer to take it off his hands for an extra fiver*, he thought. *Be doing a good deed. Helping local commerce.*

But when he peered through the peep-hole on his front door, he didn't see a pizza deliveryman. Instead he saw a couple of girls, both on the wrong side of twenty, but dressed in what Bruckner was given to understand young women wore to social occasions these days—which wasn't much. One had a teased-out mane of pale blonde hair. The other was a little thing with short red hair who couldn't seem to keep still. For that matter, neither could the blonde. The two of them were elbowing each other, giggling like lunatics.

Bruckner rolled his eyes. Students. Out to prank the loony cryptozoology professor they'd heard about, whose specialty they'd be hard-pressed to spell, much less name. Probably their jock boyfriends were hiding in the shadows, sweating their balls off in the same moth-eaten Bigfoot costumes the little darlings tried on him last Halloween. Fine. He would get rid of them, but he would have to watch his step. The girls looked drunk off their asses.

Moving carefully, he unlocked the door and eased it open. "Yes?" he growled, his gaze frigid.

The two girls stared at him as though he had just crawled out of a UFO, then broke down into shrieks and snorts, barely managing to hold each other up.

"Ladies," he said, softening his tone a bit. They were just kids, after all. Coming off like the Grinch wasn't going to help matters. "It's getting late. Can I help you?"

More giggles. The little redhead slurred into her friend's ear, "He, he, he called you a, a *lady*! You're a *lady*!"

The blonde, marginally less drunk or stoned than her companion, managed to stop laughing for a moment, clearing her throat and smoothing her t-shirt over her belly. "I...hey."

"Hey," Bruckner said frostily, recognizing this monosyllabic grunt as the basic greeting used throughout Vander. "Can we continue, please?"

"I just...we, she and I...do you know where the club is?"

Redhead broke down into shrill squeals, as though this remark were the wittiest thing she'd ever heard.

"No, I do not," Bruckner frowned. What was this, some latter-day variation on *Hey Mister, is your refrigerator running*? "It sounds like you girls have already been to several clubs."

"Yeah, it's just..." the blonde shook her head, as though trying to remember something. "You wanna come party with us?" she asked suddenly, smiling like a seven year old inviting him to her dolls' tea party.

Bruckner smiled, as kindly as he could manage. "No thank you. I'm going to bed and I suggest you both do the same."

He stepped back to close the door, but this proved to be a mistake. The girls leaped forward, grabbing him by the arms as though terrified he would get away. They pulled him, squawking in protest, out onto his front lawn.

"Stop that! What the hell are you two doing?" Bruckner was confused, even a little frightened. This had just gone way beyond a simple prank. Was he about to be robbed? He couldn't let them into the house. Dear God, no. If they saw Roc...if they opened the door to the back yard...

"Goin' to the *club*!" the redhead burbled.

"Yeah, come on! It's gonna be epic!"

"Stop it!" Bruckner had given up trying to be gentle. He was fighting back with all his force, but the girls were younger and surprisingly strong. They seemed to be trying to get him back to their car, a clunker parked askew on the road some distance from his house. He was convinced now that this was more than a joke, that the girls were meant to be a distraction while someone broke into his house. And that would be bad. More than bad. It would be like one of the monster movies he had doted on as a boy come to life.

He had to break loose from these maniacal maenads. But how? *Dear lord, being manhandled by two drunk twenty-something girls is every man's dream, and all I can think to do is get away!*

"You touched my titty!" the redhead screamed, sounding delighted.

TWENTY-TWO

"Okay, they got him," Gina said. The dark-haired bassist came running around the corner of the fence that surrounded Bruckner's back yard. She smiled. "They'll keep him busy for a while."

Diego grinned as he snatched up the canvas duffel bag he'd brought. "Poor old guy," he said. Missy and Dusty were pretty hot, but he'd dealt with them in a drunken state himself a few times; he didn't envy Bruckner.

Gina turned on the flashlight app on her phone; in its surprisingly bright light he could see her smirking. "No shit. Those dummies are lubed up enough to do him some serious damage. Hope they don't like fuckin' break his arm or shit."

It occurred to Diego, not for the first time, how hot Gina herself was, with her black hair and slim build. It wasn't just that, though; she was cool, just like you'd expect a rocker chick to be. She had surprised the hell out of him when she had suggested they simply come out to Bruckner's house and 'borrow' the emu chick. He had called her to explain their gig might be postponed indefinitely while he figured out this latest glitch from Kirby, but she didn't hesitate for a second. Not like Camila, who hadn't even wanted to hear about approaching Bruckner through his assistant. It wasn't that he didn't love Camila, it was just sometimes he got the feeling she didn't quite get him. If it were up to her he'd be working construction or something, looking for a house to buy together. Fuck that. Why couldn't she understand that pretty soon he could buy his own damned construction company?

Gina wasn't like that. It was like they were already partners in crime. She hadn't even had to think before offering her help. Flirting with her wouldn't have been cool, but he was starting to wonder if maybe there weren't something there. Shaking his head, Diego turned back to his bag, making a quick inventory.

It contained a couple of items he had just bought during a quick run to the mall: a coil of rope, to start with, tied at one end to a grappling hook that had been gathering dust at a sports supply store. Then there were two pillowcases (they came in sets of no fewer than two). One of the pillowcases would serve as a sack to hold Roc—on the off chance it didn't work, he'd have to use the duffel bag itself. He had no idea how to go about capturing a baby emu, but how hard could it be? There was also a heavy-duty flashlight and a box of live crickets from a PetPlace (he'd made a special trip out to a store where Camila didn't work). Wikipedia said emus ate a bewildering array of stuff, from grass to insects, to things with weird italicized names Diego had never heard of. He'd finally settled on the crickets as the most likely option.

As a weapon he wasn't expecting to use, he'd brought a can of mace lifted from Camila's bedroom. Finally, he'd sprung for a pack of discounted steaks (starting to turn a queasy greenish-brown), based on a vague memory of a movie he'd seen involving jewel thieves using meat to distract guard dogs. Camila hadn't mentioned the mad doctor owning dogs, but it wasn't impossible.

The plan was to get over the wall, grab Roc, then make for Diego's truck, parked some distance away—*and thank God for four-wheel drive*, he thought. He had to pick up Camila after she got off her shift, so Gina had agreed to babysit Roc until the next day, when he would hopefully have figured out exactly how the little guy was going to fit into Kirby's party.

The wall was simple fiberboard, the kind many people used to not only enclose their backyards but filter out sounds of traffic from nearby highways. It was high, but Diego had climbed higher when he was younger—and he had an idea Gina had as well.

Missy and Dusty had been instructed to keep Bruckner busy for as long as possible, after which they'd simply take off back to Missy's car and haul ass. Bruckner would probably call the cops, but wouldn't have much to give them besides a couple of drunk girls. And he might not call at all; it sounded like he was keeping his experiments strictly on the down low. Diego wondered if they themselves might not be completely legal, which was comforting in light of the theft he was about to commit.

In any case, it was time to get going. Stepping away from Gina, he threw the grappling hook. It took several tries, but he finally got it over the wall. When he pulled on the rope, it went taut.

Looping the bag over his shoulder, he nodded to Gina. "I'll be back asap," he said. "Keep an eye out; you see Bruckner or anybody else, give me a whistle."

"Wait," she said suddenly, seizing his arm. "Let me go. I can get him faster than you."

The idea of turning the mission over to Gina was appealing, but Diego hesitated, even as she was taking the duffel bag from him. "You sure? I mean, we don't know what's over there."

Gina smiled, already reaching down to unbuckle the chunky platform heels she wore. "I think I can handle the birdy. If there was anyone else in the house, they'd have come out by now. Besides, I'm more used to this than you are. I used to do urban exploration when I lived in Dallas. You just keep an eye out for trouble. Now gimme a lift, big boy."

Diego stooped and let Gina lift her bare foot into his hands. When she suddenly put all her weight on it, levering herself upward, the force of it nearly broke his grip. *She's strong*, he thought approvingly. He pushed her up, as hard as he could, sighing with relief when her weight lifted off his hands. She scrambled up the wall, holding onto the rope, the duffel bag swinging from her shoulders. Moments later, she was perched on top, waving down at him. Then she disappeared.

TWENTY-THREE

Three quarters of the way down the wall's interior side, Gina dropped the bag and then let go of the rope, landing on all fours. Adrenaline was ringing in her veins; this was cool. She hadn't done anything like this since Dallas, and not much of it then. Urban Texas was okay, but small-town Texas was for shit. She *had* to get back to a real city sooner or later; New York, preferably, but she'd even settle for San Francisco, even if it meant going back to work at her folks' restaurant. Anything was better than nursing beers in cowboy bars with Tweedle Dumb and Tweedle Retard, pretending to be punk rockers.

The band had provided some distraction, and so had Diego, with his crazy schemes to give Fatboy Kirby a "prehistoric-themed" party. Diego was cute, too. She would have made a move on him by now, but the Camila chick complicated things. She seemed pretty tight-assed, which she could tell wasn't Diego's style. Still, it didn't sit right with Gina to mess around with another girl's guy. That shit led to nothing but trouble, she'd learned that early.

Well. Time to catch a birdy.

Bruckner's back yard wasn't completely dark. He had a small spotlight fixed to the sliding door that opened onto his kitchen. It didn't provide much light, but Gina was grateful for it. Trying to chase down the bird while holding a flashlight would be a pain in the ass. Even so, she got the light out and shined it around the yard. She wanted to know what she had to work with.

The moment she turned the light on, the beam caught something tall and weird-looking. "No way," she breathed. There were two tall pillars in the middle of the yard, flanked by a boxy thing covered with blinking lights. It looked to Gina like a piece of stereo equipment. It all looked high-tech but somehow cheap, like that one English TV show about the guy with the phonebooth time-machine. It was so perfectly "mad scientist" that it tickled the crap out of her.

But what did this shit have to do with raising emus? Or ostriches, or whatever? Gina flashed the light around the yard, moving carefully. Her bare foot stepped into something squishy. *Oh, gross*, she thought, groaning inwardly. *Emu shit.*

Shining the light down on her foot, she saw she had indeed stepped in a semi-solid pile of chalky, green-flecked bird dung. It was a big pile, though. It might be emu shit, but it sure as hell wasn't from a baby emu.

A twig snapped behind her. Whirling, she just caught sight of something big—considerably taller than herself—withdrawing into the shadows. "Who's there?" she called, thoroughly spooked. No silence. Just a weird, grumbling noise that reminded her of something—a parrot? Then another sound, thoroughly inhuman, that scared the crap out of her:

"*Raaw-wwk...*"

"You'd better come out, man. I got a gun." Her bluff didn't sound very convincing, even to herself. And she had the distinct feeling that whoever it was in the shadows, it wasn't a person.

Something seriously fucked up was going on around here.

Gina snatched up the duffel bag, then moved over to the sliding door, walking slowly backwards with her eyes on the shadows. To her great relief, the door slid open at her touch. She slipped inside and pushed it shut, locking it. Originally she had intended to touch nothing, afraid of leaving fingerprints, but that birdlike growling and muttering had her spooked. Fuck it, let the cops find her prints. They weren't going to come up anywhere.

Once in the kitchen, she could hear the sound of a television in the living room, and some dim light filtered out from there. There was no sound of someone storming out to the kitchen demanding to know who was there. She could hear some faint voices from the street outside the front door, one voice raised in anger or confusion. Gina smiled. The girls were still keeping Bruckner busy, apparently. Good. The way things were going, she might need to sneak out the front door, and to hell with Kirby's supposed prize. She wasn't going back out in the yard with the muttering thing again, not anytime soon. In the meantime, she snapped on the flashlight and had a look around.

The place was a mess, though she had lived in worse. Cases of canned soda and chili stacked waist-high, shopping bags of dry goods that had never been unpacked, and everywhere books. Piles of them, old and dog-eared, that looked like they were slowly disintegrating back into their component elements of wood pulp and dust.

Gina peered quickly out the window. She thought she saw the tall shape, but once again it disappeared into the shadows. She shuddered, and turned her attention back to the kitchen.

Her sweeping flashlight beam lit up a boxy plastic thing on the floor near the door, gleaming on steel bars in windows and sides. A sharp hissing emerged from inside, and a scrabbling of claws on hard plastic.

Bingo, Gina thought, smiling. The emu was inside after all. Maybe the big shadowy thing was the mama, and they had to lock up the baby to protect it. Maybe emus were in the habit of cannibalizing their children when they got scared, like rabbits.

The question now was how to get it outside to Diego. The carrier was pretty big, obviously made for the larger breeds of dog, and a quick experimental tug at the handles told Gina she wasn't going to be able to lift it. She could theoretically drag it across the floor to the front door, but that would take time—so would calling Diego in to help her. Missy and Dusty weren't going to be able to keep Bruckner occupied forever. She wasn't going to be able to get it over the wall in the back yard.

The only option was to take the emu out of the carrier, pop it into the duffel bag, and haul ass.

Easy-peasy.

"Alright, you little booger," Gina said, kneeling before the carrier. The emu hissed and rattled around inside. It seemed bigger than she'd expected, but it shouldn't be a problem. She was pretty strong herself. She unzipped the duffel and held the open mouth of it up to the carrier door. All she had to do was let the door open and the critter run inside, then zip the zip and make tracks. Again: easy-peasy.

But when she unlatched the door and pulled it open, taking care to press the edge of the bag back up against it, shit went south quick. First, the critter wouldn't cooperate. From what Gina could see, it was hunched in the back of the carrier, hissing irritably. When she slapped at the carrier, it hissed louder. Cursing, taking a quick peek over her shoulder to make sure Bruckner hadn't gotten back yet, she hit the carrier a hard, open-handed blow, with a loud, "*C'mon!*" to provide further encouragement.

That did it. The emu slithered out of its cage like greased lightning, hitting the duffel bag and tearing it effortlessly from Gina's hand. Gina rolled onto her back, gawping and pushing herself backward with her feet. She was now confronted by something that bore no relation at all to her conception of an emu.

It was slightly less than half her own height. It reminded her of a miniature velociraptor from *Jurassic Park*, with a crest of stiff, brightly-colored feathers and a wicked hooked beak. Its forelimbs looked like stumpy wings morphed halfway into stunted, clawed hands. The thing's plumage was missing in places, leaving irregular patches of greyish-pink skin. A vague memory of a documentary she had watched on TV years before with her Dad flashed through her mind, something about how caged animals will rip out their own fur or plumage from boredom…a boredom which sometimes led to flat-out insanity.

The bird-thing turned its head, watching her with beady eyes, hissing like a teakettle. If ever an animal looked insane—no, *psychotic*—tt was this one. Gina didn't dare look away from those tiny, vicious-looking eyes. If she did, it would attack, she just knew it. She could see the duffel bag out of the corner of her eye, half its contents spilled out onto the dirty linoleum. A small canister lay just out of reach—the mace.

I've got to get it, she thought, forcing herself to calm down. She had to put all speculation on what this thing was, or how Bruckner got his hands on it, out of her mind. If I get the mace, I have a chance. No mace, no chance. Simple as that.

The canister lay inches away from her foot. She slid her leg over slightly, catching hold of it with her toes. The slight movement seemed to agitate the bird-thing; it began bobbing its head up and down, like an angry iguana.

*Slowly, slowly…*she raised her leg, pulling the canister closer and closer, until it was within inches of her hand. The bird-thing hissed throatily.

Now. Gina grabbed the canister and got it in front of her face just as the bird-thing jumped her. She pushed down the button, spraying the thing square in the face. It shrieked, falling back and clawing at its eyes with its stunted claw-hand.

Meanwhile, Gina scrambled to her feet and ran for the door to the back yard, unlocking it and heaving it open. A moment later she was sprinting across the yard. She wasn't crazy about facing whatever was out there—she was now pretty sure it wasn't the mother—but her way to the living room and front door was now blocked by a very large, hurting, angry dino-bird-thing. She could see the rope hanging down the wall, and so long as she had the mace in her hand, she was prepared to let adrenaline do the rest.

"Diego!" she screamed. "Get ready, cause I'm comin' over!"

TWENTY-FOUR

Someone was out in the back yard, screaming their heads off. Bruckner couldn't tell what they were saying, but they sounded panicked. That was enough for him.

"Get away from me!" he shouted, giving the redhead a shove that pushed her back into her friend. They had come very close to getting Bruckner into their car, and they'd gotten that far because part of him was tempted to just go with them. A very small, treacherous part of him liked this kind of manhandling, he realized. Soft, perfumed skin, boobs all but thrust into his hands for a quick feel (*We won't tell, tee-hee*).

And pray, why shouldn't he like it? It had been *how* long since he'd last gotten lucky? Plenty of the other faculty fucked around with the students, there was no question about that. When they tapped some twenty-something girl-ass, they practically put it on Facebook.

Of course, he didn't really intend to go with these zanies. The distrustful nature that had kept Thaddeus Bruckner from most human contact most of his life simply wouldn't let him. If he got in that car, he'd end up stripped naked and dumped by the side of the Texas highway—and that was a best-case scenario.

But the stunted side of him that longed to party kept him from fully pushing back, from committing. Now, hearing that scream, it was out of his hands. He had to act.

The girls were crying weakly after him, but he was already back in the house. Why had he answered the door? he asked, groaning inwardly. Why had he answered the fucking, double-damned *door*?

***

Something slammed into Gina's back, throwing her off balance so she went sprawling head-first onto the dry grass. The can of mace went flying. Whatever hit her slid daggerlike somethings into her lower back, creating an exquisite pain that made her scream like she'd never screamed onstage.

It's that thing, she thought. *The fucker got me*. Her head felt hot and her vision was trembling, her heart was banging in her ears. She managed to turn her head just enough to see it hunched over her, its wing-arms slowly extending and folding, extending and folding. The sight of it made Gina's stomach seize up. Blood or something else—tears?—flooded down its cheeks where Gina had got it with the mace.

The thing didn't look angry. Or gloating, or anything else. There was a complete lack of consciousness in its eyes that terrified her more than anything. It was going to ravage her and eat as much of her as it could hold, not because it hated her, but because it was in the hold of a bottomless hunger that controlled its every waking moment.

And then—it happened so quickly that Gina, in her pain, barely registered it—something tall and covered in darkness was looming over them. Its upper half made an impossibly quick snatching motion and the bird-thing disappeared from her back. Gina caught a glimpse of it wriggling like a worm in the bigger shadow's mouth—was that massive hooked thing a beak? Yes, a beak. Her savior was another bird-like monster, but of a different kind, vastly bigger, made for killing. A few jerks of its head and the smaller monster was gone, disappeared down the bigger one's throat.

Sobbing, Gina dragged herself forward. The pain in her back was terrible. She knew she wasn't going to be able to make it over the wall, not without help. But staying still wasn't an option, because the bigger monster was still hungry. It had to be. There was no way the smaller bird-thing would satisfy it.

Somewhere somebody was screaming, and there was a loud cracking noise. Gina didn't care. She just had to get her ass away.

TWENTY-FIVE

Diego had thought he was in fairly good shape. It was an easy mindset to get into, especially hanging out with fat-ass Kirby. Trouble was, he was dead wrong. He might not be a fat-ass, but he was a long, long way from running any marathons. Damned cream sodas.

The minute he heard Gina's scream, he seized the rope and began hauling ass up the sheer side of Bruckner's wall. Or trying to. In no time at all, every muscle in his body was aching, and he had only gotten four feet off the ground. In one way, he was grateful Gina didn't have to see this epic fail. On the other hand, Gina might be dead.

To hell with it. He let himself drop heavily to the ground and ran around to Bruckner's front door. It was swinging wide open, and Missy and Dusty were standing huddled beside it, looking scared witless.

"There's a monster," Dusty said miserably. "I think it, like ate Gina."

Groaning inside, Diego tore past the two girls, and found himself faced with an obstacle course consisting of stacks of books, office supplies, computer parts, food, and more books. Gina screamed again— she was ahead of him, somewhere. Diego ran on, taking a certain satisfaction in knocking over the stacks of paperbacks. Then he was in the kitchen, faced with the patio door. All kinds of noises were coming through it, including Gina's screams and blubbering.

"Damn it, I said get back!" Diego had never heard Bruckner's voice before, but the shouting pretty well matched his basic idea of a grouchy old dude who maybe wasn't too tightly wrapped upstairs. When he got through the door into the back yard he found himself confronted with Bruckner's back. The old guy was holding something that looked suspiciously like a shotgun. Gina was sprawled on the ground in front of him. In the dim spotlight affixed to the outer door, Diego could see blood gleaming on her back. Had Bruckner attacked her?

Puffed up with adrenaline, Diego might have tackled the old man. Problem was the thing standing about a meter before him and Gina. It was a good eight feet tall, standing on two heavy legs that ended in massive claws. It had a beak as well, a big one. But that was about as far as its resemblance to a bird went. It was more like a monster from some late-night Creature Feature.

"Damn it, Roc, g'wan! Get back!" Bruckner was brandishing the shotgun at the bird thing, more like an old coot threatening his poodle with a fly swatter than someone facing down a monster. "Roc," for its part, seemed more bemused by the screeching little creature before it than troubled. It lowered its head as though to get a better look at him, making a strange muttering noise. It lifted one foot, then set it down, lifted the other, set it down as well. It looked to Diego like it was performing some kind of weird-ass mating dance.

"Shoot it!" Diego howled.

"If I were you," Bruckner snarled, turning to glare at him, "I'd keep my mouth shut. You're in enough trouble as it—*Roc!*"

In the instant Bruckner's attention was elsewhere, the bird leaned down and snatched the shotgun from his hand. It shook its head furiously, as though it were trying to kill the gun, then threw it into the far end of the yard.

Diego ran back into the kitchen and grabbed the package of steaks from the duffel bag, ripping the plastic covering open with his fingers as he returned outside.

"Hey!" he yelled, pulling out one of the slimy pieces of meat. "Hey birdy! You want something to eat?"

The bird lowered its head, muttering again. Diego lifted the steak as high as he could, and the bird's head rose. He lowered it, squatting so that the steak nearly touched the grass, and the bird followed suit, settling its grotesque head on the ground. No question, it had gotten the meat's scent. Or maybe this was how Bruckner fed it—either way, it wanted to eat.

"Throw it!" Bruckner urged. "Far as you can!"

Diego gave him an irritated glance (*what the hell you think I was gonna do?*), then flung the steak into the shadow, then sent the second piece of meat after it for good measure. The bird turned with a squawk and ran for the steaks, while Bruckner and Diego helped Gina to her feet and back into the house.

"I hope your schedule is clear for several hours," Bruckner told Diego, his voice flat and cold. "Because you've both got a lot of explaining to do."

TWENTY-SIX

The male *Titanis* and its follower had been making a wide circuit of the prone female, getting a little closer each time. The female had gone into an almost catatonic state, barely even breathing. She was waiting for her old mate to get close enough for her to spring, but the male was cautious. The two were about evenly matched as far as size and strength, but he had tangled with her before, and had no interest in another fight if it could be avoided. The best way to avoid it would be to get the drop on her and kill her quickly.

The female's position was tantalizing. Lying with her neck stretched out along the ground made her vulnerable. All the male had to do was leap on her, using one foot to hold her still while he crushed her neck with his beak. But he wasn't quite close enough…yet.

Meanwhile, the smaller male trailed along behind him, watching his every move. Once or twice he got close enough to annoy the bigger animal, and was snapped at. If the other hadn't been so focused on the female, he might well have simply killed him.

Eventually the two were within a couple of meters of the female. Trying to get any closer without making a move would be a foolhardy risk. Screeching, feathers standing erect, the big male made a sudden rush at the female.

He lashed his head out at her neck, striking ground with enough force to send up a cloud of dust. But the female had exploded into action at the same moment, leaping up and backward, head lowered and hissing. Then the two were dancing around each other in a wide circle, heads striking at each other like grotesque cobras.

The hooked end of the male's beak drew blood, but the female retaliated with a savage kick that nearly brought him down. The male moved out of range just in time, then renewed its attack, trying to gain an advantage. But the female seemed powered by a cold fury that made her unstoppable. If the male didn't manage to bring her down soon, there wasn't much doubt of who would win the fight.

TWENTY-SEVEN

Alex stood in the nearly empty parking lot before the brightly-lit PetPlace, wondering what in hell he was doing.

She has a boyfriend, for god's sake. And she's way out of your league. You don't have a chance with her. There was no comfort in the words, but they did carry a tempting suggestion that there would be no dishonor in running now.

But at the moment, running was exactly what Alex wanted to do. The problem was, he wanted to talk to Camila even more. When he saw her come out of the shop, phone to ear and looking royally pissed off, he hesitated only a minute.

"Hey," he said, walking forward. It took a couple of "Heys" to catch her attention, but when she finally saw him, her face lit up, and his belly turned over with a sickening mixture of pleasure and the kind of pain you normally get after a night binging on tacos and really cheap tequila.

"Hey!" she cried, tucking her phone into her purse. "Ohmigod, I'm so glad to see you! Do you have a car?"

"Car? Sure, I…"

"Awesome! Can you give me a ride? Diego's not picking up."

Alex had a pretty good idea who "Diego" was. It did his stomach no good, but as an opportunity to play White Knight, it was hard to beat. "Sure, come on," he said, leading her to his rattletrap Honda.

"He's in trouble," Camila said darkly, more to herself than to him. "You have no idea. Leaves me stranded here in a fucking parking lot. I know where he is, though."

"Yeah?" Alex opened the door for her. He felt a little lightheaded. He was going to be sitting next to her in a minute. His car would be filled with the scent of her perfume…

"Yeah. So actually…can you do me a big favor?" Her attention was back with him, but there was a wheedling, calculating note in her voice now that made him nervous.

"Big favor, huh?" he asked, strapping himself in. *Just be calm. Act like you don't give a shit one way or another…*

"I mean, it's not that big, I guess, but…you can't ask me why. Not yet. Okay?"

"Okay. What is it?"

She took a deep breath, which Alex couldn't help but notice made her boobs swell in a rather fetching way. "You have to take me back to your boss' place."

"Dr. Bruckner's?" Bruckner's was the last place he wanted to go right now. It had been a long day of transcribing notes and cleaning up after Roc and listening to rants about streamers. "Why? Oh...I'm not supposed to ask."

She just smiled at him and winked, and in that moment he knew he'd do anything she asked of him.

***

"So he's *dead*. Thing One. Roc ate him?"

It was like the third time Bruckner asked about the thing in the dog carrier, which he insisted on calling "Thing One." He had helped Diego put Gina on the couch (clearing it of books and papers had taken a good ten minutes and raised a cloud of dust that still hadn't settled) and brought out bandages and antiseptic, but that was apparently as far as his hosting skills went. He stalked around the room, clenching and unclenching his fists. Missy and Dusty had fled before they even got into the house. That was probably for the best. The Sisters Airhead weren't going to do anything for their position.

"Yes, he fucking ate him," Gina spat. She was lying face-down on the couch while Diego, with no great skill, treated her wounds. She hurt, and she was sick to her stomach from all the dust in this place. Also, she was scared as hell the big thing in the yard—"Roc," apparently—was going to come smashing through the sliding door any minute and rip her head off. But all Bruckner could think about was his precious monster.

"And you *saw* this? You didn't just..." Bruckner waved his hand in a way that perfectly communicated his lack of faith in Gina's observational skills. "Imagine it?"

"I said I saw it, okay?" she snapped. "Will you just let it go?"

Bruckner turned his gaze on her. Gina told herself she wasn't scared of him, and she wasn't—mostly. The guy had to be like sixty, with no muscle tone at all and a gut to go with his scrawny arms and legs—but she didn't like his eyes. They were magnified by his coke bottle glasses, looking like frog eyes, the whites more like a sickly yellow threaded with red veins.

"You two broke into my house and released a valuable—no, a priceless scientific specimen. Irreplaceable. Thanks to you, that irreplaceable specimen is now dead. The only way to recover it is to pick through Roc's shit tomorrow for any bones that remain solid. So if I were you, young lady, I wouldn't get snotty with me."

Gina let herself lapse into a sullen silence—always her go-to position when confronted by authority figures. She wished Diego would say something, but when he finally cleared his throat and spoke up, it was with a deferential tone that made Gina sick.

"So…what are those things, anyway?"

"Not your concern," Bruckner snapped.

"Yeah, okay. So…I think we need to get Gina to the doctor, though. That thing cut her pretty deep, and the blood keeps soaking through the bandages."

"Oh, god," Gina moaned.

"We will take her," Bruckner told him. "In time. I need to think, so shut up for a minute." With that, he went back to stalking and the whole clenching/unclenching thing.

"I'm hurt!" Gina yelled. She could feel the blood seeping through her wounds. What if "Thing One" had dirty claws or, still worse, some kind of venom? She didn't think birds had any kind had venom, but it looked a hell of a lot like a dinosaur to her, and reptiles *did* have venom. Everybody knew that. She could die from her wounds, or be paralyzed for life, or god knew what.

"I'm hurt," she said again, directing it this time at Diego. She raised herself up on her elbows a little and turned to glare at him. "You hear me?" she went on, whispering it. "Let's just go!" Still he hesitated. He looked like he was thinking hard about something, the way Bruckner claimed to be doing, willing to do anything to buy himself a little more time. Maybe he was afraid of Bruckner calling the cops, but Gina didn't think that was likely. She could even understand the old guy's position, kinda-sorta. If she were raising monsters in her back yard, she wouldn't want the Five-O nosing around either.

But every minute put her deeper in danger from bird-monster cooties. She wasn't inclined to wait any longer.

"If you don't help me, I'm going myself." She kept her eyes locked on Diego's, giving him just a few seconds more to grow a set. She didn't like relying on a guy to rescue her, but she needed help, dammit. The idea of her kidneys tumbling out through the wounds in her back the minute she stood up did *not* appeal. Diego finally—finally!—gave her a tight nod, but he still looked like he was frantically processing something, trying either to figure something out or come to a decision about it. Then he got up and moved over to the edge of the room. Gina snorted in frustration. Where the hell was he going?

"Sit down," Bruckner said coldly.

"Listen man," Gina told him, her voice equally frigid. "We're going to the hospital. You want to stop me, go ahead and try. Diego..."

Before she could go on, her mouth fell open. Diego had snatched up another shotgun lying on a pile of Bruckner's junk, and was now pointing it at the old man.

Baby, she thought appreciatively. *Way to flip the script.*

"Does this place have a basement?" he asked, his voice trembling just a little.

Bruckner was staring at him, his froggy eyes looking like they were going to pop out of their sockets. "Kiddo," he said, his voice calm but just barely, "what do you think you're doing?"

"Do you have a basement or not?"

Bruckner smiled a little. It wasn't pretty. "Do I have a basement? Do *you* have a basement? Does Miss Charm over there have a basement? No, I do not, this being south Texas, where people apparently are afraid such fripperies will put their immortal souls in danger of hellfire. This house *is* built on a rather large concrete slab, if that's of any help to you."

"Okay, then, go to the bathroom. Now."

Bruckner said, "Seriously? Do you really intend to shoot me? I'm no authority on firearms, but even I can tell you're holding that thing wrong."

"Yeah, well, that makes me twice as dangerous, doesn't it?"

Bruckner stared at him, then shook his head. "Touché," he muttered, and without further argument headed for the small bathroom off the living room.

Before Gina could congratulate him, Diego swung the barrel of the gun towards her. "You too," he said.

Gina stared at him. "You are shitting me, bro."

"Look, I can't take you to the hospital right now," Diego said, hurriedly lowering the gun. "I got something to do, okay? You're safer in there with him."

"Safer with who? With Mr. Fucking Mad Scientist over there?"

"You know, I'm standing right here, kiddo," Bruckner called from the toilet. "I can *hear* you."

"Shut *up!*" Gina cried, trying to keep from screaming. She glared at Diego, imagining laser beams coming out of her eyes, frying his ass to a crisp. "Take me with you, at least," she pleaded.

Diego shook his head solemnly. "You'd slow me down. And it's gonna get dangerous. If you weren't hurt, I'd bring you, but...just get in the bathroom, okay?"

"You're going to have to carry me," she glared, crossing her arms. She didn't think he would actually do it. Didn't think he *could*. A moment later, she got the surprise of her life.

TWENTY-EIGHT

Roc wasn't happy.

First of all, he was hungry. He had been fed that night, as usual, but the cold, dead meat the strange ones gave him never really satisfied. And lately, it didn't even serve to fill his belly—he was much bigger now, and his hunger seemed bottomless. But tonight he had enjoyed a special treat; the creature that was like a smaller version of himself, the one the strange ones kept locked away, tormenting him with something he hungered for but couldn't have. To kill it, and feel the small, mangled body slide down his hugely muscled throat had felt good, unlike anything he'd ever experienced.

He wanted more. The female who had crept into the enclosure from the unknown place outside would have gone down even better, but then the oldest of the strange ones appeared and forced him back. Roc wasn't afraid of the old one, but he couldn't forget the days when he was smaller and the old one towered over him. By the time he'd overcome the feelings of deference and pulled the strange stick from his hands, he and another strange one had taken the female inside.

He was frustrated now, as well as hungry. He stamped about the enclosure with increased speed, hoping as always that the barriers that kept him inside would simply disappear. He struck at them with his beak, then turned and struck at the twin pillars that loomed up in the center of the yard. They didn't move any more than the walls did, or the box thing when he hit at that.

He screamed into the night sky, but nothing answered him.

TWENTY-NINE

"Dude, why didn't you pick up?"

"I was taking a crap," Kirby said coolly.

"You see the pics I sent you?" Diego stood by the door watching Roc stride around the yard.

"Yeah. What's it supposed to be? All I could see was like a big blur."

"It's your dinosaur, man," Diego said heatedly. He knew all too well the pictures he'd taken with his phone through the sliding door looked like shit. It was pitch black outside except for the outdoor light, and the light from the kitchen didn't help. But right now the pictures were all he had to deal with.

"I thought you said it wasn't a dinosaur." Kirby had the TV on—or was playing a game on it, and he was eating something. Something crunchy. It made him hard to hear. On Diego's end, Gina occasionally erupted with a bloodcurdling scream that made the bathroom door rattle.

It took Diego a moment to get his temper. "I was wrong, okay? So listen…do you want this thing or not? I mean, this is *real*, man. I don't know where he got this thing, but it's a real dinosaur. I think it's a T-Rex. Or like one of those things in *Jurassic Park*…a velociraptor."

"Diego, even I know those are two completely different animals. So which one is it?"

Diego shut his eyes, willing himself to calm down. "Look, you said you wanted it."

"Yeah." Kirby spoke through a mouthful of chips. Now his words were almost impossible to make out. "Sure I want it. Can you get it here?"

Diego licked his lips. "It'll cost you."

Kirby snorted. Diego couldn't tell if it was with amusement or anger. "How much?"

Out in the yard, Roc suddenly stopped his agitated stomping. He turned and stared directly at Diego. He could feel those little red eyes burning through the glass.

"Well, how much you paying me now? We said two grand."

"Two grand," Kirby agreed.

"So we say six Gs, maybe."

"Three times the original price?" Kirby snorted, then crammed a fresh handful of chips into his mouth, crunching ferociously. "Fine."

Diego took a deep breath. "So if you'll go six, you'll go twice that."

Kirby made a noise that was not quite a laugh. "Man, you're a greedy fucker. Hundred twenty, then."

"Awesome, man. I'll get back to you." With that, he hung up and thrust the phone back into his pocket. He began opening cabinets, pushing aside the crazy assortment of mismatched glasses and canned goods, looking for something.

***

"You should leave now." Kirby told the twins. They were fraternal rather than identical, but he still couldn't tell them apart and felt no particular need to. All they did was sit around his house playing video games. They were deferential to him when they needed him to be, and their company just cost him a pizza now and then, a few bottles of soft drinks. But the same qualities that made them appealing also made them irritating when Kirby wanted to be alone.

Like right now.

The brothers made no attempt to argue. They were too used to Kirby. They didn't seem happy to have to abandon their game, but did so without a word, and left without a goodbye to their host or a backward glance.

Kirby locked the door after them. Good riddance.

He went back to the couch and threw himself down. Diego had hung up on him. Nobody had ever done that to him. Like, ever.

He knew what he was doing, of course. Even now the bastard was on the phone trying to find some poor sucker willing to give him even more for the dinosaur. Or whatever the hell it was. Kirby didn't entirely blame Diego for being an opportunistic bastard; he could even admire it, in a way. Diego's mistake had been to disrespect him in his own house—well, on his own phoneline, anyway.

He peeled a slice of cold pizza off the grease-sodden box before him and took a bite out of it. Tasted like shit. He ate it anyway.

The thing in the pictures Diego had shown him might not be a real dinosaur. Kirby had no trouble believing it was just some freak ostrich or emu. But Diego sure as hell thought it was worth something. So far as Kirby was concerned, a living dinosaur was possible. His dad and mom always said that impossible belonged only in the vocabularies of lazy assholes. And Kirby Van Zandt was not a lazy asshole.

What could Kirby Van Zandt do with a living dinosaur? Hell, anything he wanted. Charge admission to see it. Or he could have it skinned for a pair of shoes, if that suited him better. The point was, it would be his. Of course the bleeding hearts and SJWs would argue that you couldn't really own an animal. Bullshit. People owned dogs and cats. What difference was there between owning a bull terrier and a living fossil? None. Most people couldn't make that stick in court, but most people didn't have the kind of legal firepower the Van Zandts did.

The SJWs would have said you couldn't own a lawyer, either. Shit. His parents owned dozens of them.

THIRTY

If Birthday Boy will pay a hundred and twenty Gs without blinking, Diego thought, *someone else will pay more.* He had some ideas. Not a museum. A private collector. They had to be out there. Shit, those people paid thousands for freaking ant-eaters. He'd seen the websites. A few emails—he'd have to be careful, set up an anonymous on Hotmail or some shit—and he'd be rolling in it.

And then—Mexico. He still didn't think Bruckner would be stupid enough to call the cops on him, but who in hell knew who the old guy was in bed with? All that scientific equipment cost money, it wasn't something you could buy on a Cowtown professor's salary. One of these Vander boys wouldn't know enough to take a chance on a mob hit, but he was a New York boy. A year or so down in Tequilaland should be enough. Word was you could live real cheap down there.

He'd have to come back for Camila eventually…maybe. She might not be into it. But that was okay. Maybe if she wasn't, it would be the best thing. This might have been a good time to explore things with Gina, but he had a feeling he'd just screwed *that* pooch big time.

Finally he found what he was looking for, hidden behind an ancient box of cereal; a bottle of bourbon, still mostly full. Good stuff, too, not the rotgut he might have expected from Bruckner. He'd figured the old guy liked a nip every now and then—who didn't? But this was hitting the jackpot.

Next he grabbed a large mixing bowl he'd spotted earlier in his search, and set it on the table. He found a dish of half-thawed steaks in the fridge, and dumped them into the bowl, along with a generous glug of the booze, saving enough for a healthy swallow of his own. Then he went to the patio door, carefully unlocking and sliding it back.

"Come on, Rocky," he called softly. "It's cocktail time."

No response. Roc was sulking, out in the shadows. Diego ventured as far as he could into the shadows, then set the bowl down and retreated into the house. Frustrated by the darkness of the yard, he looked around the kitchen for another switch that might put some more light on the subject. No dice. Finally he switched on the surge protector, just to see what would happen. This resulted in a small scatter of brightly colored lights blinking in the yard. Big deal. He sat down with the remainder of the bottle, waiting.

Eventually Roc made a reappearance, apparently attracted—as Diego hoped he'd be—by the smell of blood from the steaks, rising through the less appetizing bourbon fumes. He stalked over to the bowl, nudging it with his beak. Finally, after giving Diego a suspicious glare, he seized up the steaks, coughing as they went down.

"Yeah, that's smooth," Diego smiled, lifting the bottle in a toast. "Ain't it, big guy?"

His plan was simple. Get Roc drunk off his ass, rope his beak shut and his legs together, then pull his truck out front and get him in the back. Then…well, he'd figure it out. He knew a guy with a garage that would probably do to keep Roc secure while he made his calls.

But within a few minutes, he realized there was a problem.

Apparently Roc wasn't a bourbon man.

He went into hacking, wheezing fits, his body spasming as he gasped and strained open-mouthed at the ground. Diego guessed these were the dino-bird equivalent of dry heaves, but for whatever reason, Roc couldn't seem to bring anything up, and it infuriated him. He swatted the still half-full bowl away, squawking in rage, then went on a rampage around the yard, flapping his wing-stubs and kicking savagely at the weird-looking pillar-and-box arrangement.

Aw shit, Diego thought, watching nervously. *Hope I didn't fuck up over here.*

THIRTY-ONE

Something was wrong.

The air had a strange feeling, as though a lightning storm were imminent. But the sun was shining. Even the male knew that storms didn't come out of sunny skies.

Even so, the weird feeling in the air was doing him no good. It kept distracting him as he and the female circled around each other, each looking for the proper angle for a fresh attack. The female was distracted as well, and even more agitated, but she didn't seem surprised. Rather, the strange feeling seemed to infuriate her. She broke away from circling her opponent, running to the right. Now she was circling…nothing.

It was as though another predator—another *Titanis*, or one of the big-toothed cats that had begun roaming their territories in increasing numbers—had appeared, and the female was challenging it. But the area she circled was empty. Nothing stood there, but she hissed and lowered her head, ruffling her feathers in warning.

The male was confused, but part of him understood the female's need to challenge an invisible intruder. Nothing was visible, but it *felt* like something was. The air felt and tasted strange, and there was a weird keening coming from somewhere that hurt his ears. A moment later he had joined his former mate, circling and screeching warnings while the smaller male stood watching in confusion.

THIRTY-TWO

"Could you stop that shit, please?"

Bruckner, seated on the toilet with his arms wrapped comfortably around one knee, looked over at Gina and grinned.

"That's the Prelude from *Loehengrin*, kiddo. What, you don't dig opera?"

It actually took some effort, but Gina resisted the urge to smile back. The old guy had spread towels in the bathtub so she could lie down, and he hadn't tried anything with her—she was sure she could kick his ass even in her wounded state, but she was just as happy not to have to try.

"I'm into harder stuff, actually."

"Yeah, I guessed that. Well, we're all gonna be singing the 'Giant Terror bird is Eating My Guts Blues' if your boyfriend out there has anything to do with it."

Gina grimaced, kicking up her feet on the rim of the tub. "He's not my boyfriend. I mean, he wasn't before, and now he's not even my friend. I can't believe he did this to me."

Bruckner shook his head. "Be okay if he just did it to me, I take it."

Gina did smile at that, then let out a painful chuckle. "Ow…Jesus, don't make me laugh."

"Sorry. Well, money does funny things to people, I can tell you all about that. I mean, if it makes you feel any better, I have a feeling he's got a pretty nasty payback coming. He may not know it, but he's in way over his head. Problem is, we're probably going to share in whatever shitstorm he brings down on himself."

A loud shriek echoed from outside the house. Bruckner grimaced. "There it is. Old Roc sounds pissed. Oh, God. You sure you don't have any power on your phone?"

It was the first thing he'd asked her once Diego had put them both in the bathroom and shoved a dresser in front of the door. "No," she said ruefully, prying the phone out of her jeans and looking over the screen. "I meant to charge it this morning. Forgot. The one day I should've known I'd need it."

"Well, nothing for it," Bruckner said stoically. "Sooner or later someone will find us, and until then…."

A terrible shriek came from outside, making them both flinch. It sounded like Roc, but also…*not*. It was accompanied by another sound, a wailing howl that sounded like a wounded animal…but also weirdly inorganic, an electronic cry that pulsed on and on.

"Oh my God," Bruckner cried. He got up and held his ear to the door. "Damn it! He's got it to work! How the hell…"

Wincing, Gina levered herself out of the tub. She had no idea what was going on, but she knew whatever it was wasn't likely to be good. "What is it?"

"He's dilated a wormhole," Bruckner snapped, still listening.

"He's done what to a *what*?"

"All you need to know is, he's just put in an order for more creatures like Roc. Maybe a few cave lions and saber-toothed cats as well. Or worse things. Who did you say he was trying to sell Roc to?"

"Guy named Kirby Van Zandt. Fat little rich fuck."

Bruckner sighed as another volley of bizarre sounds blared through the door. "Well, I hope Mr. Kirby keeps some mad money in his wallet. He's going to have his pick of a whole damned menagerie in about five minutes."

THIRTY-THREE

The shining thing was back.

The mother *Titanis* screamed in fury at her old enemy. It seemed bigger now, a vast, gleaming-edged rift hanging in midair. The center of it hurt her small eyes when she tried to focus on it; it was a whirlpool of twisting, metallic colors that seemed to be trying to form a single coherent image. She danced from one foot to the other, seemingly trying to work up the nerve for a proper attack.

The males stepped back, both fighting an urge to run. Neither had seen anything like this bizarre invader. Nothing about it seemed overtly threatening, but in its way it was as fearsome as one of the other predators they shared their territory with. They felt a *wrongness* about it, much as the female had.

In the end, it was the smaller male that took the initiative. Though he feared the shining thing, the female was vulnerable while she was preoccupied with it. With a sudden squawk, he flung himself upon her, screeching and clawing at her thighs as though trying to mount her.

The female went into a rage, shrieking and twisting her neck back to try and get at her attacker. After several attempts, she managed to catch his neck in her beak, hauling him bodily over her shoulder and slamming him into the ground.

Now her frustration and blind anger had a target. She pulled him up again, shaking him the way she would a prey animal. Blood flew from his severed arteries; he made attempts to fight back, but they grew steadily feebler, until it was obvious he was dead.

With a final scream of triumph, the female flung the mangled corpse into the shining thing. It hung in mid-air, turning slowly in the spiral of weird colors like a leaf in an eddy. Then, the male's body seemed to fold in on itself, growing smaller as though being molded by enormous hands. It slid into the shining spiral, bit by bit, until at last it was gone.

The big male watched, unable to understand what was happening. He finally settled on fleeing as his best option, but then the female came at him. She moved slowly, head down in an attack position, but showing no signs of charging. The male squawked at her, but she didn't respond; she simply kept moving forward. He ran at her, and she dodged him easily, striking a hammer-blow at his head. After a few more feints, the male realized he wasn't going to succeed in bringing her down. Running was definitely the more appealing option.

But when he tried to turn, the female ran around him, blocking his path. His attempt to bite only got him a bite of his own, followed by the female hissing and stalking inexorably forward, pushing him back...

Towards the Shining Thing.

The male did not want any part of the glowing hole in the air, but the female was implacable, pushing him slowly backward until, panicking, he launched an all-out attack, hissing and tearing at the female with his beak and claws. He was desperate to get away, but the female seemed just as desperate to maneuver him into the Shining Thing. So far as she was concerned, it was simply an easy way to kill him.

Then something happened that no one had ever succeeded in doing to him; he was snatched bodily off his feet to hang shrieking and kicking in the air with his former mate. Both of them were being pulled into the Shining Thing, into a maelstrom of colors and lights and sounds. And no matter how hard he kicked and squawked, nothing seemed able to remedy that.

THIRTY-FOUR

It was the weirdest fucking thing he had ever seen.

A huge, swirling wound hung in the air between the two pillars. The edges gleamed and shone like liquid metal, while inside them was a kaleidoscope of twisting, glittering colors that seemed to be trying to form a picture. There were noises too—thundering booms, and a thin, wavering squeal that made his teeth ache. He wanted to run from the thing, but somehow he couldn't. He wanted to see what the thing would do.

Up to now, Diego had thought of old Bruckner as a mad scientist, mostly as a joke. It suddenly wasn't a joke anymore; the shining thing was proof.

Roc, for his part, had gone way beyond the liquor-fueled agitation he'd shown before. The rift—or the sounds it was making—seemed to be driving him crazy. He was running laps around the yard, squawking wildly, either not seeing Diego or simply ignoring him.

Suddenly the thing's internal rhythms seemed to reach some kind of peak; its glittering middle surged suddenly, and Diego was showered by a deluge of red liquid and tiny chunks of organic matter.

"Aw, Jesus!" Diego cried, stepping back and shaking his hands. The stuff was warm and it stunk. He had an unpleasant feeling it was composed mostly of blood. It was as though some large animal had been put through an enormous meat grinder.

But worse was to come. Two tall, shadowy figures lurched through the rift. They bore more than a passing resemblance to Roc. In fact, they looked pretty much exactly like him, just bigger—and like him, they didn't seem to be in the best frame of mind. One of them stooped down and gave a scream that made Diego's ears ache. A moment later its friend followed suit with a scream of its own.

Time to go, Diego decided. Fuck Kirby, fuck the money, fuck these things—birds or dinosaurs or whatever the hell they were. He ran for the kitchen door, sliding it back and hot-footing it through the living room without bothering to close it.

His intention was to push aside the cabinet he had used to block the bathroom door, so Gina and Bruckner could escape as well. That plan was deep-sixed by the sound of the newcomers smashing their way in and through the kitchen. Glass and small appliances were thrown to the ground and smashed underfoot; cabinets were broken open by huge beaks and their contents ravaged. Tables were overturned and chairs picked up and flung against walls. Diego grabbed the shotgun and ran past the bathroom, ignoring the shouts from inside.

No way those things'll be able to get into the bathroom, he told himself, and ran out past the blaring television through the front door…right into Camila, who stood on the doorstep with a hand lifted, poised to knock. An old Honda was parked in front of the house, a skinny kid standing beside it. He was watching Diego with a dubious expression.

"Diego?" Camila asked, staring at his red-soaked clothes and wild-eyed appearance. Then she seemed to remember something, and her face turned angry.

"We gotta get out of here," he told her, grabbing her hand. "Come on, my truck's over this way."

"Stop it!" Camila pulled away, but started at a fresh volley of shrieks and smashing from inside. "What the hell is *that*?" she demanded.

"Is that Roc?" the skinny kid asked, running up the sidewalk. "He's in the house? Where's Dr. Bruckner?"

"He's fine, look…I don't have time to explain, we just gotta…"

At that point the female *Titanis* squeezed through the doorway. She wasn't shrieking now; she squinted at them, hissing.

"Run!" Skinny Kid screamed, seizing Camila's hand and pulling her towards his car. Diego grabbed her other hand—this was hardly the time to start acting all caveman, but he was damned if this nerd was going to carry Camila off right in front of him. Camila wailed, the kid howled and Diego bellowed—over another bellow from the female *Titanis*, who was now pounding down the sidewalk toward them.

Releasing Camila's hand, Diego lifted the shotgun and tried to sight down the barrel. That was how you did it, right? He'd never shot a gun before, not even in the shooting galleries on the midway at Coney Island. The guys here in Vander liked to bust his balls about that, but fuck, how hard could it be? You aimed, you pulled the trigger. With a target this big, how could you miss?

Somehow, he managed. The bullet flew well over the *Titanis'* head, but something—the noise of the gun, or maybe the smell of it—startled her, maybe even spooked her a little. She took off up the road, shrieking the entire way, until she was lost to sight.

Ah, shit, Diego thought. *That ain't good.*

Then Roc and the other newcomer were jostling their way through the door, hissing and snapping at each other—both trying to get through at the same time, like Laurel and Hardy.

Diego hardly had time to lift the gun again before he saw Camila was already in the car, shotgun. Skinny Kid was on the driver's side, waving wildly out the window. "Come *on!*" Skinny Kid yelled. "They'll kill you!"

Screw it, Diego thought. *He's got a point.* He dove into the backseat, trying to cradle the gun. The barrel was burningly hot, so he had to settle for settling it on the seat, hoping it wouldn't scorch the fabric.

The two *Titanis* stalked round Skinny's car. Skinny was shouting at Roc like he was a trained poodle. For a moment, it actually seemed to work. At least Roc hesitated, as though trying to work out whether he'd actually seen the kid before. The other male was less impressed. It stared thoughtfully at the car, then, with a jerky up-and-down motion of its head, slammed a sizable dent in the hood. Apparently encouraged, it began laying on like a jackhammer, shaking the car while Camila screamed like a chick in a horror movie. Roc stalked over to the side, considering them through the dirty glass of the window.

"It's gonna break the window! *It's gonna break the fuckin' window!*" Camila shrieked, actually flinging her arms around Skinny's shoulders and burying her face there. The kid looked like he was blushing. Diego didn't have it in his heart to be pissed.

"G'wan, Roc! Go back to the yard! C'mon, *shoo!*" The kid waved his hand at the monster staring at him through a thin sheet of glass. He actually looked pretty fearless, though Diego noticed he didn't go so far as to roll the window down. Roc gave the car a few more experimental taps, then turned and jogged down the empty street.

Skinny hit the horn with his fist, making a short, rather anticlimactic beep. "No! Oh, you *dick!* Come back here!"

"Jeez, dude, let him go! Better down there than chowing down on us!"

Skinny pushed open his door and swung his legs out. "Don't you get it? He's free now! They all are! Where did those other two come from, anyway?" He sounded pissed now, not scared.

Diego decided to take the Fifth on that one, though he could feel Camila's eyes burning holes through him. The kid was already on his way to the house, calling Bruckner's name. It seemed like a good time to leave. He got out of the back seat, marveling at the dents that had been hammered into the chassis of Skinny's car.

Those things mean business. Thank God I got a gun.

"C'mon," he said again, making another attempt to get hold of Camila's hand through the window. Once again, she pulled it away.

"Where do you think you're going?"

It sounded like a perfect excuse to play hero, maybe save a little face. "After those things. I got a gun, remember? And a truck. We don't need to steal Skinny's."

"His name's Alex. And I'm not going anywhere with you. You want to play monster hunter? Go on. Or maybe you just want another shot at delivering them to Kirby."

Diego knew that voice. Any reasonable argument he made would be shot down immediately. It was time to go.

"Okay, listen...I'm going to try to fix this, alright? Maybe it's better you stay here."

Camila kept glaring. "I know you stole those pictures of Roc off my phone."

So much for reverse psychology. "Okay, okay, we'll talk later. Peace out, alright?"

Diego set out for the fence and his truck, the shotgun over his shoulder. He tried to whistle jauntily, like the monster hunter Camila had accused him of imitating, but after a few notes he clammed up. It was past midnight, and it suddenly occurred to him he might not live out the day.

THIRTY-FIVE

When Alex heard Bruckner bellowing behind the bathroom door, he immediately threw himself against the cabinet, trying to push it aside. It didn't budge, and it wasn't until Camila came in and gave him a hand that he was able to free his boss.

"Thank Saint Anthony," Bruckner said, slipping out of the opened space and giving Alex a warm slap on the back. "You may have just earned yourself a promotion, kiddo. I was getting the heebie-jeebies stuck in the john with Calamity Jane over there."

Alex stared in surprise at the bathroom's other occupant, a punky-looking Asian girl who lay glaring in the bathtub with her arms tightly folded across her chest.

"Hey," he said dully. The girl mouthed him a kiss, then smirked at his slack-jawed expression.

"Uhm, that's Camila," Alex said, gesturing at her.

"Nice to meet you," Bruckner said, essaying a short bow. "And this," he went on, jerking a thumb at the girl in the tub. "Is Regina. An aspiring chanteuse, and our *Titanis* thief's sometime paramour."

"Uh, *no*," Camila and Gina said, roughly in unison.

"I don't sing," Gina added. "I'm a bassist. It's just 'Gina,' too, I don't go for that fancy shit."

"My apologies," Bruckner said drily. Turning to Alex, he said, "Looks like the Terror Bird's out of the bag, kiddo. Three of them, to be exact. Our thief somehow managed to do what I've failed to do, and turned on the dilator. Apparently whatever wormhole it's locked onto is some kind of happy hunting ground for *Titanis walleri*. Personally, I would have preferred it hit Marilyn Monroe's dressing room."

"Gross," Gina muttered.

"So what do we do?" Alex asked.

"What I should have done a long time ago," Bruckner sighed. "Please tell me one of you has a working cell phone?"

THIRTY-SIX

The noises from outside his bedroom window woke Merle Hollis a long while before his customary rising time. Normally it was at least noon before he pulled his ass out of bed and headed to the living room, bleary-eyed and praying he could remember where he'd left his bottle the night before.

What he heard first was snarls and barks from Jalapeno, his wife's Chihuahua. Or rather, his *ex*-wife's chih…oh, the hell with it, the dog was his. A long, *long* way from the Redtick Coonhound he had his heart set on, but there wasn't much question Jalapeno had favored him over Erlinda, with her baby-talk and tendency to paint the poor dog's nails pink. He was a loyal little sumbitch too; when he wasn't out in the yard doing his business, he was right at Merle's heels, or next to him on the couch, cadging fries from the carry-out Merle practically lived on these days. It wasn't much of a friendship, but at least Jalapeno wasn't constantly bitching at him to stop drinking or lose some weight. Never borrowed money, either. Good dog.

The doggie-door Merle hired that Mexican kid down the street to install was the best deal he'd ever made. No more getting up at some ungodly hour so he could let Jalapeno out to do his business. There was still a lot of barking, because Big J (as the neighborhood kids called him) was about as mean as his master, and went after anybody walking down the street. But from the back yard the barking didn't carry so well, allowing Merle some much-needed additional sleep.

But this morning, it wasn't Jalapeno's barking that woke him. It was another sound, loud and screeching, something like guitar feedback and something like he'd imagine a sheet of scrap metal would make if two giant hands were to tear it in half. Some damn fool kid's idea of music, probably. Whatever it was, Merle didn't like it, and he intended to convey that fact to whoever was making it.

The sound seemed to be coming from out front, by the street, so that was where Merle headed, stumping along in his boxers and well-worn Charlie Daniels t-shirt. When he walked out the front door, he stopped cold, blinking, because what was making the music wasn't no damned record.

At first Merle thought it was a dinosaur, a T-Rex right out of one of those History Channel programs. But then he noticed the feathers and the enormous beak. Now the thing put him more in the mind of a road-

94

runner, but the biggest damned road-runner anybody had ever seen. The most heavily built, too. The Schwarzenegger of road-runners. Merle had never seen one out in the wild, but there'd been one at a roadside zoo he used to stop at back in his trucking days, to stretch his legs and give his ass a rest. It had been scrawny and half-dead, more like a starved chicken than the "predator" the hand-lettered sign on its cage proclaimed. But there was something oddly graceful about it, even so, and oddly formidable. *Elegant* was a word Merle would never use, but the way the varmint was put together seemed almost beautiful (another forbidden word). "Nice clean design," some guy standing next to Merle had told his wife, and while it irritated Merle no end to agree with a yankee (guy sounded like he was from Boston, for God's sake), he had to admit that was a good way to put it.

The thing Merle faced now had some nice clean design too, but it wasn't in a cage. It was clawing at the ground at the base of the chain-link fence that separated Merle's back yard from the street, occasionally letting rip with one of the hideous sheet-metal noises that had woken Merle up. It didn't pay much attention to the furiously yapping Jalapeno, though Merle didn't doubt its chief objective was getting through the fence and swallowing him whole. It seemed fascinated by the fence, and also a little afraid of it; every few minutes it would stop digging and give the links a heavy slam with its beak, then hop back from the resulting noise like an immense, startled jaybird.

Merle slid back through the front door, closing it carefully and locking it for good measure. He picked up his cell-phone from the silver dish on the hall table where he put it every time he came in, along with his spare change. He had no great liking for cell phones, but Erlinda had forced him to buy it about a year before their divorce—if only, he suspected, so she could keep better track of where he was. He had to admit the damned thing sometimes came in handy—like when you found a prehistoric bird-monster trying to get into your back yard and eat your dog.

As he moved through the kitchen and out through his garage, he phoned the Vander Sheriff's Office. The number was one of the few he'd put in his Contacts list—mainly because Luke Davis, the sheriff, was a sometimes hunting-buddy of his.

After three rings, Francine Conway picked up. "Vander Sheriff's Office," she said, sounding bored and also preoccupied. Probably watching movies on YouTube again, much as Luke had bitched her out for it.

"Francine, honey, this is Merle." He realized he was speaking in a hushed tone, as though the bird could hear him.

"Merle. What you doin' up this early? You grow a guilty conscience all of a sudden?" Francine's voice went wet and gulpy as she took a hit of her morning Dr. Pepper.

"Francine, is Luke there?" Francine liked to razz him, which normally he was fine with. This morning was a different matter, though.

"Out getting some breakfast. Hey Merle, do you got power?"

"Power?" For a second, Merle couldn't quite figure out what Francine was talking about. It put him in mind of the cartoons they used to run on weekday afternoons, where someone always had the power, or was looking for the power, or some damned thing. "You mean electricity? Yeah, I got electricity, why?" He realized as soon as he said it that he didn't actually know if he had power; he hadn't thought to look at the clock on his microwave or try to turn on a light.

"We've had calls all morning about people losing power. All over Vander. I guess sheriff's office must be outside the blackout zone. Or brownout, or whatever. Why they'd call us instead of the Electric Company, I got no idea."

"Look Frannie, I'm a mite busy out here…just have Luke call me when he gets in?" He hung up and stood with the phone in his hand as he looked over his choices for combat. He had a decent shotgun once, that had served him well on trips up to the hill country to shoot deer. After the divorce he'd been forced to pawn it, and never had gotten around to getting the damn thing back. The row of yard tools were mainly leftovers from the rose garden Erlinda had tried to plant once upon a time, without notable success. There wasn't much doubt which he'd use—the shovel was good and heavy. It'd give ol' Big Bird a headache, if nothing else.

A few minutes later he was back outside, the shovel over one shoulder like he was one of the Seven Dwarfs. The phone was a problem; Luke could be back any minute and he wanted to talk to him. Thing was, his boxers didn't have pockets and neither did his t-shirt. He had to settle for placing it carefully on the ground, hoping he'd hear it ring. Of course, he might not; that was the other problem. He was going to be kind of busy in just a few minutes. Waiting on Luke's call wasn't an option, any more than going to the Mexicans down the street. Merle had been brought up to believe a man took care of problems on his own land. He'd called Luke not so much as a plea for help as a purely practical nod to the future; once he killed this damned thing, somebody from the city was going to need to haul it off.

Well, he thought. *No sense putting it off any more.*

"Hey!" he shouted, squaring off with feet planted well apart. "Idjit!"

The plus-sized road-runner stopped its kicking and scratching at the fence, lifted its head to give Merle the stink-eye. Merle could just about see Jalapeno's tiny muzzle still snapping and snarling at the gap the bird had made under the fence. He had to smile at that. Big J might be a little turd, but he had the heart of a big dog. Never backed down from a fight.

The bird turned its head slightly, and gave what Merle supposed was meant to be a chirp of curiosity. A very loud chirp damn, near like to blow his eardrum out. As much as to say, "Are you back already?" Then it came at him, going from zero to a pretty fair hike in a matter of seconds.

The whole thing didn't go quite as easily as Merle had put it together in his head. He'd thought he could use the shovel as a bat, and the bird's head as a ball. He swung with a will, but the bird sidestepped him with no effort at all, and shot its head out in a retaliatory strike. Merle managed to get out of the way just in time, but at the expense of his balance. The weight of the shovel sent him toppling onto his side. A moment later he was wielding the shovel with both hands, like a fighting staff one of those martial arts guys might use, thrusting it up again and again as the bird snapped at him. The bird's beak would snap shut on it, long and hard enough to worry Merle it could snap it clean in two. It didn't seem to like the wood, though, any more than it liked the noise the fence made when kicked.

In between bites at the shovel, it clawed at Merle with its feet. Merle saw most of the blows coming and was able to twist his body to one side or another, but enough strikes landed that pretty soon he was bleeding up a storm.

Over the shrieks and Merle's curses, the sound of Jalapeno's frenzied rage was clear. A few yaps more and the dog went silent...only to start barking again, much more loudly.

Turning his head to one side, Merle saw the Chihuahua only a foot or so away, belly-down in the dust, trying to creep in close enough to give Big Bird a bite on the foot. Big J must have wriggled through under the fence; his fur was scored with stripes of blood where the ends of the wire had scratched him. He looked like a tiny, very angry wolf with enormous bat ears.

The bird hissed irritably at the dog, snapping. Merle knew one bite would be enough to bond Big J and Big Bird in alimentary matrimony. He shouted, "Damn it, Jalapeno, go on! Get back in the house! *Get!*"

That short outburst cost him his life. Big Bird turned his attention back to his victim, and apparently decided it was time to end this shit. His huge head lifted up like a jackhammer, then came down like one.

Merle Hollis went out like a candle. His last thought was, *Shit, at least the dog cared.*

THIRTY-SEVEN

Killing the strange one had felt good. The little animal that had kept snarling at Roc and making little runs at him, only to dart out of reach at the last minute was irritating, but once the *Titanis* let a few beakfuls of torn, bloody flesh slide down his throat, he was better able to ignore it.

He hadn't actually expected to kill the strange one. The creatures had been a constant in his life since his hatching, and while his instincts told him they would make easy prey, he had grown to be wary of them, and the painfully loud noises they could call out of the air. Also, they brought him food regularly, though seldom more than the cold, stinking meat he had grown up on.

The one he had just fought had brought no meat except that which it carried on its bones. Nor could it do much in the way of loud noises. It had simply attacked him...and died. This suggested certain possibilities to Roc's tiny mind...possibilities in which many of the two-legs might die.

As Roc thrust his beak into the carcass before him, the small creature ventured near him again—probably hoping to tear off a bit of Roc's kill for itself. Roc lashed out, but succeeded only in slamming its beak against the strip of stony substance that seemed so common in this place. The small animal ran off again, barking.

Roc ignored it, then lifted his head and shrieked. He didn't realize that he was calling the others like him who had suddenly appeared in the old strange one's place. The noises he made simply felt right to him. But soon he saw them approaching—the other male, and the one whose pheromones told him it was different; he had no concept of *female*, just as he had no concept of *mother*.

He didn't notice the strange shell-like creature approaching him at first. Roc had seen many of these shells since his escape, most of them immobile. Some, glimpsed in the distance, seemed to carry strange ones within them. Perhaps the strange ones fed off them in some way, like a parasite. The one approaching him now began flashing colored lights, then released a volley of honks and screeches almost equal in volume to his own. A strange one got out of the shell and began making its ridiculous squawks and howls, waving its arms at Roc.

Roc wasn't worried about it. The others were coming—he could see them running at speed towards him—and he had just learned the strange ones represented no real threat at all.

THIRTY-EIGHT

"You sure you don't want to go to the hospital?"

Gina shrugged, then winced a little at the sudden jab of pain in her shoulders. She'd been sitting on the couch flipping channels, looking for news about Roc and his pals. Most of the local stations had been out—for that matter, the power had been going in and out most of the morning. Camila guessed that had something to do with the machine in Bruckner's yard. Right now the screen was just static.

"I'll live," she said, accepting a cup of coffee from Camila. "I don't think they could do much more than the old guy did already. Just change my bandages probably. Hell, I can do that here. All they'd do after that is ask questions, and we don't need that right now."

Camila nodded, though she wasn't sure how she felt about Gina's casual use of the word "we." Was it really a good idea to get involved with this mess? Alex's boss was the scientist, after all, and the two of them were out back right now, trying to fix the time machine or whatever the hell it was that had brought Roc into this world.

Shouldn't she just leave and hope for the best?

As she picked up her own coffee and padded through the kitchen to the back yard, she knew she wasn't going to do that. She might as well call up Diego and tell him that once he caught Roc and mounted its head on Kirby's wall—or whatever he thought he was doing—she would be glad to marry him and be his little woman. Because bitching him out now wouldn't be any different from throwing away responsibility for her own life and actions.

If nothing else, she owed it to Alex to stay. Alex, and a lot of other people. After all, she had taken the pictures of Roc that had gotten this whole monster-show started. People were probably going to die because of those pictures. She would stay and see this through, she decided.

Outside, Bruckner was storming from one end of the enclosure to the other, screaming at someone on the cell-phone he'd borrowed from Gina. Alex squatted by the side of the machine that controlled the portal or time warp or whatever it was that Roc and the others had come through. He seemed to be trying to fix it, but he looked like he had no idea what he was doing.

Just as she stepped through the door, Bruckner exploded again. "Look, Dieter, I said I was sorry. What do you want me to do, get down on my knees?"

Camila decided Alex was probably better company.

"How's it going?" she asked, kneeling down beside him.

Alex gave her a miserable smile. "You tell me. You probably know more about it than I do. Dr. Bruckner told me to see what I could do, but it sure ain't much."

"Come on in, then. I made coffee."

Bruckner picked that moment to go off on another tirade. "Speaking of your boss," Camila whispered, nodding at Bruckner's gesticulating form. "Who's he talking to over there? Or yelling to?"

Alex got up and thrust his knuckles into the small of his back, stretching painfully. "An old friend of his, or colleague, or whatever. A German physicist named Dieter something. I guess he's the one who actually invented the machine."

"Yeah?" Camila said, leading him back into the house. "So why doesn't he come on down here and fix it for us?"

"I think Dr. Bruckner's trying to convince him to do just that. Thing is...I mean, I don't think Dieter likes the idea of getting his hands dirty."

"Hey you guys!" Gina called from the living room. "Get in here!"

The two ran back into the living room, pulling up short when they saw the TV. The screen showed a harried-looking young woman in a suit, speaking rapidly into a microphone. Whoever was holding the camera on her was even more harried, if not in the middle of an actual nervous breakdown. The picture was jerking up and down and from side to side. The logo of Channel 5 news was visible in the upper left-hand corner of the screen, as well as a line identifying the reporter as Casey Cameron, but between the camera-work and the shouting, wildly gesturing mob of people behind her, it was hard to get a grip on what was happening.

"After a series of power outages early this morning," Casey Cameron said, "Vander is apparently under attack by three...I don't know how else to say it, but *monsters* sounds about right."

"Aw shit," Alex said miserably.

Casey appeared to be speaking to the camera-man. "Can you move it to the left?" she said exasperatedly. One stomach-churning jerk of the lens later and they were suddenly looking at three *Titanis*, high-stepping around a suburban street in what looked like the outskirts of Vander. Two men in t-shirts and baseball hats were walking leerily around the edge of the picture, but quickly scampered off when one of the Terror Birds screamed at them.

"Sheriff Luke Davis responded to a call from Merle Hollis this morning, and suddenly found himself in the middle of a scene from a monster movie. So far it does appear that Hollis is a casualty."

"Yeah, ya think?" Gina snorted, pointing at the TV with her foot. There wasn't much doubt she was pointing at the still, red-smeared object two of the *Titanis* were fighting over. "Cause if not, that's the most tore-up looking live guy I ever saw."

"Shhh," Camila hissed.

Casey Cameron sounded close to tears. "No one seems to be sure where these creatures came from or how they got here...so far our calls for help to neighboring townships have gone unanswered."

One of the officers got too close to one of the *Titanis*. It took no more than a second for him to join Merle Hollis as pavement pizza. This resulted in even wilder camera-work and a series of deafening sobs from Casey.

"*Please* tell me those aren't our *Titanis*," Bruckner's voice said. Camila turned and saw him standing in the doorway, Gina's phone hanging from his fingers. He looked considerably more tired and worried than he had back in the yard.

"You wanna be disappointed, or you want the truth?" Gina asked.

"Where is that?" Bruckner demanded, squinting at the screen. "Where are they filming this?"

"It's out by Clark or Russell," Camila said. "I know a family out that way."

"Then we've got to get out there. There's a chance Roc will respond to me, or possibly Alex."

"What are you gonna do, whistle a mating song?" Gina scoffed.

"Those things will kill both of you!" Camila cried.

"Uhh..." Alex put in.

"Well, my...esteemed colleague Dr. Wolfschmidt," Bruckner said, staring bitterly down at the phone in his hand as though it had just bitten him, "thinks that we have a chance. A small one, it's true, but we don't have much choice.

"Apparently the work-out we've been giving the machine has had some...effects on the local environs. Basically the whole damned area— all of Vander County, likely-is now filled with dilating wormholes. So far they're still microscopic, as far as we're concerned, but here's where it gets good. Roc and his compadres have carried some kind of quantum energy in with them. It doesn't do much to them, but it sort of attracts the wormholes. Good old Dieter—who sure as shootin' is still *my* good buddy, sure as shootin', bet your ass...anyway, *Dieter* thinks that because of all this, if we just schlep the machine over and turn it on, we have a good chance of dilating a wormhole big enough to get our feathered friends back through. Without the pylons, yet. If Alex and I can get close enough we should be able to force them back through."

"Wait, though," Camila said. "Why do you even want to do this? I mean, the cops already know about Roc and the other two. Why don't you just let them finish it?"

"Yeah," Gina said. "Plus, you guys could get in some serious shit if the cops realize you're the reason the birds got loose. Shouldn't you just lay low here?"

Bruckner opened his mouth to answer, then shut it when a sizzling, shrieking noise erupted from the back yard.

"Tell me that's not what I think it is," Alex moaned.

Tossing the phone back to Gina, Bruckner headed for the back yard. "Stay here," he shouted, but naturally the girls—and a singularly despondent-looking Alex were right on his heels.

Something was waiting for them in the back yard. It had a rounded, heavy shell and a tail tipped with a spiked orb. It looked a bit like an armadillo in armor.

It honked at them.

"Oh my god, that is so fucking cute I wanna *die*!" Gina crooned, snapping pictures of the creature with her phone.

"What are you doing?" Bruckner howled, making an unsuccessful attempt to grab the phone back. "Knock it off with the snapshots, Dian Arbus, or you *will* die, that's a promise!"

"What is it?"

"A baby *doedicurus*, if I'm not mistaken. A variety of glyptodont. Early form of armadillo—will you *give* me that damned phone?!"

The *doedicurus*, apparently panicked by the fuss it was causing, took a few backward steps—and was swallowed up by a blazing disc of light that looked all too familiar to Alex, at least.

"Aww, what happened to the baby?" Gina cried, lowering her phone.

"That's what I was trying to tell you. The quantum displacement has started an escalating chain reaction. We *can't* 'just let' Vander's finest kill Roc and the other *Titanis*. If we get them back through a wormhole, the quantum upset will go away—or so Dieter thinks. But if they wind up stuffed on the sheriff's wall in the 21st century, more and more wormholes will open, and then *more*. Leading to more and more visits from large, hungry predators, not to mention people wandering into other times, or vice-versa. Just what Texas needs, a real-time re-enactment of the Alamo…with the original players!"

"Then there really will be trouble," Alex said.

"In spades, kiddo," Bruckner said grimly. "Could lead to a total breakdown of reality as we know it. And I *will* get blamed for that, no question. Bye-bye Nobel, hello Rikers. Or wherever they put naughty scientists these days."

Turning to Alex, he slapped his shoulder. "You take the ladies home, kiddo. I'll start loading the machine and extension cords into the car. Then we'll hit the road to high adventure, as they used to say in the boys' adventure novels."

"Wait a minute," Camila cried. "What do you mean 'take the ladies home?' We're coming with you!"

"That's right," Gina nodded. "We're gonna see this through. You know you're going to need help."

"Are you kidding me?" Bruckner glared. "I've already got blood on my hands. I'm not going to be phoning up your parents telling them their precious princesses were eaten by Terror Birds from the Pliocene. Besides, we don't have room in my car."

"We may have a bigger problem," Alex pointed out. "How did you get the machine here, Dr. Bruckner? I mean, when Dr. Wolfschmidt first loaned it to you?"

"Paid some guys to haul it in for me. Why?"

"Because it's a *big* mama-jamma. I can't lift it. And I don't think it's gonna do either of our cars any good."

"Good point, kiddo," Bruckner said, thoughtfully rubbing his scruffy beard. "So we need a truck."

"On it," Gina said, stabbing her finger at her iPhone. Before Bruckner got started blustering at her, she was talking to someone, one finger pressed to her ear.

"Dusty? Put Missy on. Well, I'm *sorry* I woke you, just…Missy? Hey…so you guys got back safe, huh? Thanks for making sure I was okay before you…okay, okay. Listen, can you get your brother out here? To Bruckner's? With his truck, okay? We need to move something and we need his help. What's in it for *you*? You bitch! Wait a sec…"

Bruckner seemed to be on the verge of a small stroke. "Gina! Are you sending her the pictures you took of the *doedicurus*? Is she sending…*don't you dare send that airhead those pictures!*"

"I know, right? So cute!" Gina winked and lifted a thumb at her audience. "Yeah, I want one, too. The professor says maybe we can work something out if you get Brendan out here toot suite!"

"Young lady," Bruckner said, glowering. "You may have just done this situation irreparable damage!"

"Yeah, or *saved* your ass!" Gina snorted, shoving her phone back in her pocket. "Oh, and Missy asked about you. Said she hoped her and Dusty weren't too rough on you last night. She said you were cute."

"Oh. Well..." Bruckner shrugged, not quite smiling. "Let that be a lesson to you, kiddo," he said, nudging Alex. "Muscles are all fine and dandy, but it's brains, not brawn, that really win the ladies!"

THIRTY-NINE

Leaning back in the seat beside Diego, Kirby took a long, slurping sip of his Big Gulp, part of an ongoing serenade Diego had been treated to during the long ride. Each sip terminated in a long, heart-felt "Ahh-hh," with a little click of Kirby's tongue on the roof of his mouth. Any other time Diego probably would have found this kind of funny. Just two buds on the road together. It was a nice morning, not too hot yet, no real traffic to speak of. And the fact that Kirby didn't seem at all pissed off about having been woken up at daybreak and dragged on a sudden, very extensive shopping spree was a definite plus. In fact, the chubby little bastard was in as good a mood as Diego had ever seen.

Just two good pals, sure. Eventually they'd get into the fart jokes and insinuations about each others' sexual orientation.

Two buddies. *Yeah, right.*

He couldn't take much more.

"You know that stuff's nothing but sugar," he pointed out. Not much of a burn, but he had to take what he could get.

"Yeah," Kirby said blandly. "I hope you're not thinking I'm going to pay you to be my nutritionist in addition to my dino-pimp. 'Cause, you know…I'm not.

"You're lucky I took you back at all," he went on, settling comfortably in his seat. "I know what you were trying to do, hanging up on me like that. You were trying to screw me. Sniffing around the market, trying to get a better price. Actually thought you could cold call some collectors and try to sell them a dinosaur," he chuckled, shaking his head. Another slurp, then he shook the huge plastic cup at Diego. "All you did was prove to me that you had the goods. You wouldn't have come back if you didn't."

And you knocked the price down, Diego thought wearily. *Because you knew I'd have to take whatever you offered.* And he had. Luckily, he had bigger things on his mind right now. Otherwise, Mr. Van Zandt's fat ass would have gotten his boot in it and gone bouncing down the highway.

He was torn up badly with guilt. He'd left Camila back at the mad doctor's house, and Gina—who probably did require hospital care—as well. Plus he'd just set Vander up to become a real-life monster movie. He was pretty sure there was something actionable in there, somewhere.

"All I needed this morning was your credit card," Diego told him. "And I already used it." Sure as shit he had, in a shopping spree much more extensive than the one he'd gone on with Gina. The back of the truck was loaded down with nets, rifles, boxes of shells and a collapsed metal dog-kennel. He had asked the kid at the sporting equipment store if the place stocked tranquilizer guns, but the kid just goggled his eyes at him like a freak.

"So there's really no reason for you to come with me," he went on. "In fact, it'd probably be safer for you. If you want me to drop you off, you just say the word, and I'll..."

"Wait a sec," Kirby grunted, twisting a dial on the radio.

A voice rose in the cab, so loud Diego had to restrain himself from trying to twist the radio's volume in the other direction.

"...repeat, need backup and an ambulance. I'm at Merle Hollis' place and...there is some...*thing* out here, Jesus Christ..." A loud shrieking noise followed. Mercifully, Kirby turned the radio off in favor of pecking at his iPhone.

"That's the sheriff," Kirby remarked. "Didn't sound good. What did he say? 'Earl Hollis?'"

"Merle," Diego said shortly.

"Here. 1307 Russell." Kirby's pudgy finger stabbed at the GPS' buttons until a laconic female voice advised Diego to turn left at the next light.

"Where we going?" Diego demanded, though he already knew.

"1307 Russell," Kirby said, lifting his drink in what might have been a gesture towards their destination or a toast to their mission. "Merle Hollis' house. Strap it on, son. We're going dinosaur hunting."

Slurr-rrp.

FORTY

Sheriff Luke Davis stared blankly at the scene of carnage before him. So far the huge birds had brought down two of his men; his deputy Ron Garcia and poor old Don Jeffers, whom he'd deputized right after Ron went down.

That didn't include poor old Merle, of course. God, but he felt bad about Merle. He'd called into the office while waiting for his breakfast burrito, and Francine had told him about Merle's call and he'd decided on a whim to pick up a second coffee/burrito combo-pack and go see what was up. It was unusual for Merle to be up before noon.

But when he got out to Russell, he found Merle dead, being torn three ways to Sunday by something that looked like a colossal…well, road-runner. As he sat in the car with his jaw in his lap, two more of the road-runner things came ambling up the street.

He called for back-up and instructed Ron to block off the streets as best they could. Last thing he wanted was for the good folk of Vander to see one of their own being eaten by Big Bird's cousin.

Problem was, the bird was already out of the bag. Before he'd even issued the order, cars were pulling up and people—most if not all of them armed—were gawking at the things. Getting the situation under control had been difficult, not least of all because a certain amount of shouting had been called for, and the birds didn't seem to like shouting. One damn fool tried to get too close to snap a picture, and nearly got his fool head snapped off.

Pretty soon the media arrived, which was the last damned thing he needed. He had an idea that if he weren't quite so well-liked as the town's sheriff, he would be in serious trouble.

And now came the ultimate pain in the butt.

Kirby Van Zandt had arrived, and was easing his big ass out of a truck. Not the kind of vehicle Luke thought the kid would normally be seen in; the Latino kid in the driver's seat must be one of his flunkies.

Luke knew the elder Van Zandts fairly well—as the local rich folks, not socially. Doug Van Zandt was not quite a local boy, but he was at least a born Texan. He had a reputation for taking a high hand with people, but he at least had an idea how to be civil when the situation called for it. The same couldn't really be said of Kirby's Mom, who was a New Yorker—the lowest breed of yankee in the opinion of many in town. But even Sharon was preferable to Kirby, to Luke's mind.

And well, well, looky here: Kirby had spotted Luke immediately and was making a beeline for him. Straightening his belt, Luke went to meet him. He couldn't avoid him forever. And hell, it wasn't unthinkable he was behind the appearance of the three monsters.

"Sheriff," Kirby said, proffering a sticky paw.

"Mr. Van Zandt," Luke said tightly. He decided to get right to the point. "Would you happen to know anything about these animals here?"

"Yes," Kirby said, sucking coolly at his drink. You had to hand it to the kid, he was a cool S.O.B. Apple hadn't fallen far from the tree there. "They're my property, as a matter of fact."

Luke blinked. "Your *property?*"

"I bought them. From this gentleman," Kirby went on, gesturing at the flunky, who stood by the truck looking like he'd love to just disappear into the earth.

"They're exotic birds. Very rare. I won't bore you with the details. You won't have heard of them."

"Well, are you aware that your little pets have just killed and partially eaten three citizens, two of them civilians?" *Including my deputy and my friend?* he mentally added. Luke was shaking a little.

"I'm sorry about that," Kirby said, looking so gravely sincere that Luke wanted to punch him in the teeth. "I truly am. I'm sure that once this mess has been squared away, we can work things out. My father's lawyers will be glad to step in. But right now I need your help, Sheriff."

"Oh?" Luke could feel a throbbing headache coming on. "In what way?"

"I need your help recapturing them. My friend's truck here is loaded with equipment."

"It can be loaded here to Doomsday, Kirby. I don't know how you expect me to help. Already told you my deputy is dead."

"I've already made some calls," Kirby said smoothly. At that moment a couple of trucks drove up, with OAKLAND ZOO stenciled on their sides.

"Right on time," Kirby said, looking pleased.

FORTY-ONE

Ben looked remarkably like Missy, except with formidable muscles and a broken nose. He'd shown up at Bruckner's house looking like he had the mother of all hangovers, but after being directed to the machine, he loaded it with no more trouble than if it were a cardboard box full of chicken feathers. After that, they loaded themselves into the truck and took off.

Alex had somehow managed to get himself stuck in the front seat, between Ben's sweating bulk and Dr. Bruckner's bony, nervous frame. The girls were in the back, laughing and chattering as if they were out for a day's shopping. All of them seemed in good spirits, though Missy was a little snarky about not being handed her own baby *doedicurus* upon arrival.

"Make for the park," Bruckner told Ben.

"But the *Titanis*..." Alex said, aware of the whining sound in his voice. What happened to Sunday mornings when he could sit girl-watching in the Student Union?

"We need power," Bruckner told him. "Remember that stupid-ass merry-go-round they insisted on putting up last Labor Day and never took down? Guess what that runs on. Electricity. There's bound to be an industrial-sized plug in it that we can use. Then one of us will have to get the machine going while the other finds the birds and lures them to the wormhole. *Capiche?*"

Alex nodded miserably. He had a pretty good idea whose job it would be to get the birds.

FORTY-TWO

The guys from the Zoo seemed fairly capable, but much of that façade crumbled the minute they laid eyes on the *Titanis*. Then they had all sorts of questions, which the sheriff couldn't answer and Kirby wouldn't. Diego had stationed himself as far away as he could get. He would have liked to get the hell out, but he had a feeling he'd be stopped if he started up the truck, and he sure as hell wasn't going to leave it behind.

The birds were getting noticeably more restless and aggressive. Something in their dim brains seemed to grasp that they were being held in one place, and they didn't much like it. One of them—the big one Diego thought was another male, like Roc, but bigger—had begun making runs at the Vander citizens, its beak snapping viciously. A gunshot or two brought him back in line, but inevitably some of the on-lookers had begun making a game of challenging him, running out and making rude noises before running away giggling.

The sheriff wasn't having it, but with no deputies, he couldn't do much but holler. He had told Diego and Kirby that his office had finally gotten a call from the county acknowledging their trouble—they'd seen Casey's reports on TV, apparently—but getting the cavalry to Vander was going to take a while.

"If these zookeepers can't get those varmints under control, we're screwed," Luke glared. He started to continue, but a loud scream made him shut his mouth and turn his head. The big male had managed to catch hold of the latest macho idiot, who had quite literally lost his head. The other two birds were already converging on the twitching, decapitated body. They tore into it with gusto, far more enthusiastically than they had with the other unfortunates who'd fallen to them. Something about the gory spectacle reminded Luke of something he'd seen on TV once. It had been a documentary following a pack of hyenas. One hyena, the runt of the litter, apparently, had been something of a coward, always following behind his seniors to scrounge dinner. Once he managed to make a kill of his own, he became the biggest, baddest mamajamma of the whole pack.

That was what the birds were like now; they'd gotten confident. As he was thinking this, Luke was treated to the sight of the big male turning on the crowd, who had begun inching just a little too close. He went after them, screeching and snapping his jaws. The crowd began screeching in turn, knocking each other over in their hurry to get away. A couple got knocked down, allowing the others to escape while the male began tearing into the fresh meat.

A number of people in the crowd began shooting at the male, but the other two birds got between the shooters and their colleague. A number of shots hit home, but did little damage. Worse, the birds had apparently realized the sticklike objects in their hands were the cause of the painful objects striking them. They tore them neatly out of the shooters' hands, prompting a fresh volley of yelps and running. At least three more that Luke could see didn't get away. The morning air was starting to heat up as noon drew on, and it stank of blood.

Luke's stomach felt ready to turn over.

"Sheriff, you'd better get some crowd control going here," Kirby said. "I think I've already mentioned, these animals are my property, and if they suffer any damage...."

Just as Luke was fixing to knock the little butterball down, the flunky stepped up and did it for him, landing a solid blow to Kirby's jaw that sent his drink flying. The flunky was standing over him and bellowing, "You sonofabitch! You happy now, huh? You get what you want? Huh?"

"Alright, son," Luke said, trying to pull the kid away from Kirby, who was flinching and chattering at him in a mixture of rage and abject terror. But the flunky wasn't done yet. He looked like a man who'd been sitting on a lot of guilt and anger...and who probably hadn't gotten enough sleep the last few days. He ran back to the truck and snatched a rifle out of the bed...*and you talk about a big bad mama jamma*, Luke thought. It was a full-bore elephant gun, like something out of what Luke had always thought of, with no good reason, as 'Bwana Jim' movies, the ones they played on Saturday afternoons in his boyhood.

As Kirby continued to bitch and whine (without actually getting up), the kid moved on the birds, staggering under the weight of the gun. *He might actually have a chance*, Luke thought. Assuming he knew how to shoot the damned thing. Assuming, for that matter, that it was actually loaded.

And then, finally, just as the kid was trying to sight down the barrel at the nearest bird, the cavalry came...except it was a mighty small one.

It was another kid. Just one, and pretty short on muscles. He had a gun, at least—a good old Texas shotgun—but what he was doing with it made Luke groan.

This kid *definitely* didn't know how to fire a gun.

FORTY-THREE

The figure approaching them, shouting and waving his arms, was one of the strange ones from the yard. The younger, smaller one.

Roc felt something—not actual pleasure, but more a jolt of pleasurable nostalgia. His days in the strange ones' enclosure had not been terribly pleasant, but at least they'd been simple, underlaid with a comforting routine. Out here, there was plenty of fresh meat, but also plenty of noise and smells so strange that they gave him a headache.

The other strange ones gave the newcomer a wide berth, most of them taking the opportunity to run away. The young one was squawking a noise that Roc had come to associate with himself—"Roc! Roc!" Everything else was babble, but his name called to mind familiarity in much the same way the strange one himself did.

Roc stood watching him, wondering what he'd do.

At that moment the female—he had no idea it was his mother—ran at the strange one, shouldering him aside as she screeched and lowered her head. The strange one sprinted off, but the female wasn't content with this. She wanted to add him to the kill list.

Why Roc ran at the female at that moment was a mystery even to him. He felt no affection for the young strange one, certainly. But since the arrival of the other two *Titanis*, Roc had begun feeling dominated from two sides. He didn't much like that feeling. It was time to establish some authority of his own—even if that only meant killing the strange one before his mother had a chance at him.

Then came an explosion, a noise like a thunderclap. Another strange one was standing behind them with one of the smoking sticks. The male *Titanis* lay in a feebly moving heap. Roc could smell death coming over him.

Something about the death drove the female into a frenzy. She stood weaving on her feet for a moment, then—apparently because the boy was closer—went after him. The young strange one ran like hell up the street, with the female in hot pursuit.

Titanis weren't really capable of shrugging their shoulders, but if Roc could have, at that moment he surely would have. Instead he just took off running after the wildly mismatched pair ahead of him.

FORTY-FOUR

"What the hell are you doing?" It might have been pushing it a little to say that Kirby was screaming, but he was definitely coming close.

"I think it's more like what I *did*," Diego said, shouldering the gun and then rather quickly unshouldering it. That mother was heavy. "I killed the damned bird, that's what I did."

"Don't you fuckin' talk to me that way." Kirby was in his face now, and the whole Furious Kirby experience was a little different than Diego might have anticipated. He was angry, sure; nearly incandescent. But he wasn't acting like a spoiled little kid who'd had his candy taken away. He was holding the worst of the storm in pretty good, but the look in his eyes was saying "I'm gonna kill you" in a disturbingly clear way.

"I paid for that damned thing," Kirby said icily. "You are *liable*, you bastard."

"Right now I'm *liable* to mess uppa your face," Diego said, trying his best to channel the Italian guys he'd known growing up. He was jacked up with adrenaline, ready to do maximum damage to this little prick. At the same time, he felt weirdly calm, like he was about to float away.

"Problem over here, Mr. Van Zandt?" The Sheriff had already come over to run off the gawkers who'd come over to get a look at the dead bird. The thing was a mess; the gun had hit it square in the chest, leaving it a bloody hole. It wasn't quite dead, though it was damned close; it squirmed and croaked feebly, its eyes cloudy under nictitating membranes. The crowd was doing nothing for its comfort; kids who looked old enough to know better were darting over and ripping out fistfuls of feathers for souvenirs. Others were getting in as close as they could and aiming kicks at it.

Diego almost felt sorry for it.

"No," Kirby said. His eyes were still fixed on Diego's, but he sounded calmer. Almost zombie-like. "My associate here and I are just going to go reclaim the rest of my property."

"Right," Diego said, matching Kirby's tone. *Jesus, it's like we're at the OK Corral or some shit.*

"Right now you two seem better fixed to handle this situation than anyone here, so I'm going to let you go on," Luke said, like a man picking his words *very* carefully. "But I would not advise you to go off anywhere. I've already taken down your *associate's* license plate."

He turned to Diego, handing him a card. "When you have a better idea what's what, call me. Once the boys from the county decide to get their asses over here, I can send you some backup. Meanwhile, I'll have my hands full over here." He made a face. "Heard some of these idiots talking about a 'big bird barbecue.'"

"Roger that," Diego said, taking the card and immediately feeling like an idiot. He took the card and marched over to his truck. Kirby had already gotten in.

"Just so you know, this isn't over," Kirby told him. "Once we get all this settled, I'd advise you to get yourself a good lawyer."

"Seriously?" Diego asked. "We've got prehistoric bird monsters on the loose and you want to talk suing?"

"Just the kind of guy I am," Kirby shrugged.

"Yeah," Diego muttered. "An asshole."

FORTY-FIVE

"Holy *crap!*" Ben said. Missy's brother staggered back from the huge shimmering ring of light that had opened up over Bruckner's machine like a huge neon-colored wound. Bruckner and the girls had backed away as well. Situated so near the merry-go-round, it somehow didn't look at all out of place. The outer ring flickered with numerous colors, all melting into each other. Even though it was nearly noon, the light of the wormhole burned as clearly as if it were the middle of the night.

"Incredible," Bruckner said, wiping his forehead. "It latched onto a compatible wormhole practically as soon as I turned it on." He shook his head disgustedly. "Now I'm going to have to tell that asshole Dieter he was right."

"What is that, some kind of laser light show? I saw one of those one time? Up around Austin. You know, 'Keep Austin Weird?'"

"Yeah, I know," Bruckner said, slapping Ben on the shoulder. "Look, Archimedes, I want you to keep a weather eye on that hole there. If anything tries to come through it...like a *big* something, with claws and fangs...I want you to try and steer it back in. It probably won't happen. Any of the megafauna on the other end will more likely be scared witless of it. But if it does, just yell and wave your arms."

"Yeah, okay," Ben nodded. "I get it." Camila wasn't at all sure he did. She was afraid of the wormhole; what if she and the others were pulled in somehow, and trapped on the other side? She decided to stay as far away from it as possible. She walked up past the merry-go-round, where Missy and Dusty were pretending to ride the horses, whooping and squealing.

The park was mostly empty. Word had gotten around about the *Titanis* invasion and the few people they saw were oblivious joggers. Certainly nobody had approached them or asked why they were stealing power from the merry-go-round.

Gina limped over to her. She was looking better and walking a lot straighter. The two stood quietly side by side for a while, looking into the distance, shading their eyes with their hands. A moment later Camila gasped, pointing.

"Oh my god, it's Alex! And the birds! Dr. Bruckner!"

"Heard you the first time, kiddo," Bruckner said nervously. "Listen to me," he said, cocking his shotgun. "I want you all to get into the truck and stay there. If you *won't* do that—as I know you won't—you might as well try to help steer the *Titanis* towards the wormhole. According to Dieter, once they get within a certain distance, they'll be pulled in. So just run for the hole and swerve around it."

"Uh," Camila said, remembering her anxiety of just moments before. "What about us? Won't we get pulled in too?"

"We won't be affected," Bruckner told her. "That's a definite, by the way. We're not the ones who came through in the first place. We're not carrying any loose quantum energy. The real problem is, we have no idea what the attraction distance will be. And with that," he added, "I'm going to help my assistant." He ran off clumsily towards the figures of Alex and the pursuing *Titanis*.

Camila hated to admit it, but she was starting to wish she hadn't come after all.

FORTY-SIX

Alex had a stitch in his side—a rather bad one. He kept seizing up with a stabbing pain that grew worse and worse. Texas humidity wasn't making it any more pleasant; hot sweat was running in rivers down his cheeks; his shirt was soaked and clinging to his back. His high school health teacher used to always caution him that not being overweight was not the same thing as being in shape. The old bastard was right, apparently.

The thing was, stopping for a rest wasn't an option, any more than trying to stop long enough to turn and fire the shotgun. Two very large, very angry Terror Birds were hot on his heels, screeching and clacking their beaks. Every time he thought he couldn't go any further, that he was just going to fall over and die, he heard Roc or the other bird screech, and suddenly an aching chest and sides didn't seem so bad.

He could see the merry-go-round in the distance—and a gleaming light. A wormhole. A small figure was rushing towards him, its limbs flapping wildly. Had to be Bruckner.

"Alex!" Bruckner cried. "Keep going towards the wormhole! Run *behind* it!"

Run behind it. To his exhausted mind, that just made sense. He could see the birds trying to come to a screeching halt, but stumbling cartoonishly over each other at the last minute into the hole.

Bruckner ran past him—running much more quickly and smoothly than he himself. With all the burgers he eats? That's crazy.

"Roc! Come on, ya ol' bastard!" The words were being shouted behind him. He turned enough to see Bruckner standing before the two approaching *Titanis*, shaking his gun at them and screaming curses— right before they neatly sidestepped him, continuing to run towards Alex. Then Bruckner really got pissed. His rage seemed to explode out of the air.

But apparently they weren't interested in eating Bruckner. Just Alex. And in only a few seconds they would be in an excellent position to do just that.

"Aw Jesus!" Alex cried, and that was it; he stumbled over his own feet and went sprawling on the ground, several yards from the merry-go-round. The girls were running towards him, and he tried to motion them away, tried to shout to get back…but it was like he had no air left in his lungs, like there wasn't enough air anywhere in the world to fill them.

At that moment Diego's truck appeared, screeching to a halt scant inches from his outstretched hands.

"Get away from him!" Camila cried, and for a very pleasant moment Alex thought she was shouting at Diego, telling him to get away from Alex, who was so brave. But no...she was screaming not at Diego but something else, something very large, that smelled like an uncleaned birdcage, something that was right behind him.

It didn't matter, though, because something consisting of two hard, sharp-edged blades closed on his arm just under his shoulder and lifted him effortlessly up. One of the birds. It was being almost gentle. The world veered crazily around, showing him Camila and Gina, Diego (who had a really enormous gun) and a fat little guy with a Moe Howard haircut, and the merry-go-round, where Missy and Dusty were playing ride-em-cowgirl under a blazing Texas sun. A little way off, a gigantic ring of metallic, multi-colored fire pulsed and crackled in the air.

All in all, not such a bad way to go, he thought. He would have liked to get laid first, but hell, you didn't always get a choice, did you?

FORTY-SEVEN

The mother *Titanis* shook the little two-legged being she had finally caught up in her beak, enjoying the squalls of the other two-legs clustered around her and her offspring. The abundant meat she had recently enjoyed had given her a surge of energy—much needed in this strange place.

The tiny two-legged animals were jabbering and dancing around her, apparently not realizing how weak they were in comparison to her. Even the big cats of her home territory had kept their distance from her, but these were approaching her almost as equals.

One of them came running up to her holding a stick—there was a smell coming from it, the stink of metals and smoke, and suddenly she realized she knew it.

This was the one who had killed her former mate. How it had done it she had no way of even guessing. There had been a thunderous sound, and that *smell*…and the big male had just fallen over.

She had no fondness of any kind for the male, but a deep instinct insisted she respond with rage. She had gone after another of the two-legs, the one she held now. But the real recipient of her anger stood before her, lifting the stick-thing to its face.

Now she wanted him.

FORTY-EIGHT

"Drop him!" Diego yelled at the female, trying to keep his aim steady. Much to his amazement, the *Titanis* did exactly that, letting Alex fall heavily to the ground where Gina and Camila ran to drag him to safety.

The rest of it happened very quickly.

First, the mother bird screamed at Diego, lowering her head and spreading her stubby, clawed wings. Then something small and fleshy and very solid slammed into him from the side. It wasn't until he hit ground that he realized it was Kirby. The little bastard was in a rage, pummeling him with both fists and cursing him. Of course. He had been working up to this the entire trip.

But the *Titanis* brigade hadn't finished either. Suddenly Kirby was rising into the air, just as Alex had, and for exactly the same reason. Big Mama had him, and Kirby was screaming his head off.

The Terror Bird whipped Van Zandt from side to side in what seemed like an ecstatic rage. A moment later, Roc was in his mom's face, snatching at the squalling target.

It was like watching two puppies playing with a bone. It was, however, considerably less cute, especially when small bloody pieces of Kirby Van Zandt started raining down.

"Dumbasses!" a voice screamed. Diego stared as Bruckner, breathing hard and limping a little, appeared on the scene. Holding his shotgun by the barrel as if it were a baseball bat, he took aim and swatted Roc on the back of his legs, like an unruly puppy.

"Stop *eating* people, you *schmucks*!" Bruckner screamed. "You're already gonna get me sent to jail! Let him go!" He was referring to Kirby, who was howling like a lunatic in the mother's beak, but she, perhaps because she'd already lost one prize, wasn't inclined to obey. Instead, she and Roc moved backward, step by step, towards the blazing glory of the wormhole.

"C'mon, let him go!" Diego yelled, lifting the gun and firing a shot into the air. He ran at the Mama, but a snarling, snapping Roc ran in front of her, playing defensive. Alex stepped forward, calling Roc's name, but whatever deference Roc had been willing to show him had apparently run its course. Had Alex not staggered back at just the right moment, he would have gone down.

"It's no good," Bruckner called, shaking his head and lowering his gun. "You're just gonna get yourself killed."

"You sons a bitches!" Kirby screamed. He looked much the worse hanging from Mama's beak—its sharp edges had cut him up badly and were now streaked with red. Weeping and whining, Kirby punched the bird's head again and again. From Mama's expression, he wasn't making much of an impression on her. "You get me out of this, or I swear to God, I'll bury you so deep…"

Diego and the others stood watching dumbfounded as Bruckner smacked the birds' legs again and again. Roc hissed and shrieked, but for whatever reason, they didn't seem to feel like engaging with him. Slowly, step by step, they backed towards the blazing glory of the wormhole, until its unearthly light made their plumage shine.

And then, the last miracle. The huge Terror Birds rose up into the air like pieces of flotsam before a hurricane. They moved slowly, inexorably towards the hole, squawking and kicking all the while, until they disappeared into the sizzling light, which grew in intensity until Diego found himself clapping a hand over his eyes. When he took it away the wormhole was gone.

So were the Terror Birds. And Kirby. The park suddenly seemed very quiet.

"So long, Roc," Alex said. Something in the dull exhaustion of his voice seemed to speak for all of them.

"So long, Kirby," Diego added. He felt a weird emotion between guilt and jubilant relief.

"Hey Professor, why didn't the birds go after you like they did Kirby?" Gina asked, sounding awed.

Bruckner grinned at her. "Guess when it comes to fat or lean, their choice was obvious. Hell, I'd have done the same in their shoes."

EPILOGUE

Professor Dieter Wolfschmidt turned from the decanter on the table, smiling at his guests. He carried two tiny glasses brimming with something amber-colored, and handed one each to Alex and Bruckner.

"There we go, there now, that's lovely." He had an odd accent, much softer than Alex had expected. He was as skinny as Bruckner, but far better dressed, with an odd, simian smile. Tasting the liqueur, Alex shuddered, but pleasurably. He sat back in his chair, looking out at the setting sun shining on the river. He thought he could get to like Berlin.

The last week had been unpleasant. There had been endless interviews with the police, which had not been made easier by Dr. Bruckner's sudden disappearance. Alex could only reply honestly to their questions that he had no idea what had happened to his employer. He wasn't at home and wasn't picking up calls, either at the university or his office. Luckily, the interviews didn't really go anywhere, mainly because no one seemed interested in admitting that monsters had been involved. Alex had told the police everything he had seen, as honestly as possible, until the questions just sort of dried up. He had been set free, with a warning not to leave the area.

Alex wasn't entirely surprised when the Great Man called him, a full seven days after the debacle in the park, telling him to get his ass to the airport, where a ticket to Germany was waiting for him, along with a passport, which he was supposed to have lost earlier that day and was terribly grateful to have back. Oh, and both the ticket and passport were under another name, so for right now, his name was Heinrich Donnerbrau, okay? And, "For God's sake, kiddo, don't ask any stupid questions." It all sounded highly suspect to Alex, just the kind of thing likely to get him into serious trouble. It had taken him a good ten minutes of dithering before he'd shrugged his shoulders, packed a bag, and called a cab.

But only ten minutes. He was kind of proud of that.

"Honestly, Dieter, this is piss-water," Bruckner said, making a face as he emptied the glass. "And the portions over here are for shit. Can't you offer your visitors any decent beverages?"

"Like what, some coca-cola?" Dieter scoffed, giving Alex a wink before seating himself. "You would like, maybe, a Cuba Libre?"

"All I'm saying is, would it kill you to put out a little nosh? Little cheese platter, little antipasti…"

"So tell me," Dr. Wolfschmidt said, turning his attention to Alex. "How did the rest of our dear friend's little escapade play out back in Texas? I'm not going to ask if anything's left of my poor machine."

"Oh hell no, that sumbitch is totaled," Bruckner said comfortably. "I took care of that before I left. Did you really want the local yokels trying to turn it on? Bring in a few *Homo erectus* to stir things up at the Bible Studies meetings?"

"Ah well," Dieter sighed, sipping delicately at his own glass. "And your other friends?" He smiled at Alex. "Really, after listening to Thaddeus' stories, I feel like I know them all, like characters in a knightly romance. Your lovely lady Camila, for instance?"

"She, uh…" Alex stuttered a little, all too aware he was turning red. "She and Ben kind of got friendly, after the dust settled."

Bruckner shook his head. "Of all people, right? Nice enough kid, mind you. Good hand with electronics. And he's got that Neanderthal thing going on all the chicks dig. But not the brightest star in the night sky. Oh well…I hope they have lots of fat babies. I don't envy her, Missy as an in-law, though."

"But Sir Diego?" Dr. Wolfschmidt asked, raising his eyebrows. "He wasn't heartbroken?"

"Oh, he and Gina sort of hooked up."

"Surprise, surprise," Bruckner drawled. "Before we left, we heard they were making plans to go to New York together. Probably won't last, but then, it doesn't have to. She can keep him in line, anyway."

"Then what will you do, Sir Alex?" Wolfschmidt smiled.

"I don't know…I mean, I guess go back to studying. Fall semester starts in just a few weeks."

"Really? Without your mentor?"

"Without…?" Alex looked at Bruckner.

"What's with the big eyes, kiddo? You didn't think I could come back to the US, did you? This whole junket was a favor Dieter pulled to save my butt. I doubt I'd ever get charged with murder, but I have no interest in trying to explain to Mulder and Scully how it was I came to be involved in good old boys dying at the hands of prehistoric monsters. No, Thaddeus Bruckner is going bye-bye. Say hello to Gerhardt Fassbinder."

"I can't believe you chose that name," Dieter sighed.

"But Alex, you don't have to go home, either."

"I don't?"

"Well, good old Uncle Dieter here and I are going to be collaborators. We're building a new machine…under *very* controlled conditions, you understand. Fully funded. Hell, I can't turn down an offer like that…even if the FBI wasn't after me. And I have a feeling *someone* on that project is going to need a loyal assistant. Dieter's university can easily work out some kind of transfer thingy, so your parents don't have to worry about you not getting that precious and oh-so-useful in the real world Bachelor of Science diploma."

Alex stared at the two smiling men for a long while.

"You mean, more wormholes?"

"As many as you can stand, kiddo."

"And…more monsters? Like the kind that eat you alive?"

"Would you have it any other way?" Dieter laughed.

Alex remained silent a little longer. Then, smiling, he held out his glass. "Give me a refill, and you got yourself a deal."

EPILOGUE II

The female *Titanis* glared down at Kirby for a long moment. Then, as though the sight of him made her ill, her throat began hitching and, opening her beak wide, she spewed out a torrent of gastric juices and half-digested chunks of antelope.

All of which poured on Kirby's head, soaking his shirt and shorts, both of which were already stiffened and reeking from previous downpours.

Lunch was served.

Cursing, he took off his glasses and flicked slime off his fingers. This was *not* his idea of a vacation.

He had no clear idea where he was. One minute he was hanging from the female's beak, screaming his head off. Then he seemed to be in a never-ending freefall, windmilling his arms and howling as he fell into what felt like a bad lighting effect from a psychedelic rock show. Then he was here…with the birds. He had suspicions about what happened, but they weren't anything he felt like dwelling on.

The ground here was flat and stony, studded with stunted trees and shrubs. The heat was brutal. It *felt* like Texas, but he saw no sign of human habitation anywhere nearby. Nothing like, for instance, a convenience store where he could get a bottomless cup of iced cola and a big-ass burrito.

"Raawwk!" He turned and glared sourly at the other bird, who stood watching him with its cold, beady eyes. He had been sure they were going to turn him into bird-food, but up to now they hadn't made any really threatening moves, even when he'd gotten up and started walking away. Maybe they had gotten it in their heads that he was a chick. That would explain the vomit-showers.

But his escape hadn't gotten very far. It had been his own choice to return to the birds, finally. The heat was just too intense. There was no sign of water anywhere. Walking for any distance would get him nothing but a heart attack. He was going to have to just hang with the birds, wait for something to show up. But that was okay. His dad had taught him that something always did turn up, if you waited long enough.

In the meantime, he was hungry as hell. He picked through the mess scattered around and on him until he found a fairly solid chunk, then held his breath and started nibbling. He made a face. Nasty stuff, but a man needed to eat. That was something else his dad had told him.

As he chewed, he counted off in his mind the various things he'd do to the assholes back in Vander as soon as he got a chance. They were all going to jail, there was no doubt about that. Especially the bony old bastard who had agitated the birds until they dragged his ass into the flaming whatsit into this alt-Texas Never-Never Land. The geeky guy, yeah, he was going to jail. The girls, too.

Diego was another matter. Kirby was holding a special grudge against him. Betrayal that heinous demanded a very special payback. He knew people who could be hired to do some very nasty stuff for a fairly reasonable price. He hadn't ever availed himself of these services, because they frankly made him a little nervous. They made certain jokes about his physique and certain unwholesome acts that didn't sound entirely like jokes to Kirby. But if—he checked himself. *When. When* he got home, he'd be well over that nervousness.

Maybe he'd have to hold off on Diego's spicy little girlfriend going to jail. For the moment, anyway. He could see her figuring into his plans. Definitely. He could make Diego watch.

He was so busy with these thoughts that he didn't immediately hear the footsteps behind him. The smell reached him first—a musky stench, but dry, somehow. Almost as unpleasant as his lunch. After that came a hiss, loud and throaty and threatening.

He turned and found himself confronted by a group of four figures. The one in the lead was staring down the shaft of a spear at him. They weren't human. They were tall and slender, their bodies put together in ways subtly different from his own. Their skins ranged from a dusty yellow to a pebbled green, and they looked like nothing so much as big anthropomorphic cartoon lizards from a cartoon.

The one with the spear hissed at him again. Kirby noticed that the spear was tipped with a pointed chunk of translucent stone that seemed to glow with an inner light. The other lizardmen carried spears of their own, and some wore glowing stones around their necks, though they didn't seem interested in getting between their apparent leader and the strange plump creature.

The two *Titanis* had seen the lizardmen as well. They began backing away, not fearfully but warily. They knew these creatures, and didn't like them.

That was good enough for Kirby.

He tossed aside the remains of his lunch and stood up, slapping dust off the seat of his sodden shorts. Then he smiled at the lizardmen as best he could and extended a slime-covered hand.

"Gentlemen," he said smoothly. "How you doing this beautiful morning? I don't suppose you'd be interested in a little business proposition?"

END

CHECK OUT OTHER GREAT DINOSAUR THRILLERS

SPINOSAURUS
by Hugo Navikov

Brett Russell is a hunter of the rarest game. His targets are cryptids, animals denied by science. But they are well known by those living on the edges of civilization, where monsters attack and devour their animals and children and lay ruin to their shantytowns.

When a shadowy organization sends Brett to the Congo in search of the legendary dinosaur cryptid Kasai Rex, he will face much more than a terrifying monster from the past.

Spinosaurus is a dinosaur thriller packed with intrigue, action and giant prehistoric predators.

LAND OF DEATH
by Eric S Brown & Alex Laybourne

A group of American soldiers, fleeing an organized attack on their base camp in the Middle East, encounter a storm unlike anything they've seen before. When the storm subsides, they wake up to find themselves no longer in the desert and perhaps not even on Earth. The jungle they've been deposited in is a place ruled by prehistoric creatures long extinct. Each day is a struggle to survive as their ammo begins to run low and virtually everything they encounter, in this land they've been hurled into, is a deadly threat.

CHECK OUT OTHER GREAT DINOSAUR THRILLERS

WRITTEN IN STONE
by David Rhodes

Charles Dawson is trapped 100 million years in the past. Trying to survive from day to day in a world of dinosaurs he devises a plan to change his fate. As he begins to write messages in the soft mud of a nearby stream, he can only hope they will be found by someone who can stop his time travel. Professor Ron Fontana and Professor Ray Taggit, scientists with opposing views, each discover the fossilized messages. While attempting to save Charles, Professor Fontana, his daughter Lauren and their friend Danny are forced to join Taggit and his group of mercenaries. Taggit does not intend to rescue Charles Dawson, but to force Dawson to travel back in time to gather samples for Taggit's fame and fortune. As the two groups jump through time they find they must work together to make it back alive as this fast-paced thriller climaxes at the very moment the age of dinosaurs is ending.

HARD TIME
by Alex Laybourne

Rookie officer Peter Malone and his heavily armed team are sent on a deadly mission to extract a dangerous criminal from a classified prison world. A Kruger Correctional facility where only the hardest, most vicious criminals are sent to fend for themselves, never to return.

But when the team come face to face with ancient beasts from a lost world, their mission is changed. The new objective: Survive.

CHECK OUT OTHER GREAT DINOSAUR THRILLERS

JURASSIC ISLAND
by Viktor Zarkov

Guided by satellite photos and modern technology a ragtag group of survivalists and scientists travel to an uncharted island in the remote South Indian Ocean. Things go to hell in a hurry once the team reaches the island and the massive megalodon that attacked their boats is only the beginning of their desperate fight for survival.

Nothing could have prepared billionaire explorer Joseph Thornton and washed up archaeologist Christopher "Colt" McKinnon for the terrifying prehistoric creatures that wait for them on JURASSIC ISLAND!

K-REX
by L.Z. Hunter

Deep within the Congo jungle, Circuitz Mining employs mercenaries as security for its Coltan mining site. Armed with assault rifles and decades of experience, nothing should go wrong. However, the dangers within the jungle stretch beyond venomous snakes and poisonous spiders. There is more to fear than guerrillas and vicious animals. Undetected, something lurks under the expansive treetop canopy . . .

Something ancient.

Something dangerous.

Kasai Rex!

Printed in Dunstable, United Kingdom